GW00359644

Decadence

Decadence

THE PASSING OF PERSONAL VIRTUE AND ITS REPLACEMENT BY POLITICAL AND PSYCHOLOGICAL SLOGANS

Edited by Digby Anderson

THE SOCIAL AFFAIRS UNIT

The Social Affairs Unit gratefully acknowledges the support
of the John Templeton Foundation towards the project
of which this publication is a part.

British Library Cataloguing in Publication Data
A catalogue record of this book is available from the British Library

Cover illustration:
The Arthur Rackham picture is reproduced with the kind permission
of his family/The Bridgeman Art Library

Book production by Crowley Esmonde Limited
Printed and bound in the United Kingdom

ISBN 1-904863-04-3

Social Affairs Unit
314-322 Regent Street
London W1B 5SA
www.socialaffairsunit.org.uk

CONTENTS

THE AUTHORS

Digby Anderson was Director of the Social Affairs Unit from 1980 until 2004. He is the author or contributing editor of some fifty books. He has been a columnist on *The Times, Sunday Times, Sunday Telegraph, The Spectator* and, in the United States, on *The National Review*. His most recent books are *Losing Friends* (Social Affairs Unit, 2001) and *All Oiks Now: The Unnoticed Surrender of Middle England* (Social Affairs Unit, 2004).

Kenneth Minogue is Professor Emeritus of Political Science, London School of Economics. He is currently writing a book about democracy and the moral life.

David Womersley is Thomas Warton Professor of English at the University of Oxford. He has published widely on eighteenth-century English literature, in particular on Edward Gibbon.

Theodore Malloch is CEO of The Roosevelt Group, a leading thought and strategy company. He is an intellectual entrepreneur who has been an academic, US State Department and Senate Foreign Relations economic expert, an investment banker, and high-level UN official. He has published broadly, appeared on television often, and serves on some 11 boards: university, educational, think tank, philanthropic and for-profit companies, and mutual funds.

Alexander Evans is a British diplomat. He was previously Research Director for international affairs at Policy Exchange, a London-based think tank, and an Associate Fellow at the Royal Institute of International Affairs.

Simon Green is Fellow of All Souls College, Oxford, and Reader in Modern British History at the University of Leeds. His many publications include *Religion in the Age of Decline* (Cambridge University Press, 1996) and (ed. with R. C. Whiting) *The Boundaries of the State in Modern Britain* (Cambridge University Press, 1996).

He is preparing a study of *The Secularisation of Protestant England*, to be published by Cambridge University Press.

Nicholas Capaldi is Legendre-Soule Distinguished Chair in Business Ethics and Director of the National Center for Business Ethics at Loyola University, New Orleans. He is the author of *John Stuart Mill: A Biography* (Cambridge University Press, 2004).

Christie Davies is an economics graduate of Cambridge University and has a doctorate in Social and Political Sciences from the same university. For 17 years he has been a Professor at the University of Reading. He is the co-author of *The Corporation Under Siege* (Social Affairs Unit, 1998) about environmental questions, and author of *The Strange Death of Moral Britain* (Transaction, 2004).

Peter Mullen is Rector of St Michael's, Cornhill, in the City of London and Chaplain to the Stock Exchange. He has published three novels and many books on theological matters and social affairs – including (as joint editor) *Faking It: The Sentimentalisation of Modern Society* (Social Affairs Unit, 1998). His most recent book is *Everyday Thoughts* (St Michael's Foundation, 2005).

Frank Furedi is Professor of Sociology at the University of Kent in Canterbury. His research is oriented to the study of therapeutic culture and risk consciousness. His arguments are developed in *Therapy Culture: Cultivating Vulnerability in an Age of Uncertainty* (Routledge, 2004) and *The Politics of Fear* (Continuum, 2005).

Elaine Sternberg is the author of *Just Business: Business Ethics in Action* (Oxford University Press, 2000) and *Corporate Governance: Accountability in the Marketplace* (Institute of Economic Affairs, 2004). A former investment banker, she is Principal of Analytical Solutions, and a Research Fellow at the Centre for Business and Professional Ethics at the University of Leeds.

Roger Kimball is Managing Editor of *The New Criterion* and author, most recently, of *The Rape of the Masters: How Political Correctness Sabotages Art* (Encounter Books, 2004) and *Lives of the Mind: The Use and Abuse of Intelligence from Hegel to Wodehouse* (Ivan R. Dee, 2002).

INTRODUCTION AND SUMMARY

DIGBY ANDERSON

Britain, Europe and the United States are decadent societies in a special sense of that word. They have traded in an old morality that served them well throughout their civilisation for a new, experimental quasi-morality. The old morality had well-known virtues such as courage, love, fairness, honesty and prudence. The new 'virtues' are equality, anti-discrimination, environmental concern, self-affirmation, a 'caring' attitude, and a critical mindset.

The old virtues were genuine virtues, in that they required specific behaviours of individuals. The new ones are quasi or bogus virtues in various ways. Some, such as equality, are political policies rather than features of personal conduct. Some, such as environmentalism, are arenas in which virtue may be exercised, rather than virtues themselves. Some, such as transparency in business, are ways of revealing virtue, but are certainly not virtues themselves. Some are slogans: they make rhetorical appeals to moral indignations. They merely sound virtuous. Yet others have some virtue, but they are crude and lack means of application to actual practical social settings. Finally, some actually involve what would once have been regarded as vices.

EXAMPLES

The old understanding of distributive justice, as derived from Aristotle, emphasised merit and desert. It was just that rewards in society went to those whose individual behaviour deserved them. In contrast, modern society holds that an individual's performance is so affected by environmental factors outside his control, such as background, poverty, race or sex, that justice requires governments to manipulate these factors or compensate for them, or just hand out prizes to those 'discriminated' against by them. The redemption of society used to be sought by encouraging individuals to improve. In the twentieth and twenty-first centuries, it is sought through political means, whether communism, nazism or the welfare state, affirmative action and anti-discrimination policies. Idealism was about individual achievement; it is now about, in T. S. Eliot's phrase, 'dreaming of systems so perfect that no one will need to be good'.

A similar reversal holds with the new therapeutic culture. Victorians valued, perhaps above all the other virtues, independence and self-reliance. Today, individuals are not only encouraged to seek help, but may be reprimanded for failure to use (state-provided) counselling. Again, esteem used to be something other people held – or did not hold – you in. Now it is something you hold yourself in. Indeed, the counselling services stand ready to help anyone 'suffering' from 'low self-esteem' to boost it and affirm himself. We should all have high self-esteem, whether or not we have been virtuous.

With the new environmental virtues, something rather different has happened. So passionately, indeed almost religiously, do modern environmentalists care about their cause that they can entertain no other virtues – such as economic prosperity – that might be balanced against it. The passion sometimes leads to the actual telling of untruths: a denial of the old virtue of honesty. More often, it leads to the abandonment, even disparagement, of judgement and prudence. Prudence is, in a way, the queen and the longest-serving of the virtues. The old society was very virtuous, in that it had a long list of virtues and it knew that some skill was needed to decide which virtue fitted which circumstance; what to do when one virtue conflicted with another; and how to restrain virtues from tipping over into excess and vice. The rise of the single-issue fanatic means the abandonment of the various prudential virtues of moderation, coherence and common sense.

Sometimes, modern society simply elevates the trivial or less important above the main virtue. Thus, the obsession in business with accountability and transparency. Both may be important, so that we can see that good conduct is being pursued, but neither is as important as the good conduct itself. When accountability is pursued manically and comprehensively, notably in the 'stakeholder' doctrine that a corporation is responsible to anyone and everyone – suppliers, workers, the local community, generations to come, shareholders – then, of course, the corporation becomes responsible to no one, since there is no way of reconciling competing responsibilities. As the old wisdom had it, 'no one can serve two masters'. Indiscriminate accountability leads to unaccountability.

The highest virtue in the Christian ethics that used to be so important for western civilisation was the Christian virtue of love. There is certainly no lack of talk about love today, but it has little to do with Christian love. Christian love was about will, love oriented to heavenly ends, about sacrifice, about following rules. It was sharply distinguished from natural and social loves. Modern love is about feeling – indeed the exhibition of feeling; about earthly, even fleshly, ends; about fulfilling wants; about ignoring rules; about self-fulfilment. Christian love was a theological virtue. It made no sense without the God of love. Modern love has no theology, indeed no doctrine of man. Without these, its love makes no sense.

With other old virtues, such as thrift or courage, modern society's understanding is simply less than the old society's. Courage, for example, was both admired and required, and seen to be dangerous because of its wildness and defiance. Modern society either mocks it or seeks to tame it, but increasingly, as is shown by its treatment of its armies, it misunderstands it. Thrift was good. It is now mean and bad. Yet the old thrift meant much more than hoarding. It meant stewardship and the control of greed – caring for God's endowment. The modern society's celebration of desire and its insatiable consumerism is the very opposite. Moreover, as the old theologians of thrift could have explained, it does not lead to happiness. Man was made for more than material acquisition.

As a final example, the modern society is very proud of its intellectual virtue: it is critical. Older societies were not critical; they were traditional. We are, however, critical, not least of older societies and tradition. In fact, much modern criticism in politics, philosophy and the arts is simply adversarial. It likes to throw everything under suspicion. Its goal is not truth, or the repair of inadequate or failed ideas, but subversion. Ultimately it is political. It mindlessly glorifies innovation, experimentation and destruction in the same way as it accuses others of glorifying tradition.

IT IS DIFFICULT TO BE GOOD WHEN YOU DO NOT KNOW WHAT THE GOOD IS

This book treats a very limited selection of the old, and a less limited selection of the new virtues. Its contributors seek to remind readers of what the old virtues were like, and to contrast them with the new ones. The old virtues came from different sources: the civilisations of Greece and Rome, Christianity, the traditions of the patriarchal family, and, more recently, from Victorian culture and administrative organisation. Some were in tension, and even conflict, with others, yet the old society understood and dealt with that tension: that was a virtue in itself. The contrast reveals the new virtues as far less sophisticated, as sentimental, as political rather than moral in the personal sense, and, above all, as a very poor exchange for the old. Indeed, one theme of our authors is that the new virtues – insofar as they do work – do so by surreptitiously using the old.

This exchange of well-tried genuine virtues for poor quasi-virtues may not directly affect society's behaviour. It does not necessarily mean that modern society behaves badly. It does mean, though, that its members increasingly cannot recognise what would have been regarded as good and bad behaviour. Of course, people don't have to be able to write doctoral theses on the virtues and vices to be good, but they do need to be able to recognise them in themselves and others and apply them, in order to see what it is to be courageous or loving in this or that situation. A society that recognises and applies virtues in practice may be called morally literate. Modern society is *morally illiterate*. And a society that cannot see what is good is unlikely to *do* what is good, except by accident or dying habits, using up the moral capital of the past it so rejects.

A SUMMARY AND SELECTION OF THE CHAPTER THEMES

Six old virtues are explored: prudence, courage, Christian love, thrift, disinterest, and the family virtues of authority and obedience, stewardship and succession. They are followed by a summary of six of the new virtues: distributive or social justice, the environmental virtues, the caring virtues, the therapeutic virtues, the business virtues of accountability and transparency, and the intellectual virtue of being critical.

PRUDENCE

Kenneth Minogue explains that prudence was one of the longest-serving of the old virtues, though it was variously understood at different times. Past society knew that its long list of virtues – courage, love, honesty, etc. – was admirable in the abstract, but it also knew that it needed discretion in deciding which virtue is *appropriate* in particular circumstances, and in what degree. In other words, the virtues are not just a jumble of desirable qualities (balanced by the undesirable vices) but constitute a moral organisation of life that also requires some sense of how to engage with other people. Truthfulness is an important virtue, but the tactless or 'candid' friend is not an admirable figure. Many vices result from the exaggeration of virtues – above all, the vice called 'self-righteousness'. Virtues need to be orchestrated into the spontaneities of actual social life. At various times, different key ideas were used to achieve this orchestration: ideas such as moderation, coherence and common sense. Prudence, in any of these and other ways, suggested limits – for example, how far one might go in sacrificing oneself for others, or in being truthful in revealing one's inner thoughts. It was thus a self-protective virtue, and in being self-protective it showed that no moral agent could possibly abide equally by all the virtues.

Since then, utilitarians – those who judge how good an action is by the amount of happiness or utility it results in – have tried, unsuccessfully, to replace prudence with a scientific calculation of the consequences of any act for happiness. And romantics have spurned it as too calculating. The unrealistic schemes and tempers of both communism and environmentalism in the twentieth century are examples of what happens when ideals are not tempered by prudence. Also in the twentieth century, the welfarist ambitions of democracies, along with advances in technology, resulted in prudence being absorbed by other considerations. Technology, for example, seemed to offer a solution to many moral problems, especially if they were interpreted in a utilitarian way. While the virtue of chastity might seem a policy that protects recreational sex against the dangers of undesired pregnancy and disease, in a world of contraceptive and hygienic devices it may be thought unnecessary. Modern military technology is constantly seeking substitutes for risky adventures in sheer courage. Again, prudence was often the practical virtue that children had to learn in order to save them from physical misadventure, but now government regulation spells out and enforces the precautions a prudent agent might take in subscribing to the maxim 'look before you leap'. The most recent destiny of prudence has been to suffer nationalisation, which ultimately requires that we should allow the state to do our prudence for us.

COURAGE

If prudence is nowadays scorned or nationalised, courage is misunderstood. In antiquity, and in all periods up to and including the early modern period, courage, argues David Womersley, was understood to be extreme, perhaps even flamboyant, physical bravery. Shakespeare's *Coriolanus* offers us an anatomy of this concept of courage, and dramatises its difficult relationship with the values and temperament of the peace-time world.

13

Increasingly, we confuse courage with other emotions and virtues to which it is more or less closely attached: fortitude, tenacity, resolve. We have even (in a concept such as 'cold courage') brought it close to certain forms of prudence, even though prudence is, in many ways, the opposite of courage. In so doing, we have discounted, masked or disguised from ourselves aspects of courage which were previously acknowledged to be of its very essence: its exorbitancy, its freedom from calculation, its wildness, its rejection of authority, its impatience with being dictated to in any form – in short, its antipathy to many of the human strengths we associate with a successful passage from childhood to adulthood. We have tended, more and more, to overlook the strong vein of irrational defiance in courage, and we have failed to pay sufficient attention to the fact that the impulse towards courage partakes of a refusal to accept the verdict of probability.

Our motive for so doing has been our desire to obscure the extent to which so clearly necessary and admirable a virtue as courage exists in a state of tension with, or even antagonism towards, the habits of mind and the principles of conduct which we find most useful in normal social life. As Shakespeare's *Coriolanus* again demonstrates so emphatically, societies are secured by virtues they cannot stomach. As western societies have come to be ever more effectively disciplined, as the reach of the administration of the state has lengthened and grown steadily less willing to brook any opposition to its preferences and the prudential premises upon which it is grounded, so the tension between courage and the socially useful qualities society likes to reward has grown, and so we have tried with greater determination to conceal, even from ourselves, that disparity. In doing so, we have hidden from ourselves an important but contradictory aspect of the courageous act: namely that – in spite of the fact that it often results in general social benefits – it provides, first and foremost, an intense enjoyment for the actor, so that the benefits it confers on others might be thought of as incidental rather than primary.

Societies need frequent pollination with the virtue of courage, however vigorously they may (as in *Coriolanus*) banish, mock or deplore it, or however subtly they may try to make it seem more amenable to what they take to be their priorities than, in its virtuous intransigence, it either can or should be. At the heart of courage is the principle of defiance, and this is a principle that modern western society regards in, at best, an equivocal light. So it is not surprising that the concept of courage should have come under deforming pressure and have been moved closer to tamer, more domesticated virtues.

CHRISTIAN LOVE

If courage is pre-eminently a classical virtue, love, as part of western culture, is pre-eminently a Christian one. While it, too, is now misunderstood, the misunderstanding is different: with love, the problem is that modern society wants the virtue, or a sentimentalised version of it, without the religion on which it depends.

In Christianity, Love is the principal of the three theological virtues. The term 'theological' is not idle or ornamental. The theology in the Johannine nutshell is this:

> God so loved the world that He gave His only begotten Son that whosoever believeth in Him should not perish but have everlasting life.

It was God's Love that led to His becoming man in Christ and dying for man, so that man could, if he chose, find his way back to God. To be saved, man has to return God's Love in the same fashion. Being saved will mean his union with the godhead, for union is what divine Love is about. From this theological character of Love come the characteristics of Christian Love. Christian Love is a matter of the will, not of feeling. It has nothing to do with liking. Theological Love is not the same as natural or social love. Even when this Love is explained by earthly analogy, the partial nature of such analogies should be remembered. Love is not the same as acts of corporal mercy – what are called, in modern usage, charity. St Paul explained the worth of merciful and even sacrificial acts without loving and Godward intention:

> And though I bestow all my goods to feed the poor and though I give my body to be burned, and have not charity, it profiteth me nothing. (1 Corinthians 13:3)

On the other hand, Love is not some sort of catch-all which will replace being good and doing good. And what goes for commandments, goes for creeds. The Athanasian creed puts it most succinctly:

> Whosoever will be saved: before all things it is necessary that he hold the Catholick Faith. Which Faith except everyone doth

keep whole and undefiled: without doubt he shall perish
everlastingly.

Should that not be clear, it ends,

They that have done good shall go into life everlasting:
and they that have done evil into everlasting fire.

What God wills for man by His Love is man's highest good,
union with Himself in heaven. Because God loves man as a father,
men become each other's brothers and are commanded to love each
other in the same way God loves them. This means willing each
other's highest good, union with God for ever; not doing what the
neighbour wants. Though God loves all men, God in Christ – that is,
in His Humanity – loved certain men in particular. He had a special
love for his Mother, St John (the 'disciple whom Jesus loved') and
his own people. Man, too, is called to love particular people: his
own parents (honour your father and mother; other people's fathers
and mothers won't do), his friends, those he finds himself with in
need, his own people. Since Love is a matter of will and practice,
Christian Love cannot be love of all men.

Various of these characteristics of Christian Love are especially
at odds with modern understandings of love, notably, morality subordinated to theology, love as will rather than feeling, love oriented
to heavenly ends rather than earthly wants, love as non- or unnatural, love as requiring rules to be followed, love as particularistic,
love as sacrificial rather than self-fulfilling. Modern people may,
therefore, wish to dump all or several of these characteristics.
Unfortunately, the whole edifice of Christian goodness rests on the
theology of Love. The modern advocacy of empathetic niceness and
equal rights has little to do with Christian Love. What little it has
will, of course, be lost if God is dumped. Or rather the *imperative*
character of Christian morality, which is based on a coherent doctrine of man and God, will be lost. Modern man might be able to
invent a whole new metaphysical basis for being nice to children,
helping ladies through the glass ceiling and giving to Oxfam. But
then, again, he may not.

THRIFT

Thrift is today often confused with stinginess and is equated with
meanness. The problem here, according to Theodore Malloch, is not
so much a misunderstanding of the traditional Christian (Protestant)
concept of thrift, as a half-understanding. The true origins of thrift

lie deep within the Calvinist tradition, since they were adapted to address the needs and concerns of a newly emergent sixteenth-century middle class. The theology where *worth* is determined less by the amount one spends, and more by the wisdom with which one discharges responsibilities as a *steward* over God's creation, is ingrained in the Reformation. By seeking *first* the Kingdom of God, Calvin argues that there is another restraint on excessive anxiety. In a renowned passage, Calvin expounds on the 'lay not up treasures on earth' phraseology. Built as it is into the very structure of creation, the notion of *daily bread* that sustains us – and the labour involved in providing it – is continually highlighted by Calvin. For Calvin, 'our bread' is a metaphor for *all* goods and belongings. But these are not literally *our* bread. Caring for God's endowment in a respectful and thrifty fashion is here a form of biblical obedience.

The Reformers understood the sin of greed to be a sin directly against one's neighbour. Their understanding presumed the sin of greed to be in the category of those sins that cause a break in the relation between neighbour and self. But for the Reformers, the sin in question was a transgression of the limit set for us in the world by God as creator, the consequence of which is a struggle of sovereignty over who is really in control of our lives and our future.

Modernity is trapped by a definition of the Reformation provided by the German sociologist Max Weber. Weber's treatment of the Protestant Reformation is actually based on a wrong sense of accumulation and of possessions. Weber tried to recast the sin of greed as a virtue of thrift, which is only half of the Reformers' gospel. The *calling* and *vocation* of a person was a mark of that person's election or non-election by God. Work showed evidence of productivity, as demonstrated in the parable of the talents, rather than an appetite for pleasure. Weber concluded that the result of all this working hard and spending little was savings; and these savings were always in search of new and appreciating investments. But unlike the Calvin Weber described, the other parts of Calvin espoused a different relationship between human beings and the things they possessed – a kind of communitarian understanding of what they had and held. Weber was thus only *half right* in connecting Calvin's thoughts to the rich and the later evolution of capitalism, for he missed the other and major point. For what Calvin proclaimed in his day was not what it was to be rich in goods, and so greedy, but what it meant to be rich towards God, and so generous.

For the traditional Protestant, insatiable desire is a source of unhappiness and even spiritual instability. Modern-day consumerists, however, have too often turned thrift on its head and made desire and want a source of liberation, where having more is the very definition of having arrived.

DISINTEREST

If thrift is a virtue to do with an individual's economic behaviour, disinterest is an administrative virtue, one an individual practises in public service. Alexander Evans suggests:

> Simple service is obedience. Wise and impartial advice, on the other hand, depends on a form of intellectual disobedience – disinterest...From the ancient counsellor, through the medieval fool, down to the late Victorian administrator – advice, and the integrity of those who offer it, has always been valued.

A new culture of public service emerged during the nineteenth century. Civil servants ought to be neutral: their judgement free of the vagaries and vulgarities of political fashion. Prior to 1854, public servants in Britain were highly politicised, often corrupt creatures of direct political patronage, and the nature of official appointments established a political dependency on their patrons. A systematic reform of public service was clearly required. The Weberian bureaucratic system is rule-based, hierarchical and impersonal (the office, rather than the official, matters). Personal discretion is slight: rules and precedents inform judgements.

In recent years, the nature of public service has changed. In 1971, William Niskanen's influential book, *Bureaucracy and Representative Government*, suggested that senior officials were more inclined to increase their empires and further their careers than act in the public interest. A form of sentimentality has seeped into the civil service. The belated awareness in the 1980s that much of the business of contemporary government is service delivery saw a sea-change in public-sector management. Public service became increasingly indistinguishable from customer service, and officials found the cultural change difficult. Advocates of social justice despise disinterest, arguing that without commitment social change is impossible. Social justice is the new philanthropy; social commitment the leitmotif of much state action and intervention.

Is disinterest simply another way of describing neutrality or impartiality? Neutrality is often perceived as non-participation –

whereas the administrative value of disinterest is about making judgements and being involved, without prejudice to any party. Impartiality means freedom from selfish bias or self-interest.

There is good reason to narrate and promote the virtue of disinterest. Above all, disinterest grants administrators integrity. Only civil servants with integrity can enjoy public confidence: and the nineteenth-century reforms that established western bureaucracies (as we know them) were designed to produce efficient, just and ethical public services. Selection on merit and the introduction of lifelong tenure were particularly important. This latter reform valued memory, witness and faithful advice. It is hardly surprising that many eminent British public servants were also active historians.

Today, disinterest is often disregarded. Since the late 1980s, political debate in Britain has revolved around managerialism and presumed competence in government. Passion is increasingly valued, as a glance at the public-sector jobs pages shows. Of course, disinterest has its critics. Many attack it for concealing self- or group-interest. Disinterest allows for subjectivity – indeed, it assumes just that. But it also permits judgement – if practised properly – outside subjectivity.

At their best, classical administrators have always exemplified disinterest. Their autonomy allowed them to think for themselves. They were willing to be wrong, and to learn from it. They were also willing to speak out when they were right – whatever the personal cost. Their integrity was driven by their disinterest: the wholeness of their judgement, and indeed their lives, flowed from the ability to advise rather than affirm. Disinterest is a classical virtue with a modern history. Those who practise it well are remembered for their dedication to truth. Those who no longer operate by it may well have lost virtue.

THE FAMILY VIRTUES

If thrift pertains to the economy and disinterest to administration, a concern for family, stewardship and succession are, above all, domestic virtues. Simon Green recalls just how important these virtues were. The patriarchal family, that institution which subordinated wives to husbands, children to parents, and its every living member to organic self-perpetuation, is traceable to Roman Law. Revelation and reason together extended its provisions to Christian civilisation more generally. Each pointed to the family as, literally, the first social institution; the very basis of the commonweal. It was in praise not merely of a well-ordered polity but of a progressive, commercial society that Disraeli described Victorian England as 'a domestic country'; a place where 'home is revered and the hearth sacred'.

In practice, this meant dispersed autocracy in matters both large and small: from the allocation of property and permission for marriage, down to personal nomenclature, positions at table, and even the division of private space. All these were sustained by severe sanctions if need be: English common law permitted husbands to chastise their wives with a stick as wide as their thumb. English custom allowed fathers to disinherit ungrateful children.

This patriarchal family offends our modern sense of justice, even of individuality. But we ignore its virtues both of solicitude and solidarity. They were very real. By the same conventions, husbands were responsible for their wives' debts, fathers for their children's future happiness; everything was dedicated to the family's continuing prosperity. Not for nothing did de Montaigne insist that 'there is hardly any less torment in running a family than in running a whole country'.

More significantly still, the very inequality of standing between the generations encouraged both a degree of outward devotion and an extent of inner direction among children, since lost to the affective family of contemporary preference. The loss has had more than purely domestic consequences. For by imposing obedience on the young, it sought to nurture the proper allegiances of adulthood; recognising, as Burke understood, that 'we begin our public affections in our families' and indeed 'no cold relation is a zealous citizen'. At the same time, by sustaining a disciplinary regime that implied its own eclipse – passing in adult maturity – it cultivated a very different, yet paradoxically related virtue. This was the spirit of independence.

No finer defence of the English patriarchal family has been mounted than that of the French sociologist Émile Boutmy. The family, a domestic 'monarchy by divine right' forged a 'virile race', one 'accustomed to discipline' yet also habituated to 'liberty and responsibility'. How? First by begetting sons who yearned for liberty in their own right. For liberty, not licence – they yearned to become fathers. Then, by nurturing boys who well understood that 'they did not come before their father in the affection of their mother'. The result: men were spared those 'enervating tendencies' of parental indulgence and were taught 'to count only on themselves' in life. No boomerang babies these.

And there was something else, related to property. Primogeniture not only enabled the material survival of the family; by endowing first sons beyond individual needs, it steered landlords towards the idea of social mission, and specifically the endowment of useful institutions. In pushing otherwise well-born young gentlemen into government and commerce, it spread the best kinds of aristocratic values more broadly across society. That combination, in turn, sustained not simply a small class, but a whole nation; a nation not just willing to supply the deficiencies of the state where necessary, but capable *in extremis* of resisting its pretensions to monopoly power.

DISTRIBUTIVE JUSTICE OR SOCIAL JUSTICE

The concept of distributive justice Nicholas Capaldi traces back as far as Aristotle, but it is only since the Second World War that it has become a contemporary virtue. Needless to say, the meaning of 'distributive justice' has been completely transformed in the modern context. For Aristotle, distributive justice was the assigning of responsibilities and rewards to individuals based upon merit. For the contemporary world the notion of merit (desert) has completely disappeared. The contemporary virtue of distributive justice is an attempt to reconfigure society in such a way that social roles, opportunities, assets, and responsibilities are based upon fairness.

The accounts of human nature fall into six types: the rationality model, Stoic self-mastery (rationality + habitual training), ascetic self-mastery, divine predestination, free will (plus the possibility of sin), and environmental determinism. The first five accounts all allow for the possibility of widespread failure. Moreover, any combination of these six allows for the possibility of failure to achieve virtuous status. It is only when the sixth account is held by itself that it is possible to envisage the elimination of vice.

If human beings are totally a product of their social environment, and if vice is the result of a lack of resources (political, social and material), and if there is greatly expanded wealth or resources, and if those resources are wisely distributed (or redistributed), then vice will be eliminated. Merit, or desert, is no longer a virtue if environmental (social) determinism is accepted. Charity is no longer a virtue, because it reflects an unfair initial distribution of resources, is voluntary not obligatory, and reflects a hierarchical relation between the giver and the receiver. Philanthropy is no longer a virtue for the same reasons. Magnanimity is no longer a virtue because it reflects historical accident.

The contemporary conception of distributive justice is an incoherent and unworkable virtue. There is no agreement on what things should be redistributed or equalised, i.e. no consensus on which universal facts about human nature entail normative social arrangements. Given that lack of agreement, demands for redistribution or equality remain nothing more than rhetorical masks for private political agendas. Even if it were possible to redistribute everything, so that we all started out equal, differences in ability and circumstance (for example, luck) would soon lead to inequalities. Last, in order to overcome the unegalitarian recidivism, it would be necessary to maintain the most all-encompassing social tyranny.

THE ENVIRONMENTAL VIRTUES

The modern environmental movement appears to have little use for traditional virtues. Yet, argues Christie Davies, a true environmental concern requires them. Modern environmentalism sometimes goes further and engages in what would traditionally have been regarded as vice. It is not above telling untruths if they might advance the cause. More often, it is remarkable for its lack of judgement and prudence. The classic campaign against the dumping of the Brent Spar rig in deep water, even though the pollutants had been removed from it, is a good example of lack of prudence. The rig would have lain where there is no light and a crushing pressure of water. It would have done no harm to living creatures, and indeed some might have benefited. It would not have obstructed the work of the scientists of the future. We see here a perverse environmental virtue that becomes a vice. It involves treating a part of the Earth's surface as a secular sacred space, even though it is beyond human experience and cannot damage life. It is a vice because the alternatives were worse. It was both more environmentally damaging to park the Brent Spar in a fjord, and more costly. The virtues of prudence and judgement were completely set aside in the pursuit of an absolute end that is part of a misguided search for a secular creed to replace religion and that is fuelled by a set of superstitions that ignore science. The same may be said of the opposition to nuclear power and genetically modified plants, even though they offer a net environmental gain. They have become the new devils to be expelled, because they are an affront to the new pagan nature worshipper. There is nothing new under the moon. That is why you cannot reason with environmental activists.

There are, then, no distinctive and separate environmental

virtues, merely an enhanced concern for the environment caused by new threats to it and new knowledge of it. Yet this concern is rooted in, and requires, old virtues such as prudence and thrift, and also discrimination and an appreciation of, and wish to conserve, beauty and knowledge; in the virtues of the cultivated man and the scholar. In pursuing these ends in a world dominated by the marketplace and administrative regulation, we need, of course, to call on the virtues we respect in those who work in these spheres – honesty, disinterestedness, diligence, reliability, attention to duty and courage.

THE CARING VIRTUES

Peter Mullen identifies the suppressed premise supporting the ideals of the new caring, therapeutic community as the idea that there is no such thing as truth. Whereas once one might have been received into the Catholic Church because one believed that its teachings were true, no such epistemological or fideistic strictures attend the new world of caring self-esteem, where the only justification for any *spiritual* activity is how good it makes you feel.

A presupposition of traditional religion was that we all fall short in some way or other, and that we stand in need of spiritual repair: in the old language, this realisation was cast in terms of sin and forgiveness. But a client of the new caring therapies would be outraged to be told that he was deficient in virtue or the moral aspect. Why, it would damage his *self-esteem* to be told he is a sinner! The new gospel of self-realisation is that, inasmuch as we fail to achieve the perfection of life and mood latent in us all, we do so because we are merely falling short in our application of the correct technique which, for an appropriate fee, the purveyor of the new spirituality will happily supply: it may be a 'misalignment of Yin and Yang', an unaccountable neglect of a new massage and exercise programme, or ignorance of the correct feng shui procedures when setting up a new home. So the caring therapies not only de-intellectualise traditional faith, but they de-moralise it as well. There is no truth and falsity, and there is no right or wrong. When it comes to the new caring virtues, what *is* true and good is what makes you *feel* good. In the absence of any other philosophical, theological or ethical criteria what else could it be?

Institutionalised or professional caring is a depressing affair – almost an oxymoron or contradiction in terms – and a bitter example of Eliot's warning against '...dreaming of systems so perfect that no one will need to be good'. In short, caring in the modern institutional sense is not a virtue but a paid job. And the truth is that care is not something that people can do for a wage. A carer is described as a 'professional friend', but to whom does the professional friend turn when he needs a friend?

In caring, the old religious idea that you try to act virtuously for virtue's own sake, or for God's sake, has been replaced by the new psychotherapeutic notion of virtue for well-being's sake – your own well-being. Indeed, not to look after your own health according to the current medical, dietary and lifestyle fads is regarded as irresponsible. The religious concept of *self-respect* has been supplanted by the egocentric notion of *self-esteem*. But whereas self-respect involved the peace that comes from attempting to lead a virtuous life (and its consequential blessing of a clear conscience), self-esteem means merely feeling good about yourself. Like the rest of the caring industry, it is devoid of moral content.

And the idea of *professional care* is far removed from the old commitment to *service*. To illustrate this, we need look no further than the changed nature of the institutions that provide care. Doctoring, nursing and teaching were formerly regarded as *vocations*. Nowadays these are unionised professional services, governed according to bureaucratic structures, whose moral ground comprises the modern values of universal rights, equal opportunities, monitoring and testing, and political correctness.

The old virtue of *love* or *charity* had as its goal something or someone that was not itself. That is to say, it was *religious*. The new virtue of caring is self-referential and narcissistic, and thus a devaluation of the original meaning and purpose of the commandment to love God and your neighbour as yourself.

THE THERAPEUTIC VIRTUES

In modern society, manifestations of the classical virtues of love, friendship and loyalty, argues Frank Furedi, are medicalised as a form of addictive behaviour. Kindness and altruistic behaviour towards friends and the elderly are sometimes diagnosed as the addiction of 'compulsive helping'. It appears that compulsive helpers disregard their own needs and focus far too much on helping others.

Help-seeking has become the principal therapeutic virtue, because it acknowledges the authority of the only agent of recovery – the therapist. Recovery has become a caricature of salvation. Once in recovery, the patient is saved.

Forms of behaviour that run counter to help-seeking are often castigated as symptoms of emotional illiteracy. Despite its celebration of the self, therapeutic culture is hostile to behaviour patterns that manifest the virtue of self-reliance and self-control.

Individuals who are not inclined to adopt help-seeking behaviour face considerable pressure to fall into line with the prevailing cultural expectations. After the tragic bombing in Oklahoma in 1995, the 'grief industry' invaded the city. Within a short space of time, this tragic event was 'translated into an official or authoritative language of suffering by "trauma" experts'. And although some family members of the victims 'resented the overwhelming presence of the grief industry', the psychological interpretation of the experience came to define the event. The relentless pressure to experience a tragic event according to a pre-given emotional script ensures that the public internalises help-seeking behaviour.

As the recent experience of rural Britain demonstrates, the virtue of help-seeking is zealously promoted by the therapeutic lobby. They regard the ideals of self-help, stoicism and self-sufficiency not simply as cultural norms, but as values that must be stigmatised. The ideals of rural Britain ran counter to the therapeutic virtue of help-seeking, and for that reason had to be undermined and destroyed. That is why the professional mental health response to the crisis in rural Britain took the form of a cultural crusade that sought to weaken farmers' resistance to the therapeutic world view.

The traditional ideal of the robust, independent and resilient farmer, once considered a positive virtue by the prevailing culture, was increasingly presented as a chronic flaw. Such former virtues were now depicted as a false façade assumed by emotionally primitive people, and as the indirect cause of the problem of rural stress. Mental health professionals and advocacy groups perceive the farming community as a challenge to be conquered and regard recent disasters as an opportunity to re-educate the emotionally illiterate farmer.

The act of acknowledging one's feelings and, by implication, an openness to seeking help are culturally represented as acts of virtue. In contrast, a reluctance to acknowledge the problem of the emotions and a refusal to seek help are regarded as acts responsible for both individual distress and many of the problems facing society. Help-seeking has acquired positive moral connotations akin to the act of acknowledging guilt in more traditional cultural settings.

The virtue of help-seeking is associated with the belief that people lack the inner resources necessary to help themselves. From the standpoint of the therapeutic imagination, the defining feature of humanity is its vulnerability. That is why responsible behaviour is always oriented towards being open to seeking help. Seeking help has the status of a quasi-religious obligation for the vulnerable self.

Self-discovery through a professional intermediary is justified by the assumption that individuals are helpless to confront problems on their own. According to the therapeutic version of personhood, people are not so much the authors of their own circumstances, but the victims.

The therapeutic virtue of help-seeking represents the negation of any form of genuine feeling or behaviour that can lead to a virtuous act. Worse still, this professionalisation of people's lives sends out the signal that we do not expect human beings to possess any distinct virtues.

THE BUSINESS VIRTUES

Though increasingly presented as business virtues, transparency and accountability are – at best – means of detecting and assessing the genuine virtues that business both presupposes and promotes. At worst, Elaine Sternberg argues, transparency and accountability have been advocated as means of undermining the genuine business virtues, by subverting both the activity of business and accountability itself. When business is properly understood, the virtues proper to it include most of the 'old' moral virtues and the intellectual virtues. The entrepreneur who embodies those virtues is thus a plausible model of the modern moral hero.

'Virtue' will be used here to designate a characteristic excellence: that which enables its possessor to perform its definitive function well. 'Transparency', said of systems or processes, refers to the extent to which their elements are either directly visible, or are available for inspection and scrutiny. Transparency provides no assurance that organisational objectives will be good. Nor does it necessarily aid in the performance of an organisation's functions. At best, transparency is a quality that facilitates the detection and assessment of virtue.

'Accountability' means that individuals and institutions are answerable for what they do: they must account to others for their conduct and for their use of resources. Accountability typically involves three elements: an 'agent' is accountable to a 'principal' for an 'outcome'. The purpose of accountability is to help ensure that the stipulated outcomes are brought about – irrespective of whether those outcomes are good or bad. At best an adjunct to virtue, accountability mostly comes into play to avert and correct deviation from the stipulated ends.

Accountability cannot be an intrinsic virtue of business, because it is not even a feature of many excellent businesses. Although business must be functionally responsive to whatever may influence its ability to maximise long-term owner value, business's accountability is strictly limited. Aside from their owners, to whom businesses are accountable because they belong to them, businesses are accountable only to those to whom they have specifically rendered themselves accountable, by entering into particular, typically contractual, kinds of relationships. A debt-free sole proprietor who sells services for cash is properly accountable only to himself.

Accountability can even become a vice, when stretched to extremes by the pernicious doctrine of stakeholder obligation. This demands that organisations should be accountable to all their stakeholders, where a stakeholder is everyone and anything that might affect, or be affected by, the operations of the organisation. Organisations that are accountable to all their stakeholders, or even to a few of them, are actually accountable to nobody. It is notoriously difficult to serve even two masters properly, far less an infinite number.

Demands for greater accountability are routinely used to subvert business. They not only undermine agency, but typically substitute counterproductive, incompatible or inconsistent objectives for the definitive business end, and specify inappropriate methods for enforcing accountability.

What businesses *should* be held accountable for is simply achieving the definitive business objective ethically. Business is ethical when it maximises long-term owner value, subject only to respecting those values that are necessary for the activity of business to exist. In order not to be ultimately self-defeating, business must be conducted with honesty, fairness, the absence of physical violence and coercion, and a presumption in favour of legality. Collectively, these constraints embody what may be called 'ordinary decency'. The virtues of business are not transparency and accountability, but the skills necessary for maximising long-term owner value ethically. They include, for example, a shrewd market understanding and efficient operations, and presuppose the substantive excellences that have always been necessary for productive interactions with reality.

Almost all of the 'old' virtues, moral and intellectual, are required for business. Risk-taking, courage in insisting on getting things right, fortitude and endurance, thrift and hard work are all obviously useful in helping to maximise owner value. Honesty and fairness are essential to ethical business; so is reliability, understood as honesty in action. Acknowledging errors, and allowing people opportunities even after they have failed, are both valuable in an activity that necessarily requires taking risks. Finally, the 'prudential virtues' are essential for identifying, achieving, and integrating the many different activities that contribute to maximising long-term owner value.

THE INTELLECTUAL VIRTUES

Roger Kimball identifies what is so often applauded today as 'being critical' and 'questioning' as an heir – often a wayward heir – to the Enlightenment project. That project seeks to make man autonomous by elevating human reason at the expense of the customary and the conventional. Pursuing autonomy tends, in fact, to have a deracinating effect on human experience. It leaves it impoverished and cut off from the traditions and prejudices that gave it content. It further has a perverting effect on intellectual activity by reducing reason to a tool of exposure and subversion.

Being critical tends to be an adjunct of activism, what Lionel Trilling called the 'adversary culture' of the intellectuals. That is to say, its primary orientation is negative, not affirmative. It is part of the armoury of what Paul Ricoeur called the 'hermeneutics of suspicion'. Intellectual life becomes understood as an activity of unmasking and exposure. Its goal is the subversion or transformation of the status quo, intellectually, socially, morally.

So being critical is tantamount to the politicisation of intellectual life. A fundamental tenet is that 'everything is political'. Thus the traditional integrity of that life – as in Matthew Arnold's ideal of culture as the 'disinterested' pursuit of the 'best that has been thought or said' – is systematically rejected.

Being critical tends to the hermetic. Politicised tinkering seems to go with wilful abstruseness and jargon to produce the inanities of contemporary deconstructed academic prose. Being critical, though it exalts reason, is often irrational, as in those 'science studies' which hold that science is a 'socially constructed' enterprise whose end is not truth but a perpetuation of a certain dispensation of political power. Irrational, too, is being critical's glorification of innovation. Being innovative for its own sake leads to the idea that moral progress depends on being daring.

The antidote to being critical involves two moves. First is the more intelligent deployment of criticism, in accordance with the moral and intellectual limits of 'the good for man'. Second is the acknowledgment that the human world is not the abstract world distilled by the operation of reason, but a world of appearances, a world of tangible realities that have myriad historical tendrils and interconnections. Reaffirming that world challenges not only the cult of being critical but also that scientism that glorifies technology and seeks to realise Descartes's dream of rendering man 'the master and possessor of nature'. To challenge criticism is to challenge Kant's ideal of man as an autonomous being, to recognise that man does not 'give the law to himself' – which is what 'autonomous' means – but should acknowledge his submission to the law that transcends him.

ALADDIN'S LAMP

One of the best known bad exchanges is that of Aladdin's lamp. According to at least one pantomime version of the tale, Aladdin has an old, dirty, but magic lamp, which is the source of wealth. To acquire the lamp a man disguises himself as a lamp seller offering 'new lamps for old'. Aladdin's princess wife, not knowing the value of the dirty old lamp, gives it away in exchange for a bright new one. Disaster!

The exchange of a dusty, old but well-proven morality for a bright, new quasi-morality is an even worse exchange. This book shows how good the old one was and how empty the glittering new one is. But there is something worse than the new set of quasi-virtues, and that is the exchange itself. The princess gave away Aladdin's lamp in ignorance of its magic powers. Our society has given up its priceless set of virtues in the face of ample evidence of their goodness and practicality. Indeed, it may be that it is this very goodness with which society is so uneasy. A shiny bauble morality is so much easier to live with.

PART 1

THE OLD VIRTUES

CHAPTER 1

PRUDENCE: THE ORCHESTRATION OF THE VIRTUES

KENNETH MINOGUE

THE AMBIGUITY OF PRUDENCE

Prudence is the virtue that guides us through the dangers that threaten life, fortune and integrity. Many of these dangers come from outside us, but all of them ultimately stem from our own weakness. Prudence is thus a virtue because it overcomes temptations. The problem, however, is that it may teach us to resist not merely dangerous temptations, but also risky virtues. For many acts of courage, generosity and self-sacrifice may endanger life and fortune. The striking thing about prudence, then, is that it alerts us to a civil war within the virtues, and this has been the key to its history. Some moralists have considered it the highest virtue, and others not a virtue at all.

Among the classical Greeks, *phronesis* referred to practical wisdom and, in particular, to the skill of managing cities. 'Prudence' is one possible translation of *phronesis*, which was the practical skill involved in moral and political agency. It was a virtue most at home among statesmen engaged in ruling cities, but even among the Greeks it could refer to the skill of managing a household, or one's own individual life. I find it striking that Aristotle was uneasy about extending the range of prudence from the state to the individual. 'In the popular mind', he wrote, 'prudence is more particularly associated with the self and the individual'; but he went on to suggest that this association was a usurpation of the title of prudence.[1] His point was that the good of the individual can hardly be separated from that of the city. In any case, he adds, it is not easy to know quite what is actually in one's interests. Aristotle was here putting his finger on a fundamental conflict in western politico-moral life: namely, that public duty may pull in one direction, and individual advantage in the other.

Aristotle expressed the classic view of *phronesis* in remarking: 'It is due to virtue that the end we aim at is right, and it is due to

33

prudence that the means we employ to that end are right.'[2] But prudence, here indicating merely the means to an end, easily slips over into becoming the actual object of the action, and that object will, for an individual, be self-preservation. Individual self-preservation may thus conflict with the virtues that demand self-sacrifice, and especially the virtues on which states depend. It was only with the philosophy of Hobbes in the seventeenth century that prudence, as the skill of *individual* self-preservation, became the overriding virtue from which states must rationally be constructed.

In spite of such doubts, the prudent conduct of individual life became a dominant theme of the Hellenistic world, in which a variety of moral sects – ranging from the Cynics to the Sceptics – offered guidance to the perplexed. The Stoics understood human freedom to involve the recognition of necessity, where will had to be aligned with the necessity attributed to nature. Stoic thought emphasised civic duty, but the Epicureans believed that happiness, understood as pleasure, both was and ought to be the basic *telos* of human life. Both of these doctrines were influentially revived when modern Europe came into being, and prudence was especially prominent in the ideas of thinkers who had been influenced by the Epicureans.

By far the most influential school of prudence is to be found in stories and fables. Aesop's fables have never been out of currency in European experience. The grasshopper who sings the whole summer long but has no food for the winter is rebuked by the industrious ant; the lion who spares a mouse teaches us that it is never wise to hold lesser creatures in contempt. The sun teaches the wind that it is gentleness that succeeds in getting the man to remove his coat, rather than the violence of tempests. And the arrogant hare is beaten in the race by the dogged tortoise. In this irresistible bestiary, animals play out our moral postures and pretensions, and suffer triumph or disaster. The punishment of illusion, pretentiousness and impulse is pitiless. A prudent animal never loses its sense of reality. And here was a literary form that never lost its appeal, being notably revived in the twentieth century, for example, by the American humorist James Thurber.

The coming of Christianity introduced a completely new moral world, though it never quite displaced the virtues inherited from Greece and Rome, and the history of European morals and politics is largely a dialogue between these two traditions. Christians believed that humility ought to displace pride, but the meaning of these and other terms changed as the moral atmosphere of Europe responded to the passing generations. Faith might suggest that man should take no thought for the morrow, but only at the margins was the association between prudence and reality ever entirely lost.

Aesop's world was sophisticated and cosmopolitan. It was often concerned with whether we should trust strangers, and how far. But most people, even in Europe, have lived lives of customary stability, in which hard questions of prudence arise seldom, and in which there is usually some moral adviser, such as the priest, on hand if needed. Any movement into a world of strangers required prudence. Laertes, off to study abroad, was in just such a position and needed just the kind of advice that Polonius gave him: don't lend or borrow, stick to old friends, mistrust your own first impulses and dress soberly. This is perfect advice for heedless youth. And above all, perhaps,

> Give thy thoughts no tongue,
> Nor any unproportion'd thought his act.[3]

Age knows that the spontaneity and idealism of youth can lead to personal pain. Aristotle, like Hobbes, describes prudence in terms of the experience of age and maturity. Unlike wisdom, it requires no great equipment of intelligence, but merely the common sense that learns from the bad experiences of oneself and others. The old have learned the risks of lending and borrowing, and of the impulsive passions of friendship.

Earlier times commonly believed that the world was responsive to all manner of strange spirits and powers, so that superstition may be accounted a kind of prudence. The apocryphal Irishman on his death bed, who, when asked to renounce 'the devil and all his works', replied 'this is no time to be making enemies', may have been a little undiscriminating, but he expresses an appropriate form of caution in spiritual matters. Few lives are without trials and tribulations that result from incautious conduct in earlier times. Poor Mr Bennett in *Pride and Prejudice* had married 'imprudently' in youth and had the rest of his life to repent at leisure. Such self-protective virtues stand at the opposite pole from self-sacrifice, saintliness – and from romance. Don Quixote is the very model of a man quite lacking in prudence. No doubt there are many varieties of prudence, and the rather narrow and constricting prudence recommended by Polonius must be distinguished from the 'common sense' we all must use in deploying any virtue. Indeed, reflection on prudence soon reveals that the virtues do not constitute a single coherent system of the moral life, but rather that exhibiting some virtues can be incompatible with acting on others. The man of honour, for example, cannot always be prudent: Hotspur dies, while Falstaff, who regards reputation as a mere bubble, survives. Prudence is a joker in the moral pack, and its business, on occasions, is to trump its fellow virtues.

VIRTUE AND ITS DEPARTMENTS

The core meaning of virtue is excellence, and moral virtue is moral excellence. What we admire is a human being choosing to be courageous, generous, candid, and so on, in circumstances where many people would be tempted to behave badly. All the virtues are excellences, but can we say that a person who exhibits all the virtues is a moral paragon, a perfect person? Such a paragon would hardly be human, but beyond the common-sense fact that total virtue is not possible for imperfect human beings, there is an interesting logical problem: the fact that the virtues cannot add up to a single coherent excellence because they contain internal contradictions. Different occupations – such as those of doctor or priest – have their own specific excellences, and they will sometimes conflict with other virtues. How, amidst all this conflict, can we find the good itself, that quality in terms of which all virtues are a form of moral excellence?

The hope of finding some transcending good has always been the moral version of the philosopher's stone, but in the modern state different 'moralities' are in conflict, and our admiration for one virtue will often be at odds with our admiration for another. Gandhi, Nelson Mandela, Mother Teresa and others will be revered by many as saints, but there will be no lack of critics to advance the moral case that they had feet of clay. That which makes the courageous warrior admirable may well be despised by the saintly and the peace loving. The responsibilities of the statesman may, at times, require (as Machiavelli[4] insisted) vice rather than virtue; indeed, sometimes in politics vice may actually be virtue. The confidentiality of the professional may conflict with the safety of the state. The richness, and also the incoherence of our moral admirations is a legacy of the many historical experiences that have left a mark on the way we live now. The result, however, is that no concrete decision can logically follow merely from a desire to do the right thing.

We may reformulate the problem by observing that virtues and vices are the names of abstract qualities, which means that understanding their virtuous character depends significantly on the context in which they occur. There are times when a misapplied virtue may cause more harm than good. To every virtue, in fact, there corresponds a vice that results from its foolish implementation. The generous man should not become a spendthrift, the courageous man rash; the teller of truth ought not become a 'candid friend', a tactless character. On the wall of Southwark Cathedral in London may be found a commendation for a chaplain who was 'pious without ostentation' and 'zealous with discretion'. Every structure of virtues, then, needs some higher-level guidance about how to balance our conduct. This guidance may function in two logically distinct ways, one intellectual, the other practical.

Philosophically, the virtues will be found to reveal some underlying form of intellectual organisation that might explain their virtuous character. Aristotle, for example, thought that moderation was not only a virtue in itself, but also in a sense the 'orchestrator' or 'architectonic' of all the virtues.[5] Courage, although no doubt extreme on the virtue–vice dimension, was, in terms of content, a mean between cowardice and rashness. In a different kind of way, justice appears in the *Republic* as that which orchestrates the other virtues, and is in itself a reflection of the idea of good. In classical republics, a kind of patriotism was the basic virtue, just as the solidarity of comradeship was, notionally, in communist societies. The basic Christian 'architectonic' is, one might suggest, humility (with its correlate of gratitude) while Hobbes might be interpreted as regarding logical consistency or coherence as what must follow in social and political life from the basic individual imperative to avoid violent and unexpected death. Kant also sought to understand the structure of morality in terms of logical consistency.

The second way in which the virtues must be 'orchestrated' is not philosophical but practical. To act virtuously requires not merely that one must have the quality of virtue, but that one must respond with 'common sense' to the concrete situation involved. The moral life is notoriously beset with ambivalence, as proverbial wisdom makes clear: many hands make light work, but too many cooks spoil the broth; a stitch in time saves nine, but you ought not to cross your bridges until you come to them. And so on. To some extent, the philosophical formulations may, with a different meaning, function as practical aids. To be moderate in one's virtues is sensible advice, but a general recommendation to moderation is vacuous. Hence the practical 'orchestration' of the virtues is essentially different from the philosophical. For us, the basic way in which we invoke prudence is by saying something like: 'use your common sense'. In this sense, prudence is, as it were, a virtue of virtues.

Prudence, as the conductor of the music with which the virtues enrich our lives, is taught by experience. The young are passionate idealists, and passionate idealism is the very thing against which experience warns us. It is only the old who habitually put discretion before valour. The young are also impatient, and impatience is among the strongest inducements to folly. We have seen that those in specific occupations need to temper their virtuous acts with a strong dose of prudence. To cite Machiavelli again, generosity is certainly admirable, but not if it depends upon tyrannical exaction of money from a population that will become resentful. The parent must sometimes be cruel in order to be kind. It is in such circumstances as these that prudence may lead us to talk in such a way as to suggest an actual reversal of the virtues, turning white into black. When the bureaucrat Sir Humphrey in the television series *Yes, Minister* comments about a policy: 'very courageous, Minister', he means 'don't touch it with a bargepole'.

That prudence increases with age might tempt us into extrapolation: the older we get, the wiser we get. There are, however, problems with such extrapolation, summed up as 'there's no fool like an old fool'. In the end, the rational faculties decline, and the old may discover new ways in which to be foolish. Even if this were not the case, the Karel Capek play (which later became a Janacek opera) *The Makropoulos Case* suggests that, in a human life that stretches much beyond the ordinary span, the accumulation of experience merely deranges our sense of reality.

Prudence is limited, then, in the sense that no human condition can be free from folly. Another limitation on the range of prudence emerges from changes in the way we now understand the moral life. These changes are revealed in the move we make from talk of virtues to talk of values. A virtue is a quality of human conduct widely recognised as admirable, and therefore considered to be objectively distinguished from a mere preference. Much current thought about both religion and morality rejects the idea of living in terms of a schedule of inherited virtues. We should, instead, make our own reasoned preferences (*alias* values) in navigating through life. The objectivity of long-admired virtues must give way to the subjectivity of individual judgements, valuations universalised abstractly as 'values'. It is considered that being democratic, being educated, being rational means we all have not only the right, but also the capacity to live our individual lives free from outside direction. This does not quite mean that we have achieved the moral autonomy Kant so admired; in practice, the individualist vocabulary conceals a considerable sensitivity to what governments think acceptable and unacceptable. Another source of moral judgements will be different *ethical* judgements about political policy. In a widespread politicisation of the moral life, a person's concerns about consumption of tobacco, the fate of the environment, the arms trade and human rights will often be regarded as signs of moral capacity that are more important than keeping promises, saving thriftily, and exhibiting temperance and fortitude. Certain kinds of politico-moral enthusiasm, such as animal rights and anti-abortionism, are even taken as a licence for indulging in such vices as deceit and intimidation.

Prudence as an orchestrator of the virtues, then, depends on the moral agent having the common sense to recognise what is *appropriate* in the circumstances. 'Appropriate' here indicates an individual awareness of what the situation requires, and that will vary from person to person. One cannot discuss the moral life without recognising this element of tact, indeed one might almost say 'the tactile', necessary in its implementation.

PRUDENCE AND UTILITARIANISM

In seeing prudence as an orchestrator of virtues, the modern world certainly has not forgotten its role in avoiding vices. Impulse, indulgence in appetites, thoughtless greed, showing off to impress others by taking foolish risks – these things exemplify human vices typically found in the young. Must youth forever be a hostage to impulsive follies? Might there not be some system that could save us from such folly?

This problem led prudence, in one of its roles, to migrate into whole new fields of understanding, such as probability theory, economics and public choice. Negatively, prudence is the avoidance of risk, and to achieve that we needed a more precise way of calculating risk. New statistical inquiries taught human beings how to calculate uncertainty, and the prudential man turned into economic man, seeking to 'optimise' the use of his resources, subject to the constraints of scarcity and of rules.

These developments again reveal prudence to be a virtue found at the junction of two different 'philosophies' of life. The first is that we ought to act morally and exhibit virtue in our lives, often by obeying the commands of God. The second 'philosophy' is that the whole point of life is to enjoy happiness, and achieving happiness is an art that can be theorised. In an abstract way, economics and allied disciplines attempt just that, but in the late eighteenth century Jeremy Bentham not only theorised this art as the doctrine we now call 'utilitarianism', but also believed that, in doing so, he was expounding the rationality of the moral life. The distinction between these aspects of prudence – as an *art de vivre* on the one hand, and as the secret of morality on the other – has been one of the main battlefields of moral philosophy ever since.

The most obvious way of rationalising life so as to maximise happiness is to specify the types of action that lead to happiness in the long run. A negative formulation would suggest merely that we seek ways of avoiding pain. Adam Smith attributed this idea to Epicurus and construed it as the theory that even moral value is rational only on account of its tendency to promote pleasure. In actually subordinating virtue to pleasure, rather than identifying the moral with the hedonic, Epicurus grasped the fundamental theoretical nettle that was later to lead many to reject utilitarianism as a moral theory. Jeremy Bentham responded to these ideas by formulating nothing less than a scientific system of ethics. It is true of Bentham, and even more of his successor John Stuart Mill, that utilitarianism as a supposed clarification of our moral confusions, tends to become an alternative to morality itself. This may seem merely an academic point, but its true significance was to become clear as prudence, in later generations, came to be collectivised as a matter of public, rather than individual, policy.

Benthamite utilitarianism is prudence turned into a system of life, and its ambitious claim was to regulate both morality and politics. Bentham argued that only two sorts of people could disagree with utilitarianism. One sort consisted of ascetics (mostly religious) who, by a perverse induction from the fact that pain sometimes follows pleasure, advocated the painful merely because it was painful. The second sort are the dogmatists who set up some other basis of approval, such as the law of nature, the fitness of things, the law of reason and other terms which Bentham thought merely concealed arbitrary and capricious preferences.[6]

This ambitious piece of intellectual insouciance has been the main cause of the trench warfare in moral philosophy from Bentham's day to ours. Bentham shared the eighteenth-century ambition to replace mere preference with science, and he thought he was doing so in setting up a schema by which pleasure and pain could be analysed prior to action. Bentham's rational utilitarian estimated in advance the likely consequences of his act by using seven dimensions of pleasure and pain. Pleasures and pains may vary in intensity, duration, certainty or uncertainty, propinquity or remoteness from the act, fecundity, purity, and extent (the number of persons affected by it).[7] This last dimension – extent – is an attempt to bridge the gap between the psychological egoist concerned only with his own pleasure, and the moral utilitarian concerned with the greatest happiness of the greatest number.

Utilitarianism was thus a rational system to be applied in the actual conduct of private and public life, and it emerged from the same world as the science of economics, whose ideas of opportunity cost, externalities and marginality have purported to throw much light on the art of happiness ever since the eighteenth century. Prudence in this period became the basic bourgeois virtue. Any system based on happiness (as utilitarianism was) seemed to meet the criterion for a satisfactory moral theory current at that time: namely, that morality should be rationally free standing, rather than dependent on an external religious sanction. And with the spread of commercial society, prudence was the basic virtue by which self-interest, in the widest sense, might be exercised. But in western states, the universal currency of any single moral system is a rarity. Prudence soon came to seem old and boring by comparison with the patriotic passions of some French revolutionaries, or the pursuit of glory generated by the career of Napoleon. Among romantics, the moral shaded into the aesthetic: style was the thing. Soon to emerge was the solidarism of socialist movements. The fathers may have been prudent, but the sons were romantics in revolt.

In any case, some moral philosophers argued that, while utilitarianism might well be a science of prudence, it had nothing to do with morality because conceptually it was based upon a mistake. Prudence was concerned with interests, and while their pursuit was no doubt often legitimate, it did not and could not constitute morality. It may indeed be true that pleasure is good, but to argue, as some philosophers had, that pleasure is *the* good was to commit what G. E. Moore called 'the naturalistic fallacy'.[8] Again, for Kant, morality is a categorical imperative, and the only imperative that could possibly be involved in pursuing my interests, or any other set of interests, would be hypothetical. Individual self-preservation is not an absolute moral imperative. Honesty may be the best policy, but that is certainly not what makes it a virtue. The answer to the (slightly idiotic) question 'Why should I be moral?' must be distinguished from the answer to the question 'How can I be happy?' Certainly among those of a rather puritan disposition, there is an instinctive feeling that virtue must hurt. Life is earnest, and being good cannot just be a clever way of avoiding unhappiness.

Bentham's formularisation of prudence is not, of course, made valueless merely because it cannot solve problems that have so far resisted all philosophers. His idea of the fecundity of pleasures – their propensity to go on causing pleasure repeatedly – is a valuable observation on conduct. It suggests a strong argument for basing education on authority, rather than on any supposed contemporary relevance. The child who learns a scientific principle or a poem, an episode in history or a manner of solving problems acquires something that will later be a recurring source of pleasure, and thus of value. The child who merely learns what has been thought to be relevant to the needs of his time becomes a prisoner of that epoch.

THE MODERN FATE OF PRUDENCE

Prudence might be construed as the rational pursuit of interests, but interests clash, and the question of *whose* interests becomes unavoidable. In particular, what individuals want may clash with what may plausibly be presented as the public interest. Utilitarians affirm the 'greatest happiness' principle as the abstract solution to this problem, but in practice this criterion merely leaves disputes up in the air. In any case, moral agents cannot know the future, and their judgement of consequences will often be wrong – likely to be distorted by prejudice and self-partiality. The really difficult thing to decide is how much pain for how many people might be justified for the happiness of many others. Philosophically, utilitarianism has often been rejected because of what we might call the Dostoevsky image: imagine that the happiness of the human race could be guaranteed forever at the cost of 'the torture of one little speck of creation'.[9] This is the passage that leads in to the famous story of the Grand Inquisitor, and it is suffused with a moral and religious feeling that belongs in a very different part of the moral forest from anything utilitarians are likely to inhabit. Utilitarianism remains as an interesting formulation of one of the ways in which we discuss the prudence of public policies, but it cannot be taken seriously as a foundation of moral principle.

We may, however, leave these large questions to one side, because the transformation of prudence in modern times has resulted from a quite different set of considerations. We may identify these as, first, technological changes that have given individuals much greater powers of controlling their own lives; secondly, the complexity of modern industrial societies; and thirdly, the idea that where their subjects were deficient in prudence, the state ought to supply what was needed.

Technological change has certainly transformed our subjection to many of the accidents of folly and fortune. The virtues of sexual temperance in the past were prudent reminders of the risks of sexual disease and of the consequences of unintended pregnancy. Today we have condoms, the pill and antibiotics, not to mention a relaxed social system and the equally relaxing conditions of widespread affluence. Sex as procreative, and as expressive, has in many cases become sex as recreational. Again, in earlier times, people worried about getting fatter had no option but to eat less and take more exercise. Modern scientists, however, have been working on a pill that inhibits digestion without the need for the virtue of temperance. Indeed, a little clever surgery can work wonders, both with unwanted flesh and digestive capacity. Modern warfare no longer requires quite the element of courage that once was necessary. When the Maxim gun was sold in the late nineteenth century, it was marketed as 'a labour saving device for modern warfare'. Increasing availability of similar labour-saving devices will soon make it hard to distinguish a push-button computer game of war from the real thing. One of the central drivers of western civilisation is the replacement of virtue by convenient technology.

Secondly, many elements of risk have now been taken out of the hands of individuals by public authority, because modern societies have become so complex (runs the argument) that individuals no longer have either the information or the resources to respond prudently. Public health is a notable example. Public hygiene depends on the public authority for the provision of clean water and proper waste disposal. Individuals lack the necessary information, and the resources of the authority are needed both for coordination and for the compulsion necessary to deal with the problem of free riders. The state has thus taken this problem into its own hands. Public solutions are seldom perfect, of course, because states, no less than individuals or private groups, can get these things wrong. In other words, the preference for a public over private judgement must itself be a prudential judgement. Again, it is at least convenient in large cities to have a public health authority inspecting and certifying the hygiene of restaurants. Reputation would, no doubt, in the long run sift the clean from the dirty, but regulation has a certain convenient reliability, not to say immediacy, and we have come to rely on it. It is a basic principle of civil life that law and order are most efficiently run by the state: public provision of law and order can be more efficient than the uncertainties of self-defence. School standards are another case where people would often lack the judgement necessary to ensure a suitable education for their children. Here again, however, and no doubt even more insistently than with public health, the problem arises: would you buy an educational system from the people who run education in liberal democracies today? Almost certainly not – if you were prudent. And some millions of people in western countries have come to just that conclusion: they have decided to educate their own children. It is difficult to escape the thought that modish inspectorates, pedagogic fashions and, above all, government social engineering are unavoidable whenever governments are let anywhere near education. The only saving grace of national educational systems is the right to buy one's way out.

The state has, in the last two centuries, taken over the entire domain of what economists these days call 'public goods'. The argument is that prudent public provision is more efficient than private provision could usually be. But at this point, the drive towards the nationalisation of prudence moves up a gear. The basic argument for public provision is that it is more efficient. The new argument claims that it is also more equitable in a wider sense. Such a claim to superior equity depends on the doctrine that human beings cannot live fulfilled lives without a supply of material and cultural goods, and that since capitalism cannot get these goods to the poor in adequate quantities, the state must do so. The assumption is, as with other public goods being supplied, that it is circumstances that impede universal provision. In some cases circumstances may be an issue, but in many others the crucial factor is a serious lack of prudence in many people. It is the problem of widespread prudence-deficiency to which states have been advancing a public policy solution. Such is the generation of the modern welfare state. Here the issue is not the baffling complexity of the problem to be solved, but the fact that some people are not very good at looking after themselves.

It cannot be called prudent, for example, to quarrel with one's family, given that in hard times one is likely to need their support. It is imprudent not to save against the possibility that one may have to pay for medical treatment, or the danger that one may be unemployed for some stretch of time. Getting into hopeless debt is highly imprudent, as is contracting an addiction to drugs, becoming pregnant when unmarried in one's teens, or marrying some evident brute on the basis of fleeting sexual attraction. Everyone needs provision in old age, and any prudent person would make appropriate moves long before his or her strength began to ebb. Having children can be an expensive responsibility if money has to be found to pay for educating them.

Few people in the past grew to maturity without being constantly alerted to the dangers of such evident forms of folly. Still, some people did behave in these imprudent ways, and a significant slice of what was sometimes called the 'undeserving poor' was entirely constituted of individuals behaving in this way. But they had votes, and moral sentiments have developed to the effect that the state, as protector of its subjects, ought to protect them not only from criminality and foreign invasion, but also from the consequences of their own folly. This argument was all the more convincing in that, in many cases, these consequences might follow less from evident incapacity than from simple lack of the resources. In any case, might not a constitutional incapacity to behave sensibly be construed as a kind of metabolic disorder? The result was a welfare state providing a 'safety net' to save people from many of the scrapes they got themselves into. It is, however, a standard maxim of prudence that 'truth comes by blows'. It follows logically, and it has in fact followed in practice, that the state's softening of fate's blows will increase the supply of imprudence. We thus find ourselves in a vicious circle of ever expanding prudence-deficiency, with political consequences that are important, but too extensive to be discussed here.

But we have not yet quite exhausted the ways in which prudence has been rendered – up to a point – redundant in modern life. In sketching the nationalisation of prudence, we have discussed the major issue of prudence-deficiency, but we need to remember that prudence had, from the eighteenth century onwards, come to be associated with the self-interest of the bourgeoisie. In a hostile environment, might not bourgeois prudence come to be itself regarded as a vice? Could it be that some people are excessively prudent? Might it not be the case that their greater affluence results from an antisocial concern with their own welfare to the exclusion of that of others? The conclusion might be drawn that the unnatural inequality of prudence between individuals had itself led to the social injustices of modern society. In that case, democratic governments might, in a variety of areas, see it as their duty to correct this inequality by adopting policies of redistribution in order to solve prudence-deficiency. Adapting St Augustine somewhat, we may represent the command of modern states to their peoples as: 'Give us prudence and (perhaps) chastity, but not too much.'

The problem is certainly one that agitates modern European states, for they have also been responding to the problem by transferring responsibility from the prudence-deficient to more robust third parties assumed to be more accountable. Western societies have hitherto been based on the principle of personal responsibility. That is exactly what has distinguished them from oriental despotism, in which collective disciplines are invoked. In such regimes, a whole village will suffer for the alleged crimes of an individual malefactor. This administratively convenient, though morally disreputable, practice has been spreading among us as a solution to prudence-deficiency. If the problem is one of sexual harassment among employees, for example, it may be solved by imposing penalties on employers for failing to sustain a 'safe environment'. If children play truant, the parents can be jailed, though the same parents are not permitted to discipline their children except in ways approved by the state. Again, if the patrons of hotels (or even guests at private dinner parties) lose prudent control of themselves and get drunk, the consequences can land on the head of the publican or host. Third parties are thus conscripted by the state into the business of civil enforcement.

The state has thus become a large player in the game of prudence, and it can justify its expansion by pointing to the increasing complexity of modern societies. We live, then, in a very prudent society, even if much of this prudence is done for us. Vicarious prudence doesn't, of course, come cheap, and it has led to government control of many areas (such as culture, and universities) where prudence is not involved. About 50 per cent of the entire annual wealth of most liberal democracies is spent by the government. And the rather paradoxical belief driving this remarkable development is that governments are more prudent than the people who elect them.

CAN PRUDENCE SURVIVE THE TWENTY-FIRST CENTURY?

What remains, then, of the virtue of prudence? All those government agencies are so good to us, and spread their benefits so widely, that it might be thought that the modern state had quite abolished any need for prudence. Happiness is now an explicit object of government policies. All we need do is obey the regulations and follow guidelines, and folly will be banished from our lives. But the entire abolition of prudence would require that the burden of individual self-consciousness, that famous fall in the Garden of Eden when we realised that we needed a fig leaf, should at last be taken from us. Some radical utopians such as Plato have indeed dreamed of just this. Poor Winston Smith in Orwell's *1984* lived in a society of this kind, and it was based on the idea that such self-consciousness was the root of all evil. Both money and private property were thought, rightly, to flow from it. But it is hard to imagine a human being lacking this interesting comparative dimension of consciousness. The philosopher Hobbes, in *Leviathan*, argued that the greatest pleasure for human beings was a feeling of superiority, and while the state can try to abolish the prudence that caters to this drive, it cannot abolish the propensity to think of personal advantage. Prudence no doubt will have to change its character, but being a chameleon among the virtues, it will do just that.

1 Aristotle, *Nicomachean Ethics*, Book VI, Chapter 8. I have used the Penguin translation by J. A. K. Thomson (Harmondsworth: Penguin Books, 1953), pp. 181–82.
2 *ibid.*, p.188.
3 William Shakespeare, *Hamlet*, Act I, Scene 3.
4 Niccolo Machiavelli, *The Prince*, Chapter XV.
5 Aristotle, *Nicomachean Ethics*, Book II, Chapter 6.
6 Jeremy Bentham, *An Introduction to the Principles of Morals and Legislation* (1823), ed. Wilfrid Harrison (Oxford: Basil Blackwell, 1948), Chapter II.
7 *ibid.*, Chapter IV, p. 152.
8 G. E. Moore, *Principia Ethica* (Cambridge: Cambridge University Press, 1903, 1962), p. 10ff.
9 Fyodor Dostoevsky, *The Karamazov Brothers*, trans. Ignat Avsey (Oxford: Oxford University Press, 1994), Part Two, Book Five, Section 4, p. 308.

CHAPTER 2

COURAGE: A CLASSICAL VIRTUE

DAVID WOMERSLEY

IS A COURAGEOUS ACTION ITS OWN END?

One of the most celebrated aphorisms relating to courage comes in the middle of the second poem in the third book of Horace's odes:

> dulce et decorum est pro patria mori.[1]

Today most of those who encounter this Horatian sentiment probably do so because it is quoted at the end of Wilfred Owen's 'Dulce et Decorum Est', where it is stigmatised as an 'old Lie'. Horace's line certainly enshrines a challenging idea, and the challenge it poses is brought out if we recall that, in some manuscripts, the reading is 'dulci', not 'dulce'. It is a variant that shifts the meaning towards the commonplace, since, were we to adopt 'dulci' instead of 'dulce', the line would now mean: 'It is honourable to die for one's sweet homeland.' The principle of *lectio difficilior* encourages us to prefer 'dulce' to 'dulci', but at the cost of shifting the idea expressed in this line towards the borders of paradox. One can easily see that to die 'pro patria' is 'decorum', but to say that it is also 'dulce' – 'sweet' – is to complicate the motivation of the courageous act, since to qualify it as 'sweet' implies that a courageous act of self-sacrifice is intrinsically pleasurable, and thus is, to some extent, its own end. Yet if such an action is indeed autotelic, rather than instrumental or performed on behalf of some other person or entity (in this Horatian case, the homeland), why should we admire it? Its consequences may be socially useful, but if there is a strong element of self-gratification in a courageous action, why should it command our respect?

However, considered under the rubric of psychology, Horace's pairing of 'dulce' with 'decorum' also rescues the courageous act from an internal contradiction which the variant 'dulci' would heighten. Without the inducement of an intrinsic sweetness, why would people perform acts of courageous self-sacrifice 'pro patria', when the consequences of the act would be to prevent them from participating in the ultimate good for which they were prepared to die (namely, the life of the 'patria')? Stripped of sweetness, courage could find expression only in acts of the purest altruism. But when sweetness is added – when the courageous act is rendered intrinsically satisfying – then the altruism necessary to perform a courageous action drops to a more plausible level. So Horace's doublet of 'dulce et decorum' both brings out the ethical complexity of an act of courage and makes plausible its psychology. In so doing, it introduces us quickly to the complicated questions of end and motivation, which are central to a consideration of the virtue of courage. Why do people perform acts of extraordinary courage? What ends do they have in view? What satisfactions do they derive from them? Exploring these issues will lead us towards some reflections on the place of courage in the family of human virtues, and to some conclusions concerning its relation to the social ends that we seem increasingly to regard as the proper objects to be served by all actions we call virtuous.

WHAT DO EXAMPLES OF COURAGE TELL US?

We should begin with a concrete example. Gerard Norton won the Victoria Cross in August 1944 for his gallantry in attacking German forces dug in on Monte Gridolfo, one of the key positions in Field-Marshal Kesselring's defensive 'Gothic Line' running across the thigh of the Italian peninsula. Norton's obituary in *The Times* (2 November 2004) contained the following account of his actions.

> The leading platoon of Norton's company was pinned down by flanking fire almost as soon as it had crossed the start line. Entirely on his own initiative and with complete disregard for his personal safety, Norton began to attack the enemy strongpoints in turn. He silenced the first with a grenade. Then, alone and armed with his Thompson sub-machinegun, he took on the crew of a second strongpoint from which the enemy were holding up the advance with their Spandaus. A ten-minute firefight ensued, at the end of which Norton had killed all but a handful of the enemy who surrendered.

> Bringing his platoon forward to maintain the forward momentum, Norton cleared the cellar and upper rooms of a fortified house and took several more prisoners. Finally, although weak from loss of blood due to a head wound that

had severed a vein, he led his platoon up the valley to capture
the remaining enemy positions on his company objective. He
was also wounded in the thigh during the course of the action.

There can be no question but that, on this day in northern Italy,
Gerard Norton showed extraordinary courage (in that he acted in
defiance of an immediate and life-threatening danger). He also
exhibited a number of other related but distinguishable virtues, such
as resolve, tenacity and indomitableness. It is interesting, however,
to compare the narrative of his actions with the language and premises of his citation for the award of the Victoria Cross:

> Throughout the attack Lieutenant Norton displayed matchless
> courage, outstanding initiative and inspiring leadership. By his
> supreme gallantry, fearless example and determined aggression
> he assured the successful breach of the Gothic Line at this point.

While it is undeniable that Norton's valour had the effect of
contributing to 'the successful breach of the Gothic Line at this
point', is it plausible to suggest (as does the ambiguity of the word
'assured', spanning as it does the very different meanings of 'inten-
tionally caused' and 'unintentionally brought about') that the successful breach of the Gothic Line was uppermost in Norton's mind
when he attacked the German positions? Surely his motives and
intentions were much more local and tactical than this: he wanted to
silence that machine-gun post, to clear that house. It is hard to imagine an objective as general, remote and strategic as the breaching of
the Gothic Line impelling a man to do what Norton did. And from
this we might make two inferences. First, that acts of courage tend
to be, at least in part, blind acts, performed with a view to achieving
very local objectives, and undertaken with a disregard for, perhaps
even at times in defiance of, prudential and rational calculations of
the greater good, even though it may eventually transpire that outcomes of common or general benefit (such as the breaching of the
Gothic Line) are secured as a result of courageous action. Secondly,
that when society honours acts of courage, it tends to tame them,
and conscript them to its own more general and less wild purposes.
In this respect, citations for the award of decorations for gallantry
are ostensibly acts of homage towards courageous men and women,
but are more subtly also acts of redescription, in which socially
acceptable motives are imputed to actions that, in the performance,
were fuelled by a desire to secure quite different, and much more
immediate, goals.

The career of another holder of the Victoria Cross, the Dane Anders Lassen, illustrates these points with great vividness.[2] Lassen had been raised in conditions of almost complete freedom, bordering on neglect, on his family's estate in South Sealand. Running wild in the woods and fields, Lassen acquired extraordinary skills in fieldcraft, and in the use of primitive weapons such as knives and the bow and arrow. When the Germans invaded his native Denmark, Lassen became possessed by a desire to kill as many of the aggressors as possible. As a man who served with Lassen recalled:

> Once he'd got going, he'd kill anyone. He was frightening in that way – and his view of Germans was even more personal than ours, because his country was occupied. I think he was driven by the occupation, although it's difficult to assess if the killing instinct used the war as an excuse, or whether it sprang from genuine hatred of the enemy. But I do know that if he had the opportunity, he'd kill someone with a knife rather than shoot.[3]

Volunteering to serve, he was conscripted into the Special Boat Service, and rapidly distinguished himself in a series of brilliantly effective operations for audacity, ruthlessness and tactical presence of mind. Briefly hospitalised with hepatitis, Lassen was described as follows by the man in the next bed, a padre with the Parachute Regiment:

> He was very tense, tightly coiled, a wild young boy. Very often, in my impression, he was not aware of all that he was doing. Without denigrating the bravery, I think he was one of those people who act without foreseeing the consequences. Something has to be done, so they go and do it regardless of their own safety.[4]

Driven by private, perhaps obscure and even unattractive, compulsions, and giving the impression of being still childlike or pre-adult (and hence incompletely socialised), Lassen exhibits the antipathy that exists at one level between the values which, in times of peace, we find most socially useful, and the characteristics which, in times of danger or conflict, are the most effective. Chief among those characteristics is possession of the virtue of courage. It is for this reason that so few men of the most conspicuous courage have enjoyed prominent peacetime careers. Lassen was killed on his last mission, so how he would have negotiated the transition to a world of peace must remain a matter of speculation. But, to judge from his unpredictable temper and impatience with conventional structures of command, the omens were unpropitious. After the war Gerard Norton led a life of quiet obscurity as a tobacco farmer in Zimbabwe. As Peter de la Billière writes of Charles Upham (the only combatant holder of the Victoria Cross and Bar):

> He was typical of many great wartime soldiers in that he would have had difficulty fitting into the bureaucratic, career-driven routine of peacetime military service: he was a wartime soldier, nothing more and nothing less.[5]

CORIOLANUS AS AN ANATOMY OF COURAGE

Shakespeare's most sustained exploration of the nature of courage, and of the difficult relation between those who possess it and the societies in which they find themselves, is *Coriolanus*. The hero of the play, Caius Martius (who receives the additional name of 'Coriolanus' as a result of his prowess at the siege of the enemy city of Corioles), is the foremost soldier of the infant Roman republic. His childhood was passed in the pursuit of war, as his mother Volumnia tells Caius's wife, Virgilia:

> When yet he was but tender-bodied, and the only son of my womb; when youth with comeliness plucked all gaze his way; when, for a day of king's entreaties, a mother should not sell him an hour from her beholding; I, considering how honour would become such a person – that it was no better than picture-like to hang by th' wall, if renown made it not stir – was pleased to let him seek danger where he was like to find fame. To a cruel war I sent him, from whence he returned, his brows bound with oak. I tell thee daughter, I sprang not more in joy at first hearing he was a man-child, than now in first seeing he had proved himself a man.[6]

Later the senator Cominius recalls the martial exploits of the infant prodigy:

> At sixteen years,
> When Tarquin made a head for Rome, he fought
> Beyond the mark of others; our then dictator,
> Whom with all praise I point at, saw him fight,
> When with his Amazonian chin he drove
> The bristled lips before him; he bestrid

An o'erpressed Roman, and i' th' consul's view
Slew three opposers; Tarquin's self he met,
And struck him on his knee. In that day's feats,
When he might act the woman in the scene,
He prov'd best man i' th' field, and for his meed
Was brow-bound with the oak.[7]

In one sense, the dedication of his childhood to the pursuits of war goes some way towards explaining Caius Martius's extraordinary valour in battle. At the siege of Corioles the Romans are beaten back to their trenches, and Caius Martius, almost incoherent with rage, abuses his troops unstintingly:

All the contagion of the south light on you,
You shames of Rome! You herd of – boils and plagues
Plaster you o'er, that you may be abhorr'd
Farther than seen, and one infect another
Against the wind a mile![8]

He drives them back to the walls, but is himself trapped within the gates of the city while his more prudent troops, shunning the danger, mock his ardour, saying: 'Foolhardiness! Not I.'[9] Re-emerging covered in blood, he inspires a rally among the Romans and they begin to gain the advantage. The ordinary soldiers are distracted by opportunities for looting, but Caius Martius – who claims to be invigorated rather than weakened by his wounds, for 'the blood I drop is rather physical | Than dangerous to me'[10] – returns to the fray and makes a speech to inspire his soldiers to accompany him. Invited by Cominius to pick his men, Caius Martius replies in language which, in its simplicity, illustrates the power of courage to encourage others:

Those are they
That most are willing. If any such be here –
As it were sin to doubt – that love this painting
Wherein you see me smear'd; if any fear
Lesser his person than an ill report;
If any think brave death outweighs bad life,
And that his country's dearer than himself;
Let him alone, or so many so minded,
Wave thus, to express his disposition,
And follow Martius.[11]

To which the soldiers respond in unison: 'O me alone! Make you a sword of me!'[12]

I have traced the course of Caius Martius's conduct at the siege of Corioles in some detail because it forms such a sharp contrast with both his own behaviour, and the behaviour of others towards him, which we encounter in the rest of the play. On returning to Rome, Caius Martius is nominated Consul by the Senate, and in order to take up the office must stand in the forum and solicit the support of the plebeians. Caius Martius asks to be excused this part of the ceremony:

> I do beseech you,
> Let me o'erleap that custom; for I cannot
> Put on the gown, stand naked, and entreat them
> For my wounds' sake, to give their suffrage. Please you
> That I may pass this doing.[13]

However, the tribunes insist that Caius Martius fulfil the custom of soliciting the support of the plebeians. He does so under protest, and, although he gains the votes of the plebeians, they are puzzled by his clipped and strained manner of addressing them. For his part, Caius Martius is impatient and resentful of the whole process, as he reveals in a short soliloquy mid-way through his ordeal, when he is temporarily alone on stage:

> Better it is to die, better to starve,
> Than crave the hire which first we do deserve.
> Why in this wolvish toge should I stand here,
> To beg of Hob and Dick that does appear,
> Their needless vouches? Custom calls me to't.
> What custom wills, in all things should we do't,
> The dust on antique time would lie unswept
> And mountainous error be too highly heap'd
> For truth to o'erpeer. Rather than fool it so,
> Let the high office and the honour go
> To one that would do thus. I am half through,
> The one part suffer'd, the other will I do.[14]

His patience, however, is unavailing. Incited by the tribunes, the plebeians revoke their election. In the Senate house, the tribunes provoke Caius Martius to unguarded and intemperate expressions of his contempt for the common people, and the meeting breaks up in chaos and fighting. Addressing the people once again, and accused by the tribunes of aiming at grasping 'a power tyrannical', Caius Martius explodes in rage and condemns the plebeians to the 'fires i'th'lowest hell'. In recognition of his services to the state, the tribunes do not in Caius Martius's case call for the customary punishment of execution by being thrown from the Tarpeian rock, but satisfy themselves instead with perpetual banishment, to which Caius Martius tellingly responds: 'I banish you!'[15]

As Cominius says, employing a common metaphor for political order, this *débâcle* has brought the state to the point of dissolution:

> That is the way to lay the city flat,
> To bring the roof to the foundation,
> And bury all which yet distinctly ranges
> In heaps and piles of ruin.[16]

As for Caius Martius, the shrewd senator Menenius describes his character in terms that suggest how his pre-eminence in war and his incompetence in peace are the common but discrepant fruit of a shared disposition:

> His nature is too noble for the world:
> He would not flatter Neptune for his trident,
> Or Jove for's power to thunder. His heart's his mouth:
> What his breast forges, that his tongue must vent;
> And, being angry, does forget that ever
> He heard the name of death.[17]

While this may be psychologically persuasive, it surely also makes more provoking the contrast between Caius Martius's effectiveness in battle and his political ineptitude. How can it be that, at the siege of Corioles, Caius Martius can so enthral the common soldiers that they ask him to make them his instrument ('O me alone! Make you a sword of me!'), yet be unable to solicit the citizens for their support? Volumnia cannot understand why an expert in the stratagems of war should recoil from what to her seem the kindred and similar ruses of politics:

> I have heard you say,
> Honour and policy, like unsever'd friends,
> I'th'war do grow together: grant that, and tell me,
> In peace, what each of them by th'other lose
> That they combine not there…
> If it be honour in your wars to seem

The same you are not, which, for your best ends
You adopt your policy, how is it less or worse
That it shall hold companionship in peace
With honour, as in war, since that to both
It stands in like request?[18]

But this is the perspective of the outsider, who has no personal experience of courageous action. To the man of courage, such as Caius Martius, there seems to be a world of difference between the deceptions of war and the guile of politics, to the point where Caius Martius seems to lack even the most basic political virtue, loyalty. Banished from Rome, he joins her enemies, the Volsci, and leads an army to attack his native city. With Rome on the point of capitulation, Caius Martius is prevailed on by Volumnia to desist, and in revenge for this backsliding is killed by the Volscian leader, Tullus Aufidius. The catastrophe of the play is rich in implication. The paragon of Roman courage is, in one sense, too noble for the world of politics; but, in revulsion from the uncertainties and equivocations of that world, he becomes a traitor. The political unfixedness of courage, its proximity to egoism (vividly captured in Caius Martius's retort to the citizens 'I banish you!'), and yet its enduring ability to enlist our admiration in defiance of our normal ideas of desert, resonate in the play's final moments. The paradoxical nature of Caius Martius – a man who excels in the martial field of manhood, but who also remains a child in petulant denial of the accommodations that are entailed by adulthood – shapes the play's last lines, when his antagonist, Tullus Aufidius, encapsulates the illogicality of the tribute we willingly pay to courage:

Though in this city he
Hath widow'd and unchilded many a one,
Which to this hour bewail the injury,
Yet he shall have a noble memory.[19]

Shakespeare's plays contain many depictions of courage, but it is in *Coriolanus* that he explores most searchingly the forbidding strangeness of this fundamental, but also incommensurable, virtue.

HOW DID THE TRADITIONAL UNDERSTANDING OF COURAGE BECOME CORRUPTED?

In retrospect, *Coriolanus* was, although as we have seen a paradoxical and complicated play, perhaps the last great literary work which could, with at least half its mind, admire courage as a virtue that could be acted out in good faith. Once Hobbes had postulated fear as the fundamental human emotion, it was only a question of time before the opposite of fear was manipulated into the guise of a perverse expression of its emotional antagonist. Rochester's 'A Satyre against Reason and Mankind' evinces an uncommonly sharp eye for Hobbesian consequences:

> Whilst wretched man is still in arms for Feare:
> For feare he Arms, and is of arms afraid,
> By fear to fear successively betray'd.
> Base Feare! The source whence his best passion came,
> His boasted Honour, and his dear bought Fame:
> That lust of Power, to which hee's such a slave,
> And for the which alone he dares be brave…
> The Good he acts, the Ill he does endure,
> 'Tis all from Feare to make himself secure.
> Meerly for safety after fame we thirst;
> For all men would be Cowards if they durst.[20]

After this, it seems to have been impossible for courage to be considered without some quizzical or sceptical overlay. Hobbes' contemporary, La Rochefoucauld, is positioned on exactly the same tipping point. On the one hand, his maxim 216 seems to regard courage as a substantial, distinct and real virtue:

> La parfaite valeur est de faire sans témoins ce qu'on serait capable de faire devant tout le monde.[21]

Yet its immediate predecessor, the enigmatic and complicated maxim 215, although it begins by proclaiming the apparent distinctness of 'valeur' and 'poltronnerie', ends by finding them to be almost indistinguishable in the resonant paradoxicalness of its conclusion:

> La parfaite valeur et la poltronnerie complète sont deux
> extrémités où l'on arrive rarement. L'espace qui est entre les
> deux est vaste, et contient toutes les autres espèces de courage.
> Il n'y a pas moins de différence entre elles qu'entre les visages
> et les humeurs. Il y a des hommes qui s'exposent volontiers au
> commencement d'une action, et qui se relâchent et se rebutent
> aisément par sa durée. Il y en a qui sont contents quand ils ont
> satisfait à l'honneur du monde, et qui font fort peu de chose au
> delà. On en voit qui ne sont pas toujours également maîtres de
> leur peur. D'autres se laissent quelquefois entraîner à des

terreurs générales; d'autres vont à la charge parce qu'ils n'osent demeurer dans leurs postes. Il s'en trouve à qui l'habitude des moindres périls affermit le courage, et les prépare à s'exposer à de plus grands. Il y en a qui sont braves à coups d'épée, et qui craignent les coups de mousquet; d'autres sont assurés aux coups de mousquet, et appréhendent de se battre à coups d'épée. Tous ces courages de différentes espèces conviennent en ce que la nuit augmentant la crainte et cachant les bonnes et les mauvaises actions, elle donne la liberté de se ménager. Il y a encore un autre ménagement plus général: car on ne voit point d'homme qui fasse tout ce qu'il serait capable de faire dans une occasion s'il était assuré d'en revenir; de sorte qu'il est visible que la crainte de la mort ôte quelque chose de la valeur.[22]

La Rochefoucauld's movement from asserting the polarity of courage and cowardice to finding them intertwined in the tenebrosity of that 'nuit' which 'donne la liberté de se ménager' marks a borderline in the western conversation about courage. The sceptical dismantling of courage as a substantial and distinctive virtue that seems to have occurred in the general European crisis of the mid-seventeenth century, and that entailed the dissolving of courage into its baser (but more readily explicable) antagonists, has persisted until our own day, and in defiance of much documented behaviour in the meantime that has attested to the substantial truth of the earlier attitude.

A powerful, because not over-simple, example of the dominant understanding of courage occurs in Stephen Crane's *The Red Badge of Courage* (1895). The impressionistic technique of Crane's novel leaves its meaning implicit; yet it is also unmistakable. Henry Fleming, a Union volunteer, is about to face his first action. He recalls the advice his mother gave him before he left home to fight:

> You watch out, Henry, an' take good care of yerself in this here fighting business – you watch out, an' take good care of yerself. Don't go a-thinkin' you can lick the hull rebel army at the start, because yeh can't. Yer jest one little feller amongst a hull lot of others, and yeh've got to keep quiet an' do what they tell yeh.[23]

The voice of motherly prudence has a deflating effect on Fleming, who 'had privately primed himself for a beautiful scene'.[24] It is the first of a number of encounters Fleming has with older or more experienced voices which instil in him the doctrine that courage and cowardice can flow into one another, and be separated by the merest accident or circumstance. For instance, the 'tall private' in Fleming's company reflects on the ambivalence of the group mentality in a company of soldiers – on how, like La Rochefoucauld's 'nuit', it can equally easily associate itself with both resistance and retreat:

> …if a whole lot of boys started and run, why, I s'pose I'd start and run. And if I once started to run, I'd run like the devil, and no mistake. But if everybody was a-standing and a-fighting, why, I'd stand and fight. Be jiminey, I would. I'll bet on it.[25]

In his first experience of combat, Fleming finds it to be as his companion described. There is no scope for individual heroism:

> As he ran with his comrades he strenuously tried to think, but all he knew was that if he fell down those coming behind would tread upon him. All his faculties seemed to be needed to guide him over and past obstructions. He felt carried along by a mob.[26]

The battlefield is, in this novel, the site of extraordinary constraint: 'it would be impossible for him to escape from the regiment. It inclosed him. And there were iron laws of tradition and law on four sides. He was in a moving box.'[27]

The experience of fighting entails the loss of individuality, and the soldier is fated to become 'welded into a common personality which was dominated by a single desire'.[28] Yet, when the Confederate forces unexpectedly return to the attack, Fleming is caught up in a general panic and 'ran like a rabbit'.[29] He eventually atones for his failure to stand his ground by rejoining his unit and resisting a new attack. But Crane – in this, perhaps, an unwitting disciple of La Rochefoucauld – implies that there is no moral distinction to be drawn between Fleming's shameful flight and his later resolve to stand firm. Both his flight and his staunchness were blind and automatic actions, as his unawareness of when to stop firing illustrates: 'Once he, in his intent hate, was almost alone, and was firing, when all those near him had ceased. He was so engrossed in his occupation that he was not aware of a lull.'[30] Fleming's fantasies of courageous behaviour are dispelled by the actual experience of combat – fantasies of himself in the textbook posture of the courageous:

> Swift pictures of himself, apart, yet in himself, came to him – a blue, desperate figure leading lurid charges with one knee forward and a broken blade high – a blue, determined figure

standing before a crimson and steel assault, getting calmly killed on a high place before the eyes of all. He thought of the magnificent pathos of his dead body.[31]

Given this, how free from self-delusion is Fleming's final conviction? – that his experience of battle had conferred on him 'a quiet manhood, non-assertive but of sturdy and strong blood...He was a man.'[32] And, also given this, how little surprising is it that Wilfred Owen should have responded, some twenty years later, to the Horatian conviction of the sweetness of a patriotic death by dismissing it as nothing more than a lie?

THE PROBLEMATIC RELATIONSHIP BETWEEN COURAGE AND THE SOCIAL VIRTUES

The drift in the western discussion of courage has, over the past three centuries and following the revolutionary implications in the field of ethics of Hobbes' installation of fear as the primary emotion, tended to erode its distinctive and substantial character. Increasingly we have confused it with other emotions and virtues to which it is more or less closely attached: fortitude, tenacity, resolve, even (in a concept such as 'cold courage')[33] with certain forms of prudence. In so doing, we have discounted, masked or disguised from ourselves aspects of courage that were previously acknowledged to be of its very essence: its exorbitancy, its freedom from calculation, its wildness, its antipathy to many of the human strengths we associate with a successful passage from childhood to adulthood. We have tended more and more to overlook the strong vein of irrational defiance in courage, and we have failed to pay sufficient attention to the fact that the impulse towards courage partakes of a refusal to accept the verdict of probability. Our motive for so doing has been our desire to obscure the extent to which so clearly necessary and admirable a virtue as courage exists in a state of tension with, or even antagonism towards, the habits of mind and the principles of conduct that we find most useful in normal social life. As *Coriolanus* demonstrates so emphatically, societies are secured by virtues they cannot stomach. As western societies have come to be ever more effectively disciplined, as the reach of the administration of the state has lengthened and steadily grown less willing to brook any opposition to its preferences and methods of operation, so the tension between courage and the socially useful qualities society likes to reward has grown, and so we have tried with greater determination to efface our knowledge of their disparity.

In so doing, we have hidden from ourselves an important but contradictory aspect of the courageous act, to which Horace was alert in his preference of the word 'dulce' to the easier 'dulci': namely that, in spite of the fact that it often results in general benefits, it provides an intense enjoyment to the actor, so that the benefits it confers on others might be thought of as incidental rather than primary.

Yet Samuel Johnson, with whom it is always dangerous to disagree, proclaimed that 'courage is reckoned the greatest of all virtues; because, unless a man has that virtue, he has no security for preserving any other'.[34] What does Johnson mean by this, and is it compatible with the line of analysis pursued in this essay? What I take Johnson to be driving at when he makes courage the foundational virtue is that, unless someone has the capacity for defiance, for standing apart, then, no matter how amiable he may be, his tenure of all the virtues is precarious. For 'thou shalt not follow a multitude to do evil' (Exodus 23:2). Courage is the virtue which enables us, when the need arises, to be salient and egregious. In poetry, the great example of this is Abdiel, in *Paradise Lost* – the one angel among Satan's host who, once he realised what Lucifer was about, would have no truck with him:

> So spake the Seraph Abdiel faithful found,
> Among the faithless, faithful only he;
> Among innumerable false, unmoved,
> Unshaken, unseduced, unterrified,
> His loyalty he kept, his love, his zeal;
> Nor number nor example with him wrought
> To swerve from truth, or change his constant mind,
> Though single. From amidst them forth he passed,
> Long way through hostile scorn, which he sustained
> Superior, nor of violence feared aught;
> And with retorted scorn his back he turned
> On those proud tow'rs to swift destruction doomed.[35]

Societies need frequent pollination with this virtue, however much they may mock or deplore it, or however subtly they may try to make it seem more amenable to what they take to be their priorities than, in its virtuous intransigence, it either can or should be.

1   Horace, *Odes*, III.ii.13. 'It is sweet and honourable to die for one's homeland.'

2   For Lassen, see the account (upon which I have drawn in what follows) in P. de la Billière, *Supreme Courage* (London: Little, Brown, 2004), pp. 271–300.

3   *ibid.*, p. 287.

4   *ibid.*, p. 286.

5   *ibid.*, p. 233.

6   William Shakespeare, *Coriolanus*, I.iii.5–18.

7   *ibid.*, II.ii.87–98.

8   *ibid.*, I.iv.30–4.

9   *ibid.*, I.iv.46.

10 *ibid.*, I.v.18–19.

11 *ibid.*, I.vi.66–75.

12 *ibid.*, I.v.66–76. The attribution of the final line is a textual crux. I have followed the Arden editor in giving it to the soldiers; but the argument for giving it to Caius Martius is, in certain respects, an attractive one. The encouraging potential in courage is what differentiates it from its close relation, the more ostentatious (but therefore lesser) virtue of bravery.

13 *ibid.*, II.ii.135–9.

14 *ibid.*, II.iii.112–23.

15 *ibid.*, III.iii.123.

16 *ibid.*, III.i.202–5.

17 *ibid.*, III.i.253–8.

18 *ibid.*, III.ii.41–51.

19 *ibid.*, V.v.150–3.

20 *The Works of John Wilmot, Earl of Rochester*, ed. Harold Love (Oxford: Oxford University Press, 1999), p. 61.

21 'Perfect courage consists in doing unobserved what we could do in the eyes of the world.'

22 'Perfect courage and complete cowardice are extremes which are rarely met with. The gap between the two is very wide, and embraces all other forms of courage. These latter differ from one another as much as human features and temperaments. Some men will gladly risk their lives at the beginning of an engagement, but relax their efforts and become easily discouraged as it progresses. Many are content to satisfy the commonly accepted standard of honour, and do little more. In some the power of mastering fear varies from time to time; others are liable to give way to panic; others again join in a charge because they dare not remain behind. There are those whose courage is fortified by small perils, and thereby enabled to face great ones. One man will be valiant with the sword, but afraid of musketry; another will be confident in the face of musketry, but fearful of combat at close quarters. All these

various forms of courage have this in common, that darkness, which
on the one hand exaggerates terrors and on the other conceals gallant
and cowardly behaviour alike, affords to all an opportunity of
circumspection. There is also a kind of circumspection which is
universal; for no man exhibits on any occasion all the heroism of
which he would be capable, were he assured of a safe return. From
which it is clear that fear of death does detract in some degree from
military valour.'

23 Stephen Crane, *The Red Badge of Courage*, ed. Donald Pizer
(New York: W. W. Norton and Company, 1994), p. 6.
24 *ibid.*, p. 6.
25 *ibid.*, p. 10.
26 *ibid.*, p. 17.
27 *ibid.*, p. 18.
28 *ibid.*, p. 26.
29 *ibid.*, p. 31.
30 *ibid.*, p. 71.
31 *ibid.*, p. 48.
32 *ibid.*, p. 98.
33 de la Billière, *Supreme Courage*, pp. 25–6. Cf. also Lord Moran,
The Anatomy of Courage (London: Constable, 1945).
34 James Boswell, *Life of Johnson*, ed. J. D. Fleeman (Oxford: Oxford
University Press, 1976), p. 609: 5th April 1775.
35 John Milton, *Paradise Lost*, v.896–907.

CHAPTER 3

LOVE: A CHRISTIAN VIRTUE

DIGBY ANDERSON

Thou shalt love the Lord thy God with all thy heart, and with all thy strength, and with all thy mind: and thy neighbour as thyself. (Luke 10:27)

Herein is love, not that we loved God but that he loved us... (1 John 4:10)

...[L]ove one another as I have loved you. (John 15:12)

WITHOUT CHRISTIAN THEOLOGY, THE CHRISTIAN IDEA OF LOVE MAKES NO SENSE

It might be a good idea to give the reader the conclusion of this chapter right at the outset. That way he can see why it involves lots of what might otherwise appear unjustifiably tedious theology. The conclusion is that the traditional understanding of the Christian virtue of love (henceforth usually given with a capital L) makes no sense outside a traditional conception of Christian theology. Drop the concepts of God, heaven, sin and the rest, and you will have to drop Love. Since Love comprehends the two other theological virtues, Faith and Hope, and underpins many more Christian virtues, they will have to go too. The fate of Love denied its theology will either be to wither or to be transformed into something else, something that still calls itself love but that is different from, and maybe even opposed to, Love. It might be that a secular rights-based ethics can be constructed to replace Christian ethics. But I doubt it. What seems to be happening is that Love and Christian ethics are being replaced by a populist sentimental ethics, which uses some of the language of Christian ethics but has little in common with it. It not only lacks a theology; it lacks any metaphysics or doctrine of man at all. If the civilisations of the 'West' are grounded in Christian ethics, and in some sense depend on them, the withering or perversion of Love may betoken serious trouble for them.

The doom of the West is not our concern here. Rather than defend the Christian understanding of Love or explore the consequences of its demise, I simply want to remind the reader what that understanding was, so that it may be compared and contrasted with modern moralities, which sometimes use its language and appeal to its injunctions – notably that we should love our neighbours. So let us start with a rather trivial look at what happens when Christian Love becomes confused with other understandings of love.

EARTHLY LOVE CAN ONLY BE A PARTIAL ANALOGY OF CHRISTIAN LOVE

Someone once neatly encapsulated the duty of a parish priest as to love his people into the kingdom of heaven. Once upon a time, not so long ago, about 50 years, there was a pious Christian lady. Let us call her Rosa. She was middle-aged, a spinster and somewhat theatrical. Her parish priest was also middle-aged, celibate, very sensible, very orthodox, and not the slightest bit theatrical. Rosa fell 'in love' with – or, perhaps better, 'became infatuated' with – the parish priest. She said nothing about it but, as she was theatrical, he certainly knew – as did most of the parish. As is common with infatuation, Rosa was able to convince herself that her affection was requited. It wasn't; indeed the priest was a little embarrassed and a lot inconvenienced by it. However, he had plenty of other parishioners to be concerned about, and he got on with doing his best for them.

Matters came to a head on 11 February, which was, in those days, kept as the feast of The Appearance of the Blessed Virgin Mary Immaculate. After the reading of the Epistle, the priest read the short text which followed it, the Gradual (from 'The Song of Songs'):

> The flowers appear on the earth, the time of the singing of the
> birds is come and the voice of the turtle is heard in the land.
> Arise my love, my fair one and come away: O my dove that art
> in the clefts of the rock, in the secret places of the stairs.

At the end of Mass he found Rosa, bags packed, waiting at the church door. She had arisen, departed her cleft as bidden, and was ready to come away with him. He fled back to the sacristy and, it is said, escaped to the presbytery through a window.

The tale indicates what can happen when one type of love is confused with another. It might be objected that Christianity, in this case the Church, bears some responsibility for this, since it chose the text that confused Rosa. It is from 'The Song of Songs', a book which depicts the love between God and his people Israel as like that between a bride and bridegroom. It is not an isolated instance. In both Old and New Testaments of the Bible, in the writings of the early fathers and the Saints, in both Catholic and Protestant theology, the Love of God is likened to all sorts of other human and natural loves. Why? Because there is no other way to explain it. What else but the earthly is there to explain the divine? Indeed, as a religion in which God becomes man and lives and dies on earth, Christianity is supremely involved in the earthly explanation of the divine. But this does not mean that the Love of God is identical to that of the bride and bridegroom. It is certainly not. Most analogies are partial, and this is a very partial one.

Christian teachers can happily and helpfully use such analogies, provided they and their pupils understand them to be analogies, and provided they put them in the context of what else they know about God and His overall scheme of Creation, Providence and Salvation – that is, Christian theology. The same priest who was besieged by Rosa was once preaching on the nature of God's Love. To make a certain point, he told the tale of an old and very bad-tempered lady who lived alone except for a small and yappy little dog. She was inhospitable, rarely saw other people, was selfish, thoroughly unpleasant, and never went to church. Eventually, in the fullness of time, she died. Over the following months and years several of the other parish folk – very good, kind, Christian souls – also passed away. Imagine their surprise, not to say annoyance, when they encountered the bad-tempered old lady in heaven. How had she got there? 'Well, God loves love and the lady loved her nasty little dog.' Because of that small glimmer of love she had been given life eternal.

It was, perhaps, a dangerous tale, but the priest was not trying to explain the whole of God's Love, only to point out how extreme it is and that it is a gift. On other occasions he would have been the first to show how God's Love has nothing to do with sentimentality. On this occasion he could afford the risk of sentimentality to make his particular point. He could afford it because his listeners knew their basic theology.

So if we want to know what the Christian virtue of Love is, we may certainly use analogies with other loves, and occasionally senti-mentalise it, but that does not mean that Love is like natural, human love, or that it is sentimental.

THE THEOLOGY IN WHICH CHRISTIAN LOVE IS GROUNDED

What, then, is the theology that grounds the Christian virtue of Love? It is that man was made to love and serve God and to be reunited with Him in heaven. Man is loved by God, although he has separated himself from Him. God came down to earth to die for sinful man and so to reopen the way for man back to Himself. Man is called to return God's Love,

> We love Him because He first loved us. (1 John 4:19)

Man is to love God by being obedient to Him,

> ...[T]his is the love of God that we keep His commandments. (1 John 5:3)

Man is also required to love his neighbour. And the key to all this loving is that man is asked to love in the same way that God loves,

> ...[L]ove one another as I have loved you. (John 15:12)

To know what sort of love Christians are called to, we have to know what God's Love is like, for ours has to be like His. Love is called a theological virtue. It is sometimes thought that this is just a name, but its importance is central. The three theological virtues, Faith, Hope and Charity (Love), are so called because they relate to God. No God, no Love; no Love, no Christian ethics. It is, moreover, a gift of God: no God, no giver; no giver, no gift, no Love.

How does God love? How should man love? Today we tend to view love as a strong form of liking. When we say we love someone, we mean we like them enormously. This can further mean that we *feel* strongly attracted to them. Christian Love is an act of the will. Feeling has little to do with the will; indeed it may be more or less outside our control. Thus it has little, if anything, to do with virtue. To the extent that feeling and liking are beyond the will, they have nothing to do with Love. It is true that sometimes we like that which we are called on to love, but often we do not. Love, in the Christian sense, is a matter of will, not of feelings. Since Love is of God, and of that which is good, it is said that God is the only person we can love unreservedly and directly. Love for our neighbour is perhaps best expressed as just that – love *for* him, rather than love *of* him. That is true, too, of our self-love. It should be an act, willing the best for ourselves. And 'the best' means a return to God.

This is the first of several qualifications that have to be made of Love for our neighbour. It does not mean loving bad traits in his character or behaviour, though it might mean loving him in spite of his faults: after all, it was 'while we were yet sinners that God loved us'. This immediately takes us onto difficult territory. If Love is love of the good, are we to love someone according to how good he is, as a version of Aristotle might suggest? The Christian understanding is that we should love the sinner, not the sin. And there are four inter-related reasons for loving him. The first has already been alluded to: the sinful man has a heavenly future intended for him, one purchased at great price at Calvary. Thus we love him 'into the kingdom of heaven'. Second, man stands in a unique relation to God – a relation that separates him from the rest of creation. He has been made 'in the image and after the likeness of God' and as a moral agent capable of choosing to accept or refuse Love:

> We should love one another…because we are what God's love has made us and is making of us. If men were not constituted in such a way that they were free agents, capable of choosing between good and evil…they would not be creatures capable of being uniquely related to God.[1]

The rest of creation might be entitled to our concern for its welfare. Man alone is worthy of Love (that is what is dangerous about the yappy dog story). Third, God has hallowed manhood by becoming a man himself. Points two and three can be put together:

> They should love man for being in God's image…beloved by angels, redeemed by Christ…a Temple of the Holy Ghost.[2]

Fourth, through the Incarnation, Passion, Death and Resurrection of Christ, man becomes, as St Paul puts it, the adopted son of God. That means that he must love his Father, but also that he must love his brothers. Men are each other's brothers only because they have a common Father. Deny the paternity of God Almighty as deists do, deny God Almighty as atheists do, and there is no common fraternity. How odd that the principle of fraternity, which is based on common paternity in God, should have become a slogan of the anti-Christian French Revolution.

LOVING ONE'S NEIGHBOUR DOES NOT MEAN DOING WHAT HE WANTS

For these interrelated reasons, man should love his neighbour. Once again, the obligation to Love is founded on theology. That is what makes the Revolution's adoption of fraternity so odd. It is for reasons to do with God that man should love his neighbour. So loving him cannot encompass any trait of the neighbour that is un-Godlike. Nor can it be restricted to his earthly welfare. Loving him does not mean giving him what he wants or approving of the manner in which he chooses to affirm himself. Nor should it be restricted to his earthly need. One modern use of 'love', also bound up with its near identical term 'charity', is helping a neighbour in need. This is closer to Love but distinctions must be made. Helping someone in need is not the same as helping satisfy someone's wants, and their needs have to be subjected to the same theological understanding that Love is. Even when the modern understanding of charity does not diverge from the Christian one, it is only a small part of it. Giving food to the poor is traditionally a corporal work of mercy. There is a higher form of mercy, namely spiritual, and mercy itself is merely part of Love.

What Love of one's neighbour requires has been famously listed by St Paul:

> Charity suffereth long, and is kind; charity envieth not; charity vaunteth not itself, is not puffed up. Doth not behave itself unseemly, seeketh not her own, is not easily provoked, thinketh no evil: Rejoiceth not in iniquity, but rejoiceth in the truth: Beareth all things, believeth all things, hopeth all things, endureth all things. (1 Corinthians 13:4–7)

These are the qualities of Love, and they are more important than acts of corporal mercy; St Paul writes immediately before these verses,

> And though I bestow all my goods to feed the poor and though I give my body to be burned, and have not charity, it profiteth me nothing. (1 Corinthians 13:3)

Not less, not a little, 'nothing'. This is not, of course, to diminish the importance of love for one's neighbour or works of corporal mercy. On the contrary, making love for one's neighbour part of Love of God raises it to the ultimate. In the end, such Love must be sacrificial, for that is what Christ's love is:

> He made an absolute total gift of Himself to me and spent Himself for my good.[3]

Charity loves the neighbour to lead him to God. Natural philanthropy may be worthy and beneficial, but it is limited to this life. The Christian idea of Charity is, then, supremely high, but it reaches those heights because it is about God and eternity. Remove the theology and it is less than a tinkling cymbal.

CHRISTIAN LOVE MEANS OBEYING COMMANDMENTS

Another way in which Christian Love is far from the modern understanding of love-as-feeling is in Christ's insistence that to love is to obey God's commandments. Because we think of love as a feeling, we tend to think of it as very different from following rules. Indeed, we sometimes see it as liberating us from rules. That is not the Christian understanding. The Love-Liberationists are fond of quoting St Augustine's injunction, 'Love and do what you will.' They would do well to study the lines that precede it:

> Such is the force of love, that, as you can see, it alone separates, it alone distinguishes the actions of men...A father beats his boy, a seducer of boys caresses. If you but name the two actions, who would not choose the caresses and decline the blows? But if you take note of the persons whose actions they are, it is love that beats the boy and iniquity that caresses him. See then what we are insisting upon: that the deeds of men are discerned only by reason of love...A short precept therefore, is given you: Love and do what you will.[4]

St Augustine again:

> Two loves, therefore two cities. There is an earthly city made by the love of self even to the point of contempt for God, and a heavenly city made by the love of God even to the point of contempt for self. The earthly city glories in itself, while the heavenly glories in God. The earthly city seeks glory from men; but conscience bears witness to the fact that God is the greatest glory of the heavenly city.[5]

We have come a long way from feelings and being nice to people. There is still further to go. Love means obedience, and that obedience is to authority and orthodoxy.

There is a view of Christianity as a supremely 'female', soppy religion, in which all you have to do is love. It was an intimation of this version of Christianity that so disgusted the philosopher Nietzsche, who held that Christianity is essentially a spineless, fawning, weak and wet religion. The consequences of this transformation are profound, and for Christianity very dangerous indeed. For instance, that tale about the old woman and her dog seems to be getting very close to the idea that everyone goes to heaven; after all, who has not loved something once in his life? The Church called this Universalism and labelled it a serious heresy. It is sentimentally seductive to suppose that no one will go to hell. But this wholly upsets the traditional teaching on freedom, responsibility and the eternal consequences of human choice.

Not only is Love heavenward; it and orthodoxy have clear ideas of who is set to go there. One of the creeds of the undivided Church, the *Quicunque vult* spells it out, at its beginning:

> Whosoever will be saved: before all things it is necessary that he hold the Catholick Faith. Which Faith except everyone doth keep whole and undefiled: without doubt he shall perish everlastingly.

It goes on to list the character of the Faith, which is largely the doctrine of the Trinity. Returning to the Last Things and especially judgement, the judgement of the Almighty and All-loving God, it ends:

> They that have done good shall go into life everlasting: and they that have done evil into everlasting fire.[6]

Not a drop of soppiness there. God loves all men. He loves them so much that He gives them freedom, freedom to love Him or not. If they choose to refuse His love, and distance themselves utterly from Him, then they consign themselves to hell. He does not put them there. His judgement merely accepts their decision. The priest who told the story of the old woman knew this, and so did his congregation. They said the *Quicunque vult* together. It was precisely because they understood the overall scheme of the 'divine economy' that they could be given the story without it being a licence for Universalism.

All this can be summarised very easily. Christianity is not a child's list of notebook ethics. It is a full-blown religion with an idea of what man is, God is and what the world is for. Its Love belongs in this realm. It only makes sense in this realm. And this is the measure of the modern popular misunderstanding. What passes for good, and even Christian behaviour, today is a fraction of what is involved in Christian Love. Sometimes it may even be opposed to it.

CHRISTIAN LOVE AND CHRISTIAN HUMILITY ARE NOT SUPINE BUT HEROIC

At this point a small digression might be in order, starting with that famous quotation from St Paul above, about Love and relating to the alleged wetness of Christian Love. St Paul denounces vaunting and puffing up with pride. An essential part of Love is humility. Surely this is truly wet. What a strange notion it seems that men, even supremely gifted men, should be humble. Humility is certainly not on Aristotle's list of virtues. But then Aristotle's list was essentially about social, not theological virtues. And the only way humility makes any sense is when it is treated theologically. The reason why even the saints are humble is precisely that their great gifts are gifts of God and are nothing for them themselves to feel proud about. Humility is the natural relation of fallen man to Almighty God, even of gifted fallen men. Of course, it should not go so far as to deny such men's gifts – that would be ingratitude indeed – or to incapacitate man from seeking great achievement. That also would be untruthful, denying the gifts of God. Two other points might be made. One is that any consideration of Christ's earthly life, and that of the saints, shows them to have been far from 'wet' men. Jesus Christ's earthly life is nothing if not heroic. The man who stands before Pilate is indeed a king, if not in the way the Jews, and earlier the disciples, expected. Athanasius, Augustine and Ignatius were scarcely wimps. But they, and St Paul himself, knew where their heroism came from. Point two: they were also destined for glory. If man should be humble, it is because his destiny is to be glorious, to enjoy God forever in Heaven. That is no low view of man. Nor is it confined to the future. The future is forever breaking in on the present. From baptism onwards, and especially in the sacraments, above all in the Mass, man on earth is caught up in life eternal, and hence in glory.

Again and again one comes back to the simple precept that nothing about Christian virtue, about Love, humility or any of the other moral teachings of Christianity, makes any sense when shorn of theology: that is, of a Christian view of God and man and of the scheme of salvation.

CHRISTIAN LOVE CANNOT BE REDUCED TO, OR ADEQUATELY EXPLAINED BY, HUMAN LOVES

One of the sharpest and briefest analyses of loves related to Christian Love is C. S. Lewis's *Four Loves*.[7] It is such a good analysis, and so germane to our topic, that a largely uncritical summary is due. Lewis, considering the love of nature, says that, although nature never taught him that there exists a God of glory and infinite majesty, it did give the word 'glory' a meaning for him. Similarly, he learned a proper understanding of the word 'fear' from 'ominous ravines and unapproachable crags'. Nature, too, can arouse longings, so it can help someone on the way to Love of God. Of course, if itself deified, it may also lead in the opposite direction, as can love of one's country, class, school or regiment. When it becomes a religion, it is a demon; yet it may help towards religion if it is treated appropriately. It also needs supplementing. Lewis does not spell out the supplement, but it would seem to be the consulting of doctrine in a church through a sacred text. So these loves can do more than act as the analogies we discussed above; they can be preparation for Christian Love. This love is that of appreciation.

Then there is the love called affection, a sort of comfortable fondness. It is a humble love and one that springs from familiarity. We 'grow' fond of the old man, the shopkeeper, or the dog; even of inanimate things, like the armchair. We take the objects of our affection for granted. There is little appreciation of them, at least until we are parted from, or deprived of them. Yet the objects of affection are so diverse and apparently haphazard that it can lead us to appreciate goodness on a very wide scale. Affection is like Love in its humility (it is not puffed up), in the way it 'suffers long', and its capacity to open our eyes to goodness in strange places resembles humble sanctity. Yet it is double edged. Affection can be a sickly sentimentality, which is a false love. Affection asks little or nothing. We need it, but do nothing for it. We know we have to do something for erotic love or friendship; affection we expect. It is costless. That makes it the opposite of Love.

Eros is the love of lovers, the love that lovers are 'in'. It can take people over, quite suddenly – unlike most affection – and people can 'fall in it'. Eros is like Love in its total commitment:

> It is as if Christ said through Eros, 'Thus – just like this – with this prodigality – not counting the cost – you are to love me and the least of my brethren.'[8]

The analogy of God and Israel with the bride and bridegroom is well chosen. It prepares us for understanding the overwhelming, sacrificial nature of God's Love. But if Eros is made into a god, he too becomes a demon. He is so important that worship of him justifies all manner of things that would otherwise be seen as obviously evil: he was so much in love that he lied, he neglected his work and his parents...The love becomes more than an extenuating circumstance: it becomes an 'authority'. And Eros is the father of jealousy, suspicion and resentment.

It is odd that Lewis does not make married love one of his 'Loves'. Obviously it is distinct from Eros, at least for most couples. He does mention it, however, and it follows the same pattern. Marriage, of course, is likened to the relationship between Christ and His Church. That is the high element. Yet attending to its everyday cares and anxieties may well have kept more couples away from their prayers than the more carnal aspects of Eros. Marriage, especially modern marriage, is greedy. It wants all its members' time and attention. It can thus be the enemy of all sorts of other loves, especially love of friends and, of course, Love of God. Samuel Butler memorably said that

A man's friendships are, like his will, invalidated by marriage.[9]

Lewis argues that friendship itself can subvert Love. He recognises it as a great love, but then suggests that what can be a school for virtue can also be one for vice. Friendships can become coteries, cabals, conspiracies, gangs and mutual admiration societies. One can argue – and I have[10] – about whether these are perversions or logical consequences of true friendship. And the same question can be raised about Christian marriage, but not about Eros or affection. I would grade the various natural loves to make true friendship and Christian marriage much closer to Love than affection and Eros. This matters. It also matters that some of the troubles that exclusive pursuit of the natural loves brings are worse than others. But the point need not be laboured here. What Lewis shows is that the natural loves are a preparation for Love, but an inadequate one. He also shows how, when they are not encompassed with Love, they may lead away from and subvert Love. Most important of all, these distractions and subversions may look like, and certainly often employ the language of, Love itself. What modern society is facing is an explosion of false and distracting loves and an utter confusion about what to call them and how to recognise their falsity. Once again, we return to the unique and unavoidable use of the theology of Love. Not only does it complete the inadequacies of natural loves at their best, but it is the standard by which we can differentiate their best from their worst. In modern society, this theology is largely lost or trivialised, and thus both Love itself and the understanding of it are imperilled.

CHRISTIAN LOVE IS NOT LOVE OF ALL MEN

One reason why friendship's claim to be a virtue is sometimes attacked is that it is regarded as particularistic: it singles out one person to be especially loved. We love our friends more than we love other people. There are those today who would interpret Christian ethics as universalistic: that is, we should love all men. The most used – and abused – textual licence for this is the parable of the Good Samaritan. The lawyer who approaches Christ asks what he must do to inherit eternal life. Jesus asks him what the Scriptures say. He replies with the words discussed earlier in this paper about loving God and then one's neighbour. Told that this is correct, he then asks 'And who is my neighbour?' Jesus proceeds to tell the parable: a man on a journey is attacked, robbed, stripped and left for dead. Various of his own people pass by and ignore him. Then someone from a people despised by his people stops and takes care of him. The moral that contemporary commentators like to draw is that Love prevails over barriers of class, religion and race. We must love all men. Often implied is 'all men equally'. Hence, loves which, as it were, single out this person before that for loving are not good loves, especially if this is done on the basis of what one universalist calls 'tribalism'. If Christian Love can be interpreted in universalistic terms, then it can be used to bolster worldwide declarations of human rights and all the other modern obsessions with equality.

The first test of whether Love is to be particularistic or univer-sal is 'What is God's Love like?' And the immediate answer is 'universal': He loves all men. A little reflection, however, shows that God-as-man, Jesus, shows an especial Love for His Mother, Mary Magdalen, Lazarus, St John ('the disciple whom Jesus loved'), the inner core of the Apostles, Saints Peter, Andrew and John, the Apostles and His own people, the Jews. And rather more reflection on the Love of His Father shows that Almighty God, while He certainly works on a large plan and loves all, 'sees and thinks of individuals'. Newman puts it – in a meditation – like this:

> Thou art careful and tender to each of the beings Thou hast created, as if it were the only one in the whole world...as if Thou wast waiting on it and ministering to it for its own sake.[11]

This is surely a quality of Love that any child, spouse or Christian will know. From both considerations, that of the Son on earth and the Father, Newman derives the injunction that of course we should love some more than others. Of course, after God, family, friends, co-religionists and neighbours come first. This is because Love is not a feeling or a declaration, still less a theory of rights, but a practice. In a passage that might have been written as a prescient rebuke to the egalitarian theorists and universal declarationists, he writes:

> There have been men before now, who have supposed Christian love was so diffusive as not to admit of concentration upon individuals; so that we ought to love all men equally.
> And many there are, who...consider practically that the love of many is something superior to the love of one or two; and neglect the charities of private life, while busy in the schemes of an expansive benevolence...Now I shall here maintain, in opposition to such notions of Christian love, and with our Saviour's pattern before me, that the best preparation for loving the world at large, and loving it duly and wisely, is to cultivate an intimate friendship and affection towards those who are immediately about us...
>
> [H]ow absurd it is, when writers...talk magnificently about loving the whole human race with a comprehensive affection, of being the friends of all mankind...This is not to love men, it is but to talk of love. The real love of man *must* depend on practice...
>
> It is obviously impossible to love all men in any strict and true sense. What is meant by loving all men is to feel well-disposed to all men, to be ready to assist them, and to act towards those who come our way, as if we loved them. We cannot love those about whom we know nothing; except...we view them rather in...faith than love. And love, besides, is a habit, and cannot be attained without actual practice, which on so large a scale is impossible.[12]

The Love of the Good Samaritan is commended by Jesus, not because he professed a love of all men, but because he practised love on the one person he found near him – him 'who comes our way'. Of course God loves all, and those who love and obey Him must be 'ready' to love *any* man. But practical Christian Love, and there is no other kind, cannot be love of *all*.

THE TEST OF A CHRISTIAN'S LOVE IS THE CHARACTER OF GOD'S LOVE AND THUS THE CHARACTER OF GOD

There is much that may be disputed in this. But this is not the place for any such arguments. I said I did not propose to defend the Christian understanding of Love. I have simply tried to show that there is a Christian understanding of Love – one that is complex and rich. It also stands in marked contrast to many popular understandings both of love and Christian Love today. The test of whether a love is truly Christian must be whether it resembles God's Love, especially that shown by Christ on earth. This makes it theological. One other way of making this point – the only one that matters – is this: the Ten Commandments are arranged with the most important first. The first three are about man's relation to God and are thus sometimes called the vertical commandments. The other seven are horizontal. They are about duties to fellow men. They follow from, and depend on, the three vertical commandments. Nietzsche was right when he pointed out the considerable consequences of the death of God. Chief among these is the loss of rationale for the horizontal commandments. Modern society could try to build an ethics of its own based on purely earthly considerations. But it will be starting from scratch. Such an ethics can have nothing to do with Christians' understanding of Love for, as St Paul so nicely put it on their behalf (Philippians 3:20),

Our conversation is in heaven.

POSTSCRIPT 1

I have presented this analysis of the Christian virtue of Love as a simple reminder of what was standard doctrine. By that I mean what most mainstream Christian commentators would have agreed to be doctrine. Lest this claim be doubted, I would mention that, having written the paper, I belatedly looked up 'Love' in the highly standard textbook, *A Dictionary of Christian Spirituality*, published as late as 1983.[13] The main points are clearly stated there: that we love in response to God's Love and as He loves; that the test is that we obey His Commandments; that nowhere in the New Testament are we commanded to 'Love all men' which would, 'make love too general to be particular, immediate, practical'. It also discusses the difficulties and limits of using earthly love as an analogy of Love.

POSTSCRIPT 2

It would be interesting to apply the analysis of this chapter to other Christian virtues and vices. A brief consideration suggests that many, if not all, would yield similar results. Take, for instance, another theological virtue, Hope; one of the deadly sins, Gluttony; one of the key Christian concepts, Forgiveness; and one of the key disciplines, Chastity. In none of these is much of the original Christian sense present in modern usage.

1   Basil Mitchell, *Morality: Religious and Secular* (Oxford: Clarendon Press, 1908), p. 128.

2   Thomas Traherne, *Centuries of Meditations* (Bertram Dobell, 1908), Second Century, quoted in Mitchell, p. 127.

3   St Bernard, 'Sermon iii' in *Circumcisione*, PL 183, Col 138.

4   St Augustine, 'Homilies of the Epistle of John to the Parthians', in William A. Jurgens, *Faith of the Early Fathers* (Collegeville, MN: Liturgical Press, 1970–79), Vol. 3, pp. 125–6.

5   St Augustine, *City of God* (Harmondsworth: Penguin Books, 1984), Book 14, Ch. 28, p. 593.

6   Translation of the *Quicunque vult* in *The Book of Common Prayer*.

7   C. S. Lewis, *The Four Loves* (London: Collins Fontana, 1963).

8   *ibid.*, p. 101.

9   Samuel Butler, *The Way of all Flesh* (London: Bestseller Library, Paul Elek, 1958), p. 315.

10 Digby Anderson, *Losing Friends* (London: Social Affairs Unit, 2002), pp. 104–6.

11 J. H. Newman, 'The Providence of God' in *Meditations and Devotions of John Henry Newman* (London: Burns and Oates, 1964), p. 92.

12 J. H. Newman, 'Love of friends and relations' in *Selected Sermons, Prayers and Devotions; John Henry Newman*, ed. J. F. Thornton and S. B. Varenne (New York: Vintage Books, 1998).

13 'Love' in *A Dictionary of Christian Spirituality* (London: SCM Press, 1983).

CHAPTER 4

THRIFT: A VICTORIAN VIRTUE WITH CALVINIST ORIGINS

THEODORE MALLOCH

These days no one wants to be considered a *cheapskate*. Frugality is about as popular as chastity or abstinence. But it wasn't always so.

A recent, and telltale, Yahoo word search on 'thrift' produced few results: a newsletter on 'simple living', an offensive guide called *Cheap Stingy Bastard* on so-called 'good' deals, *The Complete Tightwad Gazette*, the somewhat satirical *Cheapskate Monthly*, numerous addresses for actual thrift shops, and the frugal 'tip' of the week – saving cans. This is *not* the virtuous thrift of an earlier and more respectful era.

Modern definitions of thrift are not nearly as good as the 1828 one provided by Webster:

> Economical in the use or appropriation of money, goods or provisions of any kind; saving unnecessary expense, either of money or any thing else which is to be used or consumed; sparing; not profuse, prodigal or lavish. We ought to be frugal not only in the expenditure of money and of goods, but in the employment of time. Prudent economy; good husbandry or housewifery; a sparing use or appropriation of money or commodities; a judicious use of any thing to be expended or employed; that careful management which expends nothing unnecessarily, and applies what is used to a profitable purpose; nothing is wasted. It is not equivalent to parsimony, the latter being an excess to a fault. Thrift is always a virtue.[1]

While Gertrude Himmelfarb was certainly correct in describing the transmutation of virtues to values[2] and the 'de-moralization' of society generally, she was less complete when it came to the religious origins of some of the key Victorian virtues, such as thrift. The Victorian contributions and moral framework, in both Britain and America, were, as she noted, essential, not only for the good life of individuals, but also for the well-being of society. But where did this seemingly foreign, now distant notion of thrift originate?

THE ORIGINS OF THRIFT

The true origins of thrift lie deep within the Calvinist tradition, where they were adapted to address the needs and concerns of a newly emergent sixteenth-century middle class. Thrift had become necessary in a society that had risen above bare subsistence, and where people were engaged extensively in the practice of trade and manufacturing. The theology where *worth* is determined less by the amount one spends, and more by the wisdom with which one discharges one's responsibilities as a *steward* over God's creation, is ingrained in the Reformation. This Judaeo-Christian lineage is itself traced back to the saga of the patriarch Abraham, where in Isaiah 51:2 it is recorded,

> Look to Abraham your father, and to Sarah who bore you;
> for I called him alone, and blessed him and increased him.

Calvin's *Institutes of the Christian Religion*[3] and his many *Commentaries*[4] are replete with interpretation of scripture on nearly every doctrine. The virtue of thrift plays prominently throughout the entire corpus of his work. His reading of Matthew 6 is particularly noteworthy in this regard. Believers ought to rely on God's Fatherly care, to expect that He will bestow upon them whatever they feel necessary, and ought not torment themselves with unnecessary anxiety. He forbids believers to be anxious or to seek in a manner that looks around and about them, without looking at God, on whom *alone* their eyes ought to be fixed. Calvin says,

> Beware those who are never at ease, but when they have before
> their eyes an abundance of provisions; and who, not admitting
> that the protection of the world belongs to God, fret and tease
> themselves with perpetual uneasiness.[5]

By seeking *first* the Kingdom of God, Calvin argues another restraint on excessive anxiety. He states, 'It is a gross and indolent neglect of the soul, and of the heavenly life'[6] that leads men to fail, and to moderate their cares and desires. In a renowned passage, Calvin expounds on the 'lay not up treasures on earth' phraseology with a fiery warning:

> This deadly plague regains everywhere throughout the world.
> Men are grown mad with an insatiable desire of gain. Christ
> charges them with folly, in collecting wealth with great care,
> and then giving up their happiness to moths and to rust, or

exposing it as a prey to thieves…They are blind and destitute of sound judgment, who give themselves so much toil and uneasiness in amassing wealth, which is liable to putrefaction, or robbery, or a thousand other accidents: particularly when God allows us a place in heaven for laying up a treasure, and kindly invites us to enjoy riches which never perish.[7]

The notion of *daily bread* that sustains us, and the labour involved in providing it that is built into the very structure of creation, is highlighted continually by Calvin. 'Yet our Lord commenced with bread and the supports of an earthly life, that from such a beginning he might carry us higher.'[8] Calvin is teaching his followers to endure patiently, to accept humility and not to be 'intoxicated by a false confidence in earthly abundance'.[9] This understanding of thrift is radically different from some Scrooge-type figure portrayed in a Dickens novel. For Calvin, 'our bread' is a metaphor for *all* goods and belongings. But these are not literally *our* bread. As Calvin states,

> It is so called, not because it belongs to us by right, but because the fatherly kindness of God has set it apart for our use.
> It becomes ours, because our heavenly Father freely bestows it on us for the supplies of our necessities. The fields must, no doubt, be cultivated, labor must be bestowed on gathering the fruits of the earth, and every man must submit to the toil of his calling, in order to procure food. But all this does not hinder us from being fed by the undeserved kindness of God, without which men might waste their strength to no purpose. We are thus taught, that what we seem to have acquired by our own industry is His *gift*.[10]

Caring for God's endowment in a respectful and thrifty fashion is here a form of biblical obedience. Some would contrast this with the Baconian notion that the world is ours to exploit. Calvin actually taught that the commandment in the first chapters of Genesis would instruct us to 'build and to keep' which suggests a proper balance, not a mandate to pillage. This *balance* is part of the role of thrift to distinguish between what we *want* and what we *need*. It is also a balance between oneself and the world. Rooted in gratitude, such a cycle of thrift outlasts itself and is also profoundly tied to transcendence.

The Reformers understood the sin of greed to be a sin directly against one's neighbour. Their understanding presumed the sin of greed to be in the category of those sins that cause a break in the relation between neighbour and self. The theory of economic scarcity rather than abundance, upon which these theological claims rest, may indeed be very outdated. But for the Reformers, the sin in question was a transgression of the limit set for us in the world by God as creator, the consequence of which is a struggle of sovereignty over *who* is really in control of our lives and our future. Hence the sin of greed is really the sin of 'desiring a life subject to human control over a life of vulnerable trust'[11] in God.

WEBER'S ERROR

Modernity is trapped by a definition of the Reformation provided by the German sociologist, Max Weber. Weber's treatment of the Protestant Reformation[12] is actually based on a wrong sense of accumulation and of possessions. Weber tried to recast the sin of greed as a virtue of thrift, which is only half of the Reformers' gospel. Sociologically, Weber looked at the coincidence of wealth in the Reformed countries and concluded that a certain kind of theology seemed to breed people who did not desire enjoyment, but instead preferred a desire for gain. While it was true that Northern Europeans – and those of them who migrated to North America, for that matter – worked to meet their basic needs and accumulated savings, the reason for this seems far removed from the sin in question. For in Calvinism, for the first time, *work* was given a religious character and became an ethical demand. A person worked not to live, but because God commanded it.

The *calling* and *vocation* of a person was a mark of that person's election or non-election by God. Work showed evidence of productivity, as demonstrated in the parable of the talents, rather than an appetite for pleasure. Weber concluded that the result of all this working hard and spending little was savings; and these savings were always in search of new and appreciating investments. But unlike the Calvin Weber described, the other parts of Calvin espoused a different relationship of human beings to the things they possessed – a kind of communitarian understanding of what they had and held. Geneva was actually flooded by poor refugees for this very reason. Calvin believed that, just as the rich had a responsibility to the poor, so too the poor had a mission to the rich. The poor were the receivers of God, the vicars of Christ, the solicitors of God who offered the rich an opportunity to rid themselves of monetary slavery, an opportunity to be saved from greed.

Weber was thus only half right in connecting Calvin's thought to the rich and the later evolution of capitalism, for he missed the other and major point. What Calvin was preaching in his day was not what it was to be rich in goods, and so greedy, but what it meant to be rich towards God, and so generous. He did not legislate generosity in a strict calculation or a defined sum, but rather called his followers to take the *rule of love* as their guide. This was no form of asceticism, but rather a life of lived thrift as a virtue. It was, first and foremost, a life of gratitude, for all that they had been given not finally to have or keep, but to hold and employ as stewards, until, in Calvin's words, 'such time as they came to behold the face of Him whose love had never let them go'.[13] The meaning invested in the idea of religious calling, first by Luther in a more infantile form, and then systematised by Calvin, should be understood as, above all, a life of gratitude.

MODERN-DAY CONSUMERISM

For the religious, insatiable desire is a source of unhappiness and even spiritual instability. Modern-day consumerists, however, have too often turned thrift on its head and made desire and want a source of liberation, where having more is the very definition of having arrived. The historian Christopher Lasch, in *The True and Only Heaven* (using Nathaniel Hawthorne's phrase) traced the story of how, since the eighteenth century, capitalists have made insatiable desire less and less of a vice and more and more of a virtue.[14] In one view, it is what drives the engine of economic growth and expansion. In consumer societies, former virtues like thrift and self-denial are perceived as vices because they lead to economic stagnation. They are called 'miserly', and people who follow them are seen as shrivelled and unable to enjoy the fruits and pleasures of this life. Thrift in itself does not produce wealth, but its opposite – profligacy – destroys wealth. The term 'spendthrift', no longer much in use, suggests a wasteful polar opposite to thrift. Notions of restraint are no longer part of modern culture, and nor is the shame of an earlier era of too much debt. One could even ask in our world of abundance if thrift has outlived its usefulness. The materialist who lives to consume more and more would likely have to answer in the affirmative.

The over-heated economy, it is said, is impeded by such virtues as thrift, and thrives precisely on avid consumers who know *no* limits to their desire. In such a moral universe, desire is the *only* real absolute. Where nothing is forbidden it is because nothing is sacred. And nothing is sacred, except personal and unlimited desire. The unleashing of unquenchable appetites leads inevitably to corruption and decay, personally and collectively. It is not only objectively, but indeed statistically proven to lead to immoral behaviour, and therefore existential misery. We see and gauge the loss of sacred meaning because we are created to live under a sacred canopy. Accepting moral limits and accepting the challenges to our pride and complacency come from taking a sacred moral code seriously: the Jewish people were God's chosen people not because God let them do whatever they wanted. His Ten Commandments were conceived not as a form of repression, but as a call to self-sacrifice in the name of that which is most fully human.

Few modern illusions have, in fact, caught the imagination as overwhelmingly as the myth of the Hollywood-invented so-called 'American Dream', with its emphasis on high consumption, compulsive acquisition and instant gratification. In their book *Affluenza: The All-Consuming Epidemic*, authors John De Graff, David Wann and Thomas Naylor describe a 'painful, contagious, socially transmitted condition of overload, debt, anxiety, and waste resulting from the dogged pursuit of more'.[15] This metaphor of a disease is an apposite characterisation of a malignant condition that is eating into the entrails of America. The insatiable urge to acquire things, whether or not they are needed, has, it is suggested, reached epidemic proportions. It has caused severe social and cultural dislocations and has warped the basic values of American society. One of the most corrosive impacts of this too robust consumerism is on human relationships. In a throw-away culture, the notion of planned obsolescence and the attitudes formed in relation to products eventually get transferred to people, too. Just as things are discarded after casual use, so people are cast off if they lose the capacity to participate in the cycle of consumption. In a consumerist culture, therefore, one's status is linked in large part to one's ability to *buy*.

VIRTUE AND THE MORAL LIFE

As a counter to consumerism, normative philosophers have long taught that through virtue man achieves genuine happiness. The full flourishing of human beings depends on a moral life. Here the virtue of thrift is paramount. Aristotle thought that habits of doing right always looked at the *median* as the best course. He saw both the deficiencies and the excesses as vices to be avoided. His advice, in essence, was to tend towards that extreme to which one is least prone.[16] In thrift, that would mean the ideal is to be generous. Avoiding, on the one hand, cheapness and, on the other, extravagance.

The median is a generous life. This implies that a person of thrift does not exclude generosity, but rather encompasses it. Jack Templeton has written eloquently about combining thrift and generosity in a book under that title.[17] As he recommends it:

> Thrift is not so much a matter of how much we have, but of how we appreciate, value, and use what we have. Everyone, regardless of income level, has opportunities to exercise the virtue of thrift. We practice thrift by monitoring how we spend our time and money and then by making better decisions.[18]

The parable Jesus told of the talents is indicative of ethical behaviour on thrift. To recap, it begins with a wealthy man, going on a long journey, who chooses three servants to look after his resources or talents (currencies) in his absence. While he is gone, each will be judged on proper behaviour. He gives the first servant five talents, the second two talents, and the last, only one talent. While he is gone, the first servant puts his master's talents to immediate work. In fact, when the master returns, the servant has turned the five talents into ten. The second servant was just as successful, turning two talents into four. The master is very pleased with the results of such thrift and stewardship. Each has shown himself to be a true steward of the assets entrusted to him. He is not, however, pleased with the third servant, who has been motivated not by stewardship, but by fear and lethargy. The third servant has done nothing with the talent. He had simply dug a hole in the ground and buried it for safekeeping. The master punishes him by taking the only talent he had and giving it to the servant who had amassed ten talents. The *moral* of the parable is shockingly clear: focus on what you have been given. It points unquestioningly to hard work, industry, and the wise use and investment of all resources.

Thrift, in this famous and oft-quoted passage, is not just a better reading of the 'bottom line'. 'Rather, it is part of a spiritual and cultural understanding of how we are to use our time, our talents, and our resources. Creating a culture of thrift means embedding this virtue in a larger framework of personal responsibility, discipline, purpose, and future-mindedness.'[19] This is perhaps best summarised in the words of the founder of Methodism, John Wesley, when he said, 'Make all you can; save all you can; give all you can.'[20] The noun *thrift* comes from the verb 'to thrive', which in turn comes from the Old Norse, *thrifask*, 'to thrive'. The basic meaning, then, excludes both poverty and excess. The thrifty person, as a thriving person, has a reasonable concern with both the present and the future. Thriftiness is not stinginess. Thrifty people show a respect for both their own and others' future and financial stability. They are very mindful of the needs of others. They neither hoard nor engage in conspicuous consumption. They do not buy in excess, but they do plan for their financial future. Savings are here not only part of salvation; they are also works of sanctification.

THE CONSEQUENCES OF MODERN SELFISHNESS

In James Collier's *The Rise of Selfishness*, the blame for terminal decline is assigned to the transition over the last century from a community-oriented citizenry to an overly self-oriented citizenry. This is a book by a self-confessed liberal, who now believes that all the wonderful 'progressive' programmes pushed by government and the media failed really to produce progress.[21] Significantly, he argues that the Victorian ethos – the ideas, attitudes and ideals that characterised Britain and the US in the latter half of the nineteenth century – has been abandoned, to our detriment. As he says,

> The Victorians had roots; they had obligations; they had responsibilities. The essence of Victorianism was self-discipline and responsibility. Every man had a responsibility to his wife and children, to his forebears, to his community, to his nation, to his race, and he was expected to take all of these responsibilities seriously and to put them ahead of his personal self-interest. Having a strong sense of national and racial identity helped a man accept his responsibilities, but self-discipline was necessary too. Parents raised their children with this in mind, not hesitating to apply external discipline, including corporal punishment, when needed. Thrift was a virtue, and waste a sin. People paid first for what they wanted to buy, not later. There were no credit cards. A man chronically in debt was a man whose honor was in jeopardy. Temperance and self-restraint also were virtues. A man constitutionally unable or unwilling to postpone self-gratification was held in low esteem.[22]

The most dangerous consequence Collier sees in the *transition* over the last hundred years from Victorian virtues to a wholly self-centred population is the utter destruction of the family. He looks at the trends – children growing up without fathers, working mothers putting consumerism ahead of proper parenting – and he warns, 'we have seen an abandonment of parental responsibility which is unmatched in human history'.[23] The disregard for law and the contempt for authority have sprung from the trend to more selfishness. But the long-term impact is greatest on the essential building block of society – the family.

> Increasingly younger people reject marriage, divorce easily, abandon their children, have fewer friends and see less of them...How do we explain this? In part it may have to do with the intense involvement with the media, which provide a substitute for human interaction...But at bottom, the increasing fragmentation of people is a consequence of the long-term turning inward to the self as the primary concern of life.[24]

Another real consequence of the loss of thrift as a virtue is evidenced in the dilemma of old age. Can one support oneself? What is the role of personal savings, accumulated over a lifetime? Is there a value in not being a burden to others? In the current welfare-state mentality most of this decision-making has been passed over to the state. In that sense the welfare state has removed actions from consequences.

HEROES OF THRIFT

Are there any heroes of thrift from whom we moderns and post-moderns can learn? Sir John M. Templeton, the famous but humble investor of the century and the founder of mutual funds, in the course of his generous, philanthropic life has come to very interesting conclusions. Studying the teachings of the laws of the spirit, he suggests, benefits humanity in even greater measure than studying, for example, the laws of chemistry. He cites Matthew Arnold, who believed that the decreasing influence of the Bible from the nineteenth century on could be reversed, if only the ideals, hopes and laws expressed in the poetic and allegorical language of the scriptures could be explained experimentally. In that way, dogmatic theology could be replaced by empirical theology, and the nexus between science and religion could be made more evident. If everyday people could understand religious principles in their own language, rather than in ancient metaphors, they might take them more seriously. Believing, for instance, that self-reliance depends on making decisions for oneself, rather than depending on others, would build a stronger person and society. Furthermore, according to Templeton, concentrating the mind on positive and productive things would lead to greater material success and greater wealth, which themselves flow from spiritual growth and progress.[25]

In the 1870s the world deemed a gifted Scotsman, Samuel Smiles, author of the best-selling book *Self Help*,[26] an international celebrity. Translated into many languages and inscribed on walls around the world, his words held great sway for decades, but are now largely forgotten. At his death the funeral cortege was nearly as long as Queen Victoria's. The wisdom of Smiles is absorbing. Strength lies in an ethical dimension, which Smiles called 'character'. It meant much more than mere obedience to regulations or business ethics. His other books, *Character* (1871), *Thrift* (1875) and *Duty* (1880), give a flavour of a remorseless advocacy of virtue. Together, they form a library of wisdom about the virtue of thrift in building character and bonding individuals in noble pursuits.[27]

Earlier still, in colonial America, another noted stalwart of thrift was the revolutionary statesman, inventor and publisher, Benjamin Franklin. As one of the best known and most widely admired figures in American history, his wit and charm made him most endearing. His practical intelligence and commitment to virtues, especially thrift, were well known; he viewed industry as admirable. Franklin's contribution to modern political thought should not be underestimated. The range of his ideas spans letters, essays, pamphlets, political documents and an annual Almanac. His pithy sayings are celebrated and are of lasting value, even in our present age. Some of those most pertinent to thrift are:

> He that builds before he counts the cost acts foolishly; and he that counts before he builds, finds he did not count wisely.
>
> Patience in market is worth pounds in a year.
>
> An egg today is better than a hen tomorrow.
>
> All things are cheap to the saving, dear to the wasteful.
>
> Light purse, heavy heart.
>
> Ere you consult your fancy, consult your purse.
>
> Gain may be temporary and uncertain, but ever while you live, expense is constant and certain.

Buy what thou hast no need of, and ere long thou shalt sell
thy necessaries.

Beware of little expenses; a small leak will sink a great ship.

And the best known,

A penny saved, is a penny earned.[28]

These three heroes of virtue can teach us a great deal of
wisdom about wealth, savings and the virtue of thrift.

MODERN THEORIES AND INSTITUTIONS

In modern-day management theory, financial and investment strategy
there is little mention of thrift. The term is either used pejoratively
or simply excused altogether. There are a few exceptions, though:
Thomas Stewart, the management guru, recently suggested in
'12 Management Tips for Slow Times', that thrift, 'that quaint
Calvinist virtue could be the "first-mover" advantage of the 21st
century.'[29] He advocates thrift. Since profits are down and demand
sags, Stewart says, 'Companies should turn to austerity.'[30] He says,

> The future no longer belongs to the irrationally exuberant,
> but to companies that demonstrate, quarter in and quarter out,
> the ability to produce and sell more without burning through
> people, capital, and other resources. The grand strategic
> challenge, the one real leaders set for themselves, is to use lean
> times like this to transform a company into an organization
> that knows in its bones how to do more with less – not just
> now, but forever.[31]

Here corporate frugality is a means to an end, as well as the
vision, or story, of what the company is, where it is going, and why
it's worth the pain to get there.

Another place we encounter thrift today is in the history of savings banks. The concept of savings banks can be traced back to
1810, when a parish minister in a small Scottish town encouraged
thrift in his congregation and began to collect more than tithes.[32]
Similar institutions sprang up in Australia, New Zealand and
America, largely with a religious impetus. By the 1850s these thrift
banks had become involved in an activity that is now highly prized:
mortgage finance. Later trends included self-reliance and planning
towards saving for retirement, education, and of course more
sophisticated investment advice. Most of the advances made in
savings over the last two centuries would probably be beyond the

comprehension of the early founders of thrift institutions. But the reasons for savings, rooted in the concept of thrift, remain the same – to serve communities, to grow, and to help people and families grow and preserve their wealth. The wealth management and complex, diversified portfolios of the 21st century are a long way from rural, church-based savings, but the rationale remains virtually the same.

This brings us to the so-called *paradox of thrift*. There is a debate raging in many countries around the world about whether people are saving enough for their own good. The importance of saving is rarely debated. But since it involves the sacrifice of consumption today for the sake of benefits in the future, it is difficult for a household, a business, or a government to decide on the proper or appropriate rate of saving. Saving behaviour has important national and macroeconomic implications that ultimately affect all citizens far beyond the realm of their own domestic financial management. It influences the overall performance of an economy, and therefore national prosperity and economic growth. No less a figure than Adam Smith, in his *Wealth of Nations*, argued the virtue of saving as the key to economic progress.[33] Contrast this with John Maynard Keynes who, in his *General Theory of Employment, Interest, and Money*, regarded a high savings rate as anything but a virtue, as something that actually undermined prosperity.[34] His argument became the basis of the celebrated 'Paradox of Thrift'. Economists have debated for decades about some magic number or formula for the level of savings in a given country. While there are many sides and positions, most see today's savings rates as too low. Furthermore, there is general agreement that there are often economic obstacles to the way the financial and tax systems function, which bias individuals and companies towards consumption and away from saving. Removing these inefficiencies and obstacles is, it is argued, paramount, so that people and companies can make clear, rational and informed choices about what is the appropriate level of savings.

DEMOCRATIC MORALITY

Hopefully this makes it clear that economics cannot be so easily separated from morals and character. 'Ordinary integrity', Edmund Burke wrote, 'must be secured by the ordinary motives to integrity.' Thrift, honesty, and ingenious effort are rewarded in economic life. For Burke, the vast majority work principally out of self-interest, to benefit themselves and their families. There is nothing wrong with this state of affairs; it is merely a condition of ordinary human nature. Competition puts a premium on industry, thrift, honesty, and ingeniousness, for the slothful, the spendthrift, the known cheats, and the stupid fall behind in the economic contest of free enterprise.[35]

In the end, it is true that, more than anything else – more than any specific values or virtues – it is a reluctance to speak the language of morality, and to apply moral ideas to social policies that separates us from the Victorians. The Victorian virtues, rooted in the Protestant Reformation – work, thrift, temperance, respectability – are, as others have suggested, quite modest, even mundane. They rest on no special breeding, status, talent, wisdom, grace, or money. They are, in the ultimate sense, *democratic*.[36]

The Victorians have too often been condemned as materialist, racist, self-righteous, hypocritical, imperialist, and even (worst of all) earnest. Yet, as the latest treatment now shows, these

> sturdy, steadfast Britons, confronted the most tumultuous challenges: the incredible rise of industrialism, the rapid spread of railroads, the shift from farm labor to work in mines and mills, the teeming swarm to city living, the soul-wrenching clash of new scientific ideas with ancient religious beliefs, and ultimately, the burden of empire.[37]

The Victorian premium on the self – self-help, self-interest, self-control, self-respect and self-discipline – allowed for a truly liberal society. It upheld the self, *not* selfishness, in the context of the family, the other mediating 'little platoons', and the State. That society of middle-class adherents anchored in democratic capitalism believed in, and required nothing less than, a moral citizenry. Do not sell thrift short, for thrift, as a Victorian virtue with deep-seated Calvinist origins, ultimately made possible *both* capitalism *and* democracy.

1 Webster's Dictionary, 1st Edition, 1828.
2 Gertrude Himmelfarb, 'From Victorian virtues to modern values' AEI Bradley Lecture Series, 13 February 1995, p. 1. The longer book treatment is, *The De-Moralization of Society* (New York: Vintage Books, 1994).

3 John Calvin, *Institutes of the Christian Religion* (Westminster: John Knox Press (1559 translation), 1960).
4 John Calvin, *Commentaries* (Grand Rapids: Baker Books, 1974).
5 Calvin, *Commentary* on Matthew 6:31–43.
6 *ibid.*
7 *ibid.*
8 *ibid.*
9 *ibid.*
10 *ibid.*
11 *ibid.* Christopher Dawson, the social historian, speaks highly of Augustine's social ethic in *Progress and Religion* (Washington, DC: Catholic University Press of America, 2001), when he says, 'In the West, under the influence of Augustine, Christianity became a dynamic moral and social force.'
12 Max Weber, *The Protestant Ethic and the Spirit of Capitalism* (New York: Penguin, 1965). Simon Schama provides a historiographical critique of the connection drawn between specific tenets of Calvinist theology and a study of spending habits in Dutch society in his tome, *The Embarrassment of Riches: An Interpretation of Dutch Culture in the Golden Age* (New York: Vintage Books, 1997). Paul Marshall's thesis in *A Kind of Life Imposed on Man: Vocation and Social Order from Tyndale to Locke* (Toronto: University of Toronto Press, 1996) provides an alternative and different interpretation on Weber and Locke.
13 Calvin, *Commentary* on Matthew 6:31–43.
14 Christopher Lasch, *The True and Only Heaven: Progress and Its Critics* (New York: W. W. Norton, 1991).
15 John De Graff, David Wann, and Thomas H. Naylor, *Affluenza: The All Consuming Epidemic* (San Francisco: Berrett-Koehler Publishers, 2003).
16 Aristotle, *The Nicomachean Ethics* (Oxford: Oxford University Press, 1998).
17 John Templeton, Jr, MD, *Thrift and Generosity: The Joy of Giving* (Philadelphia: The Templeton Foundation Press, 2004).
18 *ibid.*, p. 41.
19 *ibid.*, p. 42.
20 *ibid.*, p. 6.
21 James Collier, *The Rise of Selfishness in America* (New York: American Philological Association, 1991).
22 *ibid.*
23 *ibid.*
24 *ibid.*

25 Robert L. Herrmann, *Sir John Templeton: Supporting Scientific Research for Spiritual Discoveries* (Philadelphia: Templeton Foundation Press, 1998), p. 30.

26 Samuel Smiles, *Self Help* (Oxford: Oxford University Press, 1995).

27 *Character*; *Thrift*; and *Duty*, all by Smiles, were reproduced by Indy Press, 2003.

28 On Benjamin Franklin, see: Alan Houston (ed.), *Franklin: The Autobiography and other Writings on Politics, Economics, and Virtue* (Cambridge: Cambridge University Press, 2004). The best *new* treatments of Franklin are: Walter Isaacson, *Benjamin Franklin: An American Life* (New York: Simon and Schuster, 2003); and Gordon S. Wood, *The Americanization of Benjamin Franklin* (New York: Penguin, 2005).

29 Thomas Stewart, '12 management tips for slow times' *Business 2.0*, 1 February 2002, p. 1.

30 *ibid.*, p. 1.

31 *ibid.*, p. 2.

32 Savings banks are described at length in Report of ASB Bank Ltd., 2001.

33 Adam Smith, *The Wealth of Nations* (New York: Prometheus Books, 2003).

34 John Maynard Keynes, *The General Theory of Employment, Interest and Money* (New York: Prometheus Books, 2002).

35 *The Best of Edmund Burke: Selected Writings and Speeches* (Washington, DC: Regnery Publishing, 2000).

36 Himmelfarb, 'Victorian virtues', p. 15.

37 A. N. Wilson, *The Victorians* (New York: W. W. Norton, 2003), p. 224. This is a critique of the well-known work by Lytton Strachey on eminent Victorians, which pictured them as stupid and prudish.

CHAPTER 5

DISINTEREST: AN ADMINISTRATIVE VIRTUE

ALEXANDER EVANS[*]

Disinterested intellectual curiosity is the life blood of real civilization.

G. M. Trevelyan, *English Social History* (1942)

Nothing is less sincere than our mode of asking and giving advice. He who asks seems to have a deference for the opinion of his friend, while he only aims to get approval of his own and make his friend responsible for his action. And he who gives advice repays the confidence supposed to be placed in him by a seemingly disinterested zeal, while he seldom means anything by his advice but his own interest or reputation.

François De La Rochefoucauld (1613–80)

Simple service is obedience. Wise and impartial advice, on the other hand, depends on a form of intellectual independence – disinterest. This sometimes requires the strength of character to stand up to leaders who are about to make bad decisions. From the ancient counsellor, through the medieval fool, down to the late Victorian administrator – advice, and the integrity of those who offer it, has always been valued. But the values held by advisors have varied. Even so, it is perhaps telling that all the best counsellors in history combined an unerring eye for truth with the ability to present it – often bluntly – to their masters. Not for nothing in Moghul India was a good grand vizier cherished. The fate of an emperor was often intricately intertwined with that of his lead officials. Officials determined actual revenues and implemented (or obstructed) orders. One's spymasters guaranteed information free, or so they claimed, of adulteration. Masters of revenue, guardians of secret information, determinants of policy, and guarantors of justice, the most senior advisors played a critical role in making the Moghul Empire work.

[*]Alexander Evans is a British diplomat. The views here are his own and do not represent British government policy. This chapter is dedicated to Kathleen Kazer.

Max Weber, writing on bureaucracy, predicted many of the characteristics of the modern age.[1] Bureaucrats, hidden behind thick town walls or facing the people when dispensing justice in far-flung villages, quickly multiplied. A new culture of public service emerged during the nineteenth century. At its heart lay an attempt to depoliticise advice. Civil servants ought to be neutral: their judgement free of the vagaries and vulgarities of political fashion. By granting their mandarins tenure, modern European states significantly advanced the fight against corruption. It is, perhaps, ironic that the Victorian age – an age of hypocrisy – saw the establishment in Britain of what was, perhaps, one of the most able bureaucracies in the world. It certainly proved less corrupt than many of its European counterparts. It is also notable that the British administrative system – defined between the 1870s and 1930s – drew on an imperial tradition that had been applied for longer in India and Ireland.[2] Ironically, the first European civil service was set up in India by the East India Company. To prevent corruption and favouritism, promotions within the company were based on examinations. The system then spread to the United Kingdom in 1854, and to the United States, with the Pendleton Civil Service Act, in 1883. Reform in the US was stimulated by a presidential assassination – President James Garfield was murdered by a frustrated office-seeker.

Prior to 1854 public servants in Britain were highly politicised, often corrupt creatures of direct political patronage. The nature of official appointments established a political dependency on one's patron. However able, officials were unlikely to exercise independent judgement – not least since many posts were available for outright purchase, which led to the onerous task of recouping one's investment. This brings to mind a Pakistani newspaper editor who, in November 1999, was explaining the background to General Musharraf's coup in Pakistan. You realise, he said, that the previous civilian governments had short tenures – while the cost of standing and winning a seat in the National Assembly had risen. Any parliamentarian, therefore, had to recoup his costs, with interest, in the shortest time possible, thereby further fuelling corruption.

A systematic reform of public service was clearly required. The Northcote–Trevelyan report of 1854 on *The Organisation of the Permanent Civil Service* set out what could be done. Although slowly and only partially implemented, the reforms established a competitive entry examination, promotion on merit, and independence based upon continuity of service. The Weberian bureaucratic system

95

is rule-based, hierarchical and impersonal (the office, rather than the official, matters). Personal is slight: rules and precedents inform judgements. Of course, organisations are rarely that rational – and much depends on the political direction given to them, and the personal characters of those who serve within them.

Similar reforms had taken place in British India, although there largely as a result of the Indian Mutiny (1857), after which India was transferred from a private guild into a public institution under the British Crown. Up to that time, the Honourable East India Company's Civil Service had formed the general administrative cadre of civil servants in India.[3] From 1858, it was superseded by the Indian Civil Service. This was also influenced by the Northcote–Trevelyan report. Here too, the principle of entry by competitive examination was well established by the late nineteenth century. From 1893 onwards, for example, the Indian police recruited its top officials mainly through an annual competitive examination held in Britain.

In the early twentieth century, the British civil service grew rapidly. Largely thanks to Liberal governments, the total grew from 50,000 in 1902 to 161,000 in 1920. In 1976, at its peak, it had grown to three-quarters of a million, before falling again to 459,600 in 1999. And the British were not alone in massively increasing their bureaucracy. The US saw its federal service grow from 53,000 at the end of the civil war to 166,000 by 1891. By 2002, it had risen to 1.9 million. The French – the creators of the Napoleonic state – had 2.3 million civil servants in 1999.[4]

In recent years, the nature of public service has changed further. The rise of market politics and the decline of statism (though it continues to raise its head), along with the rise in public cynicism about aloof, patrician and supposedly powerful mandarins, has diminished the standing of civil servants. In 1971, William Niskanen's influential book, *Bureaucracy and Representative Government*, suggested that senior officials were more inclined to increase their empires and further their careers than act in the public interest.[5] Niskanen's work directly contributed to the critique of officialdom that fed into the New Right during the 1980s.

No longer a gilded élite, the brightest and best of today's civil servants have to contend with the fact that many who are more able than they are choose to work in the private sector. There has been a marked change in the competencies demanded of officials. Once it was solely intellectual and administrative skills that were prized;

now interpersonal skills have come to be an integral part of a senior manager's toolkit. Sentimentality, after a fashion, has seeped into the civil service, though the emphasis on human skills, at least, is no bad thing. The belated awareness in the 1980s that much of the business of contemporary government is service delivery saw a sea-change in public-sector management. Semantics aside, public service became increasingly indistinguishable from customer service – and officials, used to distance, found the cultural change difficult.

Today, officials retain some of the Weberian virtues.[6] Many retain lifelong tenure. A generous pension scheme (albeit to be revised in 2013) is an added incentive to remain in public service. Political impartiality remains prized, notwithstanding episodic sniping from critics on both the left and the right.[7] Even so, many public officials (personally) tend to be statists – after all, tax revenue feeds their budgets. Simultaneously, the civil service is institutionally reasonably cautious. It carries a streak of small-c conservatism that has its advantages (again, Weberian values of rationality and informed judgement) and its disadvantages (the system is resistant to change – a challenge amidst a complex world of public policy and the need for cross-government working practices).

So the *Zeitgeist* has changed. Although some British civil servants (diplomats, for example) remain Crown rather than civil servants, they are all now servants of the people. And though bureaucrats may not be forced to be partisan, they are encouraged to be passionate. Disinterest runs directly counter to a set of agendas that have gained currency since the 1960s. Critical theorists, feminists, queer theorists, postcolonialists, indigenous rights advocates – all argue for a politics of disposition rather than disinterest. Doubt is not enough. Only commitment to critical (read directed) thinking will do. As Emile Cioran notes:

> Once man loses his facility for indifference he becomes
> a potential murderer. Sceptics who propose nothing are
> humanity's beneficiary; believers its nemesis. We mistrust
> swindlers, tricksters etc. but believing in nothing it is not
> they who betray man; they leave man to apathy, despair, or
> uselessness; to them humanity owes the few brief periods of
> prosperity it has known.[8]

Interest is much to do with social justice. Advocates of social justice despise disinterest – without commitment, they argue, social change is impossible. And today, as citizens we are all meant to be interested. We are encouraged to feel commitment to others – albeit a generalised social commitment, rather than a personalised moral commitment. Social justice is the new philanthropy; social commitment the leitmotif of much state action and intervention. The danger is that self-expression overcomes the commitment to the common good. A focus on the private replaces public responsibility, and risks follow from resulting indulgent spontaneity.[9]

The decline of tenure for civil servants (there is no longer such a thing as a 'job for life'), the increasing mobility of young professionals, and a greater plurality of ethical groundings have all undermined the former foundation stones of a public-service ethic. Disinterest is no longer part of the job description, although impartiality usually is. These values are now formally policed. Regulators set standards, as well as promote and police them. In an increasingly atomised and privatised environment, professionalism alone is no longer trusted to deliver. The implicit social contract has to be articulated, formalised, imposed.

The classical virtue of the impartial administrator is, in fact, a relatively modern invention for the British. It flourished, briefly, from the 1850s to the 1950s, but the public-service ethic it partly represents has been challenged ever since. It draws, of course, on earlier traditions – some of which are dealt with below.

THE INTELLECTUAL HISTORY OF DISINTEREST

Establishing the intellectual provenance of true disinterest is no easy task. It has clearly always been valued by some. One obvious beginning is Biblical. Solomon, second son of David, and King of Israel until his death sometime between 938 and 916 BC is the archetype of wise leadership.[10] Solomon was but eighteen when he became king, but he reigned wisely for forty years. The wisdom of Solomon, of course, is best known through the anecdote in which he has to judge which of two women is the true mother of a baby. Solomon recommends the baby be cut in half. The false mother does not object, while the true mother offers up the child if only it can be spared. What appears to be disinterest, and even crass stupidity, is in fact an inspired act of judgement. Stories of speaking truth to power – and of those who advise the powerful both truthfully and not – are ubiquitous. Good and false counsel figure in countless battles and lives of kings.

Ancient Chinese society valued counsel. A conservative, authoritarian system depended on its mandarins. Ancient Chinese society was traditionally divided into four classes: the scholar-administrator, the farmer, the artisan, and the merchant. The scholar-administrator was at the apex of this system – and was expected to prove his worth through competitive examination.[11] The Imperial Service Examination was introduced during the Sui Dynasty (581–618), and endured for more than 1,300 years until the Qing Dynasty (1644–1911).[12] Held at both national and provincial levels, the Chinese system of selecting bureaucrats may well have influenced later attempts by the Victorians to institute a system based on merit rather than patronage. The top two or three hundred officials each year were the product of the national imperial examination.[13] Graduates were called *jinshi* ('presented scholar'); some three or four thousand ruled China in the late eighteenth century – by then a country of 300 million.

The Chinese system had something of disinterest about it. Heavily determined by Confucianism, the scholar-administrators enjoyed high status and were considered guardians of moral virtue. Their virtue was defined, in part, by their distance from personal gain. Not for them the vulgarity of the merchant, or the disarray of the marketplace. But to what extent was their presumed moral virtue a reality? Did the Confucian imperial administrative system generate (or sustain) a moral order at odds with periods of chaos in Chinese history, or was it simply a veil for a hypocritical system, in which personal gain was concealed as public good?

To answer this, we have to determine whether the power of the *jinshi* derived from their moral status as guardians of Confucian knowledge, or from their control over regional levers of power. It was more likely the latter – the mandarins became renowned for their corruption and ultra-conservatism, and over time their Confucian training was blamed for corroding imperial power.[14] However, individual tales of administrators who lived up to their morals survive. During the Ming dynasty, an able official called Hai Rui (1515–87), despite twice failing the national imperial examination, rose on merit to become secretary of the Ministry of Revenue. In 1565 he wrote a scathing memo to the reigning emperor, Shizong, charging him with corruption. The Emperor was incandescent with rage, and ordered Hai Rui to be brought before him at once. Only then did he learn that Hai Rui was standing by the court entrance, with a coffin ready for his body. The Emperor realised immediately that killing Hai Rui would only validate the (true) charges of corruption, so he had him imprisoned and tortured instead. In due course, charges were preferred, and Hai Rui was sentenced to death – only to escape and be rehabilitated following the death of the Emperor. Hai Rui's tomb is a tourist attraction in modern China. A play based upon his life was perceived to be a covert attack on Chairman Mao. It was feared that the character based on Hai Rui could be associated with Marshal Peng Dehuai, a former defence minister who spoke out in 1959 against Mao's brutal policies. Perhaps more fascinating yet is the way in which Hai Rui's contemporaries saw him as the successor to another official, Bao Zheng (died 1062). Zheng was honest, and particularly reputed for his ability to defy influential officials. Indeed, Hai Rui's nickname was 'Lord Bao of the South'.

In Europe, from classical times, a king's advisors included mentors, counsellors, and fools. The term mentor derives from the counsellor entrusted with educating Odysseus' son Telemachus in Homer's *Odyssey*. Ever since, the idea of learning has been intimately linked with the ideal teacher. The mentor teaches us to be ourselves, and teaches us about ourselves.[15] He may seek to imbue us with certain values, but too much (or too little) moulding of character often proves dangerous.

And a king's lead advisor's power has always been noted. Take the most powerful chess piece – the queen. On a chess board she is all powerful, capable of moves denied even to bishops and the (curiously limited) king.[16] The queen in chess derives from the Muslim vizier. A vizier was a high-ranking religious and political advisor, generally to a king or sultan. The ancient game of chess came to Europe from Asia, brought by the Moors. Nobody quite knows where exactly it originated – but most probably either in China or Persia. The Moors learned chess from the Persians after they invaded Persia in the eighth century. The Moors later invaded Spain, and thus the game was introduced to Europe – and Christianised, with the powerful Muslim vizier (advisor) translated into the medieval queen. Medieval queens often acted as counsellors or *de facto* regents, so it is understandable that the Persian confidante becomes the Christian queen.

Later on, there are a number of empirical traditions that exemplify disinterest. Both the fool and the jester (in their medieval and literary incarnations) illustrated plain speaking, devoid of self-interest. The fool has a far deeper pedigree than the jester – although jesters are but one variation on the fool.[17] The role of the fool is to be found in most cultures, and has a documented past as far back as the Egyptians, who brought pygmies from Central Africa to entertain the king. Henry VIII had fools at court.

The court jester made his first appearance in medieval courts around 1200 – although the institution existed in ancient China. The jester was the real-life equivalent of the literary medieval fool.[18] Court jesters were able to speak their mind, when all others about them at court had to keep their counsel. Jesters were, through humour, able to challenge the king's policies, and possibly influence them through anecdote, proverb or ridicule. Comic actors of Rome played a similar role, and were regularly suppressed because of the influence they were perceived to have on public opinion. Several famous tales of jesters live on to this day. For example, Yu Sze, court jester to the Chinese Emperor Shih Huang-Ti, saved countless lives with humour. The Emperor had built the Great Wall of China, and thousands had died in its construction. He then ordered the wall painted, which would again have resulted in a heavy death toll. Yu Sze used humour to persuade the Emperor otherwise, when all the Emperor's mandarins dared not.

Across the Muslim world, the Sufi Mullah Nasruddin is well known for his populism, humour and wisdom. In what is probably an apocryphal tale, he spent time at court with a king. One day the King happened to glance at himself in the mirror, and wept. He could see how old he looked, and this depressed him. Other members of court, unsure as to precedent, also cried. When the King finally stopped crying, so did all those at Court – apart from Nasruddin, who continued to bawl like a baby. Why, asked the King, have you not stopped crying? Nasruddin straightened up and replied: 'Sire, you looked at yourself for but a moment and you cried. I have to look at you all the time.' Nasruddin, who probably lived somewhere in Anatolia during the 13th century, is a recurring figure in contemporary Muslim folk stories. His itinerant status as wandering scholar and stooge allowed him to speak the unspeakable.

Shakespeare's plays featured both wise fools and foolish jesters.[19] He used the fool to explain, narrate and comment on the world as revealed through the play. *Twelfth Night* sees an example of a wise fool – Feste. Feste is detached, intelligent, curious, and gets on with everybody. He comforts Olivia as she mourns her brother's death, explaining that he is in heaven. Meanwhile, Sir Andrew Aguecheek is the classic jester: the slapstick fool who falls for anything Sir Toby Belch suggests.[20] The jester finally died out as a court institution in about the sixteenth or seventeenth century in China, and the early eighteenth century in Europe. It is interesting to note that, around the same time, there was a growth in printed social commentaries, and a broader segment of the elite began influencing policy. Criticism, advice and satire in print displaced oral and performing traditions like that of the jester.[21]

One of the first mentions of disinterest in English appeared in a 1612 essay by Francis Bacon. In 'The Charge Touching Duels' Bacon criticised the impassioned nature of the duellist, and recommended that the state abolish duelling. In doing so, the duellist would see 'the law and rule of state disinterest him of a vain and unnecessary hazard'.[22]

But disinterest has not always been well regarded. Its twin meanings do not help. On the one hand, it can mean 'What is contrary to interest or advantage; disadvantage' while on the other, it can be altogether more honourable: 'Indifference to profit; want of regard to private advantage; disinterestedness'. But the virtue of disinterest – a virtue so critical to public service – rests with the latter meaning. Today, disinterest is often disregarded. Distance is not fashionable, while intimacy, warmth, and engagement are.

Even where the tradition has persisted, it is under threat. The Indian Administrative Service (IAS) is one example. The successor to the British imperial system, the IAS remains a gilded elite in India. In the 1990s, it numbered fewer than 5,000 of the 20 million government employees across India. Recruitment is via a rigorous examination system. In 1988 only about 150 out of approximately 85,000 candidates were appointed to the IAS. Economic liberalisation in India since 1991 has transformed the Indian economy. Through something similar to the British consumer revolution of the 1980s, Indian society has been changed. In part as a result of this, corruption – sometimes a problem, but one that the IAS had largely escaped during the 1950s and 1960s – has crept in. IAS officers have gained a reputation for being staid, conservative, and, sadly, too often corruptible or open to political influence.

In the United States, where the bureaucracy deliberately contains many more political appointments (election, rather than selection, is often preferred) problems of *parti pris* officialdom exist. The result: a political system that relies increasingly on the courts to adjudicate, because elected officials are not disinterested enough – at least for those who did not vote for them. Even so, the American system also values advice: the President is given wide scope to appoint advisors on a range of issues. One President, JFK, understood the value of good counsel: 'The men who create power make an indispensable contribution to the Nation's greatness, but the men who question power make a contribution just as indispensable, especially when that questioning is disinterested, for they determine whether we use power or power uses us.'[23]

THE DECLINE OF DISINTEREST

Disinterest did not suffer a sudden death. But it is in decline, as an order based upon precedent, rules and intellect is gradually replaced by one that values passion, sentiment and social action. Since the 1960s, the West has changed utterly. Across the West the culture wars have been lost. In Europe – unlike America – we find ourselves intellectually and often spiritually adrift.[24] In a culture that stands for nothing, we fall for everything. And as a result, social and political life has become both more pragmatic, and more partisan. The pragmatism is driven by the politics of consensus: on a market economy, social liberalism, a measure of state intervention, and so on. Since the late 1980s, political debates in Britain have pivoted around managerialism and presumed competence in government. But politics has also become more partisan.

Since the 1970s, the frustration of successive government with a slow and (perhaps inevitably) small-c conservative bureaucracy has encouraged a slew of minor changes. First came greater politicised policy planning in the 1970s. Then came the Thatcher era, which saw Thatcher and a group of her closest advisors seek to translate the public services from the Sir Humphrey-like gatekeepers of public policy into the delivery mechanism for a government agenda.[25] Harold Wilson himself had five special advisors. Edward Heath distrusted the Treasury and brought in commercial brains from Bovis, Sainsbury's and Marks & Spencer. Thatcher, interestingly, relied less on special advisors than others – but her style was more direct. Today there are around 80 special advisors, as against the 40-odd under John Major. Many of these exist to manage the media, rather than lead on policy.

Moreover, take advertisements for contemporary public-sector jobs. One often now finds 'passion' or 'impatience' cited as values.[26] Emotive language is ubiquitous in contemporary job advertisements in Britain. Yet the emotional intelligence increasingly sought by employers is not about emotional excess: it calls for empathy, not zeal.

A SYNONYM FOR NEUTRALITY?

Is disinterest simply another way of describing neutrality or impartiality? Neutrality is often perceived as non-participation – whereas the administrative value of disinterest is about making judgements and being involved, without prejudice to any party. As Elias Canetti put it, one can never be neutral in other people's wars. 'In wars that do not concern me', he added, 'I am always on both sides.' Impartiality means freedom from selfish bias or self-interest. Indifference is usually cited as a lack of interest. But disinterest is – peculiarly – about interested disengagement. Impartiality – as a form of behaviour, rather than a moral virtue – captures a little of what this essay means when it discusses disinterest. But the appeal of disinterest is that it accepts how *involved* we all are, without compelling us to attach ourselves to individual policies or positions.

The International Committee of the Red Cross operates in line with strict neutrality. The principle they work by is: in order to continue to enjoy the confidence of all, the Movement may not take sides in hostilities or engage at any time in controversies of a political, racial, religious or ideological nature. 'Neutral, impartial and independent' claims their website, and this has been true of much of their work.[27] And yet this fails to capture their involvement in relieving humanitarian situations. The ICRC does intervene – albeit clinging to these principles while doing so. Unsurprisingly, their operations – as with charities that operate in a similar fashion (like Médecins Sans Frontières) – have come under threat since September 11. The War on Terror permits little by way of neutrality: mass casualty terrorism, and the western response, offer clear moral choices that each of us needs to make. The very concept of neutrality has come under severe strain as a result.

In the wake of the latest invasion of Iraq, jurists have wrung their hands over the breaking down of international ethical norms like humanitarian neutrality. Suicide attacks on the United Nations headquarters, and deliberate killings of charitable workers from CARE and Médecins Sans Frontières show just how far such norms have broken down.[28] In a world in which little is taken as a given, such norms can no longer be taken for granted. Fairness is not a fair-weather virtue, but one that demands moral grounding, not moral grazing. The dilemma for international aid workers and civil servants has, perhaps, been the most acute: to withdraw, which accepts the suspension of neutrality, or to persist, which risks lives.

Financial journalists also face clashes of interest. Should a journalist who holds a chunk of BT stock (or even half a dozen shares) pass judgement on its performance without mentioning his holding? Should he accept generous gifts from companies he writes about? Some newspapers have an internal monitoring system (dusty notebooks in editors' desks); others (like the *Financial Times* Lex column) do not permit writers to hold any stock directly.[29] And rising concerns about possible influence reflect declining faith in the integrity of individuals. Professional disinterest, it appears, demands integrity and judgement – yet today this is considered elusive.

THE VIRTUE OF DISINTEREST

There is good reason to narrate and promote the virtue of disinterest. Above all, disinterest grants administrators integrity. Only civil servants with integrity can enjoy public confidence: and the nineteenth-century reforms that established western bureaucracies (as we know them) were designed to produce efficient, just and ethical public services. One dictionary definition of integrity begins with 'wholeness'.[30] Disinterest is a sign of integrity: the ability to come to a judgement based on evidence, and not to succumb to florid rhetoric.

And administrators remember. Again, the innovation of lifelong tenure for civil servants in 1854 helped professionalise the British civil service. This reform valued memory, witness and faithful advice – values that Milan Kundera would fiercely defend decades later as central Europe laboured under Soviet tyranny.[31] It is perhaps unsurprising that many eminent British public servants were also active (and sometimes professional) historians. Modern historians value disinterest. Driven by intuition, disinterest and good judgement, this school of history is now criticised by postmodernists.[32]

Many of these polymaths echo China's original scholar-administrators. Sir C. P. Lucas (1853–1931) managed a multi-volume *Historical Geography of the British Colonies*. And A. B. Keith (1879–1944), who was called to the bar, wrote a major treatise on *Responsible Government in the Dominions* and still found time to become a sometime Acting Professor of Sanskrit at the University of Oxford. Michael Oakeshott, who so extraordinarily combined a commitment to organic conservatism with a dissolute personal life, described conservatism as being '...not a creed or a doctrine, but a disposition'.[33] And it is disposition – rather than dogma – that drove classical administrators. Many shared a commitment to duty and to service. This can appear quaint to many young administrators today – we understand the ethic, but the ethic itself has since been 'privatised' by virtue of being personalised.

There is a legitimate debate as to how detached officials should be: they need, after all, to have the drive to carry government policy through. Here, perhaps, lies the greatest contemporary dilemma: how to deliver changes in public policy, without compromising the principles that underpin public service. None of this is helped by a welter of surrounding debates that are often on points of advantage, rather than of principle.

All statesmen have drawn on advisors: some prove better than others. Fitfully loyal to their masters, the best advisors have always sought to inform rather than influence – to be honest, rather than seek honours. It is comforting to discover that the Privy Council – viewed by some as an anachronistic element in Britain's unwritten constitution – values independence of advice. Contemporary Privy Counsellors have to affirm their loyalty to the Queen, and the oath they take on appointment includes a commitment to giving good counsel. The oath includes: 'You will in all things to be moved, treated and debated in Council, faithfully and truly declare your Mind and Opinion, according to your Heart and Conscience.'

Of course, disinterest has its critics. For one, it is easy to confuse with impartiality – not quite the same virtue. As G. K. Chesterton wrote, 'impartiality is a pompous name for indifference, which is an elegant name for ignorance'. Edward Said also criticised the 'fiction of scholarly disinterest', arguing that it concealed hard coded value systems.[34] But his argument was partial and ahistorical: 'the West writes the rest' is based upon a specific moment in world history, neglects non-western sources, and fails to account for similar world views held outside the West.[35] Disinterest allows for subjectivity – indeed, it assumes just that. But it also permits judgement – if practised properly – outside subjectivity.

Disinterest is an integral part of good decision making. Public policy – or indeed life – built only on *a priori* assumptions, rather than evidence, history or precedent is a recipe for chaos. It allows the insidious creep of propaganda, rather than principle – which took place, for example, in totalitarian bureaucracies that never valued dissent. We should always remember that 'the most dangerous propaganda is the kind which is not recognised as such at all, either by its audience or even by its perpetrators. It is the steady drip, drip of aggressive, prejudiced or materialistic ideas which those competing to be social leaders project through all the media in their fight for personal success.'[36]

Our polymath administrative predecessors have much to teach us. Elias Canetti, one of the few twentieth-century writers to write with intense integrity, wrote in 1946 that '[l]earning has to be an adventure...What you learn at a given moment ought to depend on chance meetings, and it ought to continue in that way, from encounter to encounter, a learning in transformations, a learning in fun.'[37] Classical administrators – from the counsellor, via the fool, through to late Victorian officials – were exemplars of this advice. The autonomy they were granted allowed them to think for themselves. At their best, they were willing to be wrong, and to learn from it. They were also willing to speak out when right – whatever the personal cost. Men like Hai Rui and Bao Zheng are remembered because of their dedication to truth. Their integrity was driven by their disinterest: the wholeness of their judgement, and indeed their lives, flowed from the ability to advise rather than affirm.

1 Dirk Kaesler, *Max Weber: An Introduction to His Life and Work* (Chicago: University of Chicago Press, 1989).
2 See Alan Beattie and Patrick Dunleavy, 'New perspectives on the British imperial state', *Political Studies Association Conference Proceedings* (1995), pp. 120–9.
3 Philip Lawson, *The East India Company : A History* (London: Longman, 1993).
4 For a useful history of the French civil service, see Roger Grégoire, *The French Civil Service* (Brussels, International Institute of Administrative Sciences, 1964).
5 William Niskanen, *Bureaucracy and Representative Government* (Chicago: Aldine Atherton, 1971).
6 See Richard Chapman, *Ethics in the British Civil Service* (London: Routledge, 1988).
7 One example is David Richards, *The Civil Service under the Conservatives, 1979–1997: Whitehall's Political Poodles?* (Brighton: Sussex Academic Press, 1997).
8 E. M. Cioran, *A Short History of Decay* (New York: Viking Press, 1976).
9 Paul Lichterman, *The Search for Political Community: American Activists Reinventing Commitment* (Cambridge: CUP, 1996), p. 35. Lichterman discusses this in the context of green activism, but the point holds true for public servants.

10 'All of Israel...feared the king because they saw that the wisdom of God was in him to make justice. King Solomon was king over all of Israel' (I Kings 3:28–4:1).

11 See Metropolitan Museum of Modern Art, 'The Scholar-Administrators of China' www.metmuseum.org/toah/hd/schg/hd_schg.htm

12 Wellek Xiong, 'Ability out of fairness', *Shanghai Star*, 23 May 2002.

13 Wang Bing-zhao, Xu Yong (eds), *The Study of the Imperial Examination System in China* (China: Hebei People's Press, 2002).

14 Wolfgang Franke, *The Reform and Abolition of the Traditional Chinese Examination System* (Harvard University pamphlet, 1960).

15 See Brenda Whitney, 'Mentors: benevolent fools or goddesses of power?' *Critical Quarterly*, October 2004 , Vol. 46, 3, p. 111.

16 See Marilyn Yalom, *Birth of the Chess Queen: A History* (London: HarperCollins, 2004).

17 Jon Spayde, 'Medieval Fools', *Utne Reader*, May 2002, Issue 111, p. 69.

18 Beatrice Otto, *Fools Are Everywhere : The Court Jester Around the World* (Chicago: University of Chicago Press, 2001).

19 See Robert Goldsmith, *Wise Fools in Shakespeare* (Michigan: Michigan State University Press, 1968).

20 See both Frederick Ward, *The Fools of Shakespeare* (Folcroft, PA: Folcroft Library Editions, 1973) and Sandra Pyle, *Mirth and Morality of Shakespeare's Holy Fools* (Lewiston, NY: Edwin Mellen Press, 1998).

21 Although satire is also a long-standing tradition. See Charles Knight, *The Literature of Satire* (Cambridge: CUP, 2004).

22 Sean Gaston, 'Derrida and disinterest', *Angelaki: Journal of Theoretical Humanities*, Vol. 7, 3 December 2002, p. 116.

23 John F. Kennedy, Speech, Amherst College, 26 October 1963.

24 One key difference is Europe's comparatively low levels of religious practice, commented upon in Robert Kagan's *Paradise and Power: America and Europe in the New World Order* (London: Atlantic Books, 2003).

25 See Andrew Blick's *People who Live in the Dark: Special Advisers in UK Government 1964–2004* (London: Methuen Publishing, 2004).

26 Take the advert for a Director for Local Government Performance and Improvement (*Guardian*, January 2005), which includes the phrases: 'Are you passionate about public service? Are you impatient about improving local government delivery?' and concludes by stressing 'the desire to make a difference'. See http://jobs.guardian.co.uk/browse/finance/public-sector/vacancy-865687.html

27 See www.icrc.org/

28 See, *inter alia*, CNN, 'Truck bomb kills chief UN envoy to Iraq', 20 August 2003, and BBC News, 'MSF suspends work in Afghanistan', 3 June 2004.

29 A. Evans, 'How independent should financial journalists be?', *The Banker*, May 2001.

30 Concise Oxford Dictionary (7th edition, 1982).

31 Milan Kundera, *The Joke* (London: Faber, 1983) pp. 244–5 and *The Book of Laughter and Forgetting* (New York: Penguin, 1981) pp. 7–8.

32 See Keith Jenkins, *On 'What is History?'* (London: Routledge, 1995) and Richard Evans, *In Defence of History* (London: Granta, 2001).

33 Michael Oakeshott, 'On being conservative' in *Rationalism in Politics and Other Essays* (Indianapolis: Liberty Press, 1991), p. 407.

34 Edward Said, *Orientalism* (New York: Vintage, 1979).

35 Ian Buruma and Avishai Margalit, *Occidentalism: The West in the Eyes of Its Enemies* (New York: Penguin, 2004).

36 Oliver Thompson, *Mass Persuasion in History: A Historical Analysis on the Development of Propaganda Techniques* (Edinburgh: Paul Harris Publishing, 1977), p. 132.

37 Elias Canetti, *The Human Province* (London: Andre Deutsch, 1985), p. 75.

CHAPTER 6

THE FAMILY VIRTUES: AUTHORITY AND
OBEDIENCE; STEWARDSHIP AND SUCCESSION

SIMON GREEN

TWO ENGLISH ODDBALLS

Even by the highest standards of his caste, Merlin Charles Sainthill Hanbury-Tracy, 7th Baron Sudeley, is no ordinary eccentric. Devoted beyond duty to his sovereign, he proudly serves as Vice-Chancellor of the Monarchist League. An unashamed patriot, he determinedly reigns as Chairman of the Monday Club. Eschewing all conventional forms of gainful employment, he is Patron of the National Association of Bankrupts. Yet his first loyalty remains to his family – its past, present and future. Still squire of the manor, the poignantly childless peer and joint author of *The Sudeleys: Lords of Toddington* pointedly lists his heir in *Who's Who* as fellow 'kinsman' Desmond Andrew John Hanbury-Tracy. Above all, though, he is loyal to his family's past: this otherwise unblemished churchman – a leading light in the Prayer Book Society – publicly records his principal pastime as 'ancestor worship'.[1]

By contrast, Christopher Simon Sykes, the more obviously talented issue of a no less distinguished family, looks, at least on the surface, to be a thoroughly modern aristocrat. A much published photographer and journalist, he is also something of a society figure. He carries no arcane social and political baggage; not even membership of the Conservative Party. Man about town and a natty dresser, he enjoys the good things in life; and a few of the bad things, too. But Christopher (now in his mid-fifties) is still devoted to Sledmere, the Sykes' ancient family home. Just listen to him speak:

> Pluck me from my bed, blindfold me, drop me anywhere in the world and I could pick out the smell of Sledmere from a thousand others. This is the house where my family have lived for 250 years. It is where I was brought up and spent my adolescence. Though I left it when I was eighteen, I still feel attached to it as if by some invisible umbilical cord. I do not

live there yet my roots are there. For good or bad, it inhabits my soul.[2]

These are no idle words; still less, the shallow apology of a man who got his housing free. Remember, Christopher Simon Sykes is a third son. He does not live at Sledmere. Nor has he for nearly forty years. That privilege belongs to his eldest brother, Tatton. Moreover, this distinction among siblings was something he learned the hard way. Tatton had to tell him. Shortly after the death of their father in 1978 Christopher 'nonchalantly' informed the new squire of Sledmere that:

> '[B]y the way I'm coming up for the weekend and I'm bringing a couple of friends.'
> 'Who said you could do that?' he asked me with some surprise.
> 'I don't have to ask', I replied indignantly, 'it's my home.'
> 'Not any more it isn't', he told me, firmly, 'it's *my* home now. You'll always be welcome here…but from now on you must ask me if you want to come and stay, not just presume you can.'[3]

Surely, the stuff of irreparable family rupture; except that it proved otherwise. True, Christopher initially 'stalked off in a fury'. But when he 'thought about it' he realised that 'Tatton…was right'. He was 'head of the family' and Sledmere '*was* now his home'. That meant it was 'time for the rest of us to move on'. This was 'a difficult task'. But it was also a 'necessary transformation'. With its completion, the Sykes clan lives on. And Sledmere is reborn. That matters more than Christopher's personal preferences.[4]

THE PRIORITY OF THE HOUSEHOLD

Most of us, in all probability, would not so much condemn as fail even to comprehend such seemingly antediluvian personal priorities and proprietorial arrangements. After all, few any longer feel sacredly *defined* by their ancestry. Still fewer would happily live according to the constraints which such a definition must invariably entail. To be sure, anecdotal family history preoccupies many. As Llewellyn Powys once observed:

> Each family, however modest its origin, possesses its own particular tale of the past which can bewitch it with a sense of insistent romance as can ever the tradition of kings.[5]

By extension, more thoughtful citizens continue to value the institution of the family more generally. Thus Pope John Paul II: 'As the family goes, so goes the nation and so goes the whole world in which we live.'[6] But if amateur genealogy is now a more popular pastime than ever, only a handful engage in such research for the purpose of *revering* those members of their extended family who have gone before them. For every obscure devotee of personal lineage, there are surely many more quietly content to establish the very obscurity of their forebears as a way of underlining the full extent of their own, unaided achievements in life. Olive Lloyd-Baker's heroic insistence, made in conversation with the then Poet Laureate, that 'an ounce of heredity is worth a pound of merit', may have tickled John Betjeman pink.[7] It would, however, leave 'Essex man' cold. He prefers to think, with Frank Sinatra, that he did it all 'his way'.[8]

By the same token, few of us conceive of our souls in terms of some bricks and mortar we have long since ceased to inhabit. Indeed, few now plan their lives by reference to a peculiar place in the order of lineal inheritance. Most Americans fondly believe that they have not done so since a cherished revolution abolished the hated institution of primogeniture in the New Republic.[9] Frenchmen – at least Frenchmen of a certain kind – characteristically trace liberation from that same curse to the gradual imposition during the nineteenth century of the Napoleonic Code throughout 'the octagon'.[10] Even in England, the sway of entail – that binding, legal arrangement for the settling of land and property on first sons, the institution that even recently enriched Tatton and deprived Christopher Sykes – has greatly declined since the First World War.[11] More to the point, the massive growth – both in the absolute size and proportionate wealth – of the middle classes that has been common to all the advanced economies since the Second World War has, at one and the same time, both increased the extent and diminished the significance of proprietary succession throughout contemporary society. For, as inherited property has become more common, so it has altered in nature. To come into land today is seldom to acquire the presumed social responsibilities, still less the immediate political privileges, that once followed – in England anyway – almost as a matter of course.[12] It is simply to deploy one of the many possible forms of capital. This still confers considerable material advantages on the individual beneficiary, and that still offends egalitarian, distributionist sensibilities. But it scarcely defines personal identity or establishes the basis of social relations.[13] To that extent, the rich really are now just richer than everyone else.[14]

Whether this is for good or ill is a question best considered elsewhere. For now, suffice it to note that, for the best part of its history, 'the family', so called, thrived not merely as a non-contractual, but also as an essentially authoritarian system of social relations – one that subordinated wives to husbands in the marriage construct; also children to the *paterfamilias* in the legal rights of fatherhood; and finally every living member to the overriding end of its organic perpetuation. Similarly, it should be noted that property played a crucial, constitutive role in this way of being. Indeed, it would scarcely be an exaggeration to insist that the two institutions were, until quite recently, conceived as indispensable bulwarks of social order that stood, or fell, in their intertwined destiny. This was because the family had its life in the home – that peculiar institution that served both as the source of all authority and as the unique repository of unconditional love. And the home required property for its establishment. Put another way, domestic virtue presupposed private space, be it ever so great or ever so humble – the acres of Sledmere or 'the right to shut a door against another person'.[15] Why? Because no less than the observance of rules or the expression of affection, the capacity to objectify (and own) nature was understood to be a vital prerequisite not merely of privacy, but also of identity: what distinguished human beings from animals. By extension, the succession of property through the generations was conceived as something analogous to biological descent – in effect, what distinguished the family from the pack. For that reason, the father-headed family and, with it, the grid of inheritance, were never the preserve of the privileged few. They were once the lot of us all: in the household.

The notion of *paterfamilias* is traceable to Roman law.[16] For much of subsequent European history – to say nothing of non-European traditions – its rules and regulations were peacefully incorporated into the broader social conventions of Christian civilisation.[17] So much so that de Tocqueville famously remarked upon its peculiar absence in nineteenth-century America as proof that 'the family...properly so-called...had ceased to...exist' in that novel democracy.[18] This was almost certainly an exaggeration. However, that so careful a social commentator should have been moved to say it at all proves just how closely our forbears associated family life with fatherly rule. Their essential purpose everywhere was to define the legal rights of the household exclusively in its head. The Bible justified this state of affairs as God's command. Reason pointed to the necessity for sovereignty in the domestic, as in any other, social bond. Tradition more broadly sanctioned such arrangements, enforcing a customary obedience of wives to husbands, and similarly the proper *piety* of children for parents. Each presumed the logical priority of the household as – literally – the first social institution: the institutional model upon which all other necessary, and civilising, human organisations were based.[19]

Seventeenth-century contract theory did little to undermine that commonly conceived certainty. Much of its underlying political teaching was corroborated, even as its social analysis was qualified, in the more substantial findings of eighteenth-century 'civil histories'.[20] All the while, the fundamental relations of pre-modern life proclaimed its continuing urgency. Up until very recent times, industry, trade – even government – remained as much aspects of domestic kinship as impersonal relations. Indeed, indenture and servitude ensured many more were actually subject to the authority of the family than any of the various census figures ever revealed.[21] Thus it was in praise, not only of a well-ordered, but also of an impeccably modern, commercial society, that Disraeli described Victorian England as: 'a domestic country'; a place where 'the home is revered and the hearth sacred'.[22]

That doctrine occasionally gave way to a fact that observant critics knew well enough. Hobbes even went so far as to remark that:

> whereas some have attributed the Dominion [of the family]
> to the man only...they misreckon in it.

For, whatever the law might say, 'there is not always that difference in strength, or produce between the man and the woman'.[23] Which was no doubt true, many times over. Yet Malmesbury's most famous son may have missed the more important point. For, whatever the vagaries of nature, the patriarchal household was rarely bereft of sustaining social sanctions. English common law permitted husbands to chastise their spouses according to a 'rule of thumb', that is, with a blunt instrument the width of this digit, well into the twentieth century.[24] Both legal authority and domestic custom allowed fathers to disinherit ungrateful daughters. Actually, 'to disclaim all...potential care, propinquity and property of blood', leaving them, as Lear left Cordelia, with 'thy truth, then, [as] thy dower'.[25] Not just daughters, either. When young Robert Cecil announced his intention of marrying the inappropriately bourgeois Georgina Anderson in 1858, his father (the second Marquis of Salisbury) promptly cut him off for good. Albeit, in this instance, with less harrowing consequences. The prospect of poverty first obliged the importunate youth to hawk his earnest thoughts on contemporary questions to a grateful *Quarterly Review*. Today, these form the basis of his reputation as a major nineteenth-century political thinker. Then Robert's elder brother died, comparatively young. So the disobedient boy succeeded by right, as third Marquis, in 1869. His statue still stands outside Hatfield House, a tribute to the greatest statesman of Queen Victoria's later decades.[26]

His was an unusual case, scarcely less so than Cordelia's. Imaginative literature, and even the historical record, more frequently record an institution characterised by unrighted capriciousness and blighted by unresolved injustices. But that, too, may be less damning a criticism than most modern authorities presume. It has now become so common to condemn the patriarchal family for its presumed enormities – for the sheer inequity of such unequal and unaccountable domestic relations – that contemporary sensibility has become virtually blind to its redeeming virtues. Yet these were considerable; and probably no less valuable. After all, the privileges of husbandry, properly so called, also entailed profound responsibilities. At their most stark, the very same laws that prevented married women from holding property separately from their spouses also made the head of the household legally responsible for all those debts which his wife accrued. These nearly ruined the Sykes family in the middle of the nineteenth century.[27] More typically, the dominion that a father exercised over his offspring presupposed his continuous dedication to their present and future well-being, its fulfilment achieved at no mean cost. Hence de Montaigne's pained insistence that: 'there is hardly any less torment in running a family than in running a whole country'.[28]

FROM OBEDIENCE (NATURALLY) TO INDEPENDENCE

More significantly, the inequality of standing between the generations encouraged both a degree of outward devotion, and an extent of inner direction in the young that have been all but lost in the permissive, affective family of contemporary preference. It is by no means obvious that this loss is best understood as progress. Something in our very nature compels us to think of children as having responsibilities towards their parents which extend beyond mere contractual right; responsibilities, in effect, due to parents simply in recognition of the biological bond itself. For that reason, our sense of filial obligation is only ever ambiguously related to the concept of justice. It is also about honour, as the Bible had it, or *pietas*, as the Romans believed. Dishonour and impiety are expressed in that 'refusal to recognise' as legitimate related demands that 'do not arise from consent or choice'.[29] They were once discouraged by something more than just the indistinct claims of nature. Not only family law, but the full weight of social convention actively condemned any such juvenile delinquency. And not just for the sake of parental ease, but rather in the belief that precisely because the family was the first institution, disobedience in the home presaged disloyalty to society more generally. And from there it was but a small step to treason against the nation. As Burke put it, 'we begin our public affections in our families. No cold relation is a zealous citizen.'[30]

The universal presumption of obedience in youth was conceived as part of a common learning process. Valuable in itself, such knowledge was, above all, necessary for the acquisition of the proper allegiances of adulthood. To that end, it was both generally valued and widely disseminated. In the era before universal, compulsory education, the relevant responsibility for its inculcation was almost entirely delegated to domestic authority. This, social as much as legal, burden was sustained by complex customs of parental authority and juvenile submission: beginning with such weighty concerns as propertied descent and permission to marry, and proceeding on to such seemingly trivial matters as personal nomenclature, positions at table, and even the precise deployment of private space. Those conventions characteristically emphasised the virtues of paternal governance and filial respect. These qualities were sometimes elevated at the expense of more natural intimacy between the generations. Sometimes, but not always: Thomas Bagehot positively 'worshipped' young Walter, 'the greatest treasure of his life'. And that before the *Economist*'s future editor had published a word.[31]

Moreover, the very assertion of such authority was, of necessity, time bound. As such, it was only ever understood in terms of its eventual eclipse. Thus, it actually formed part of the cultivation of a quite other, yet paradoxically related, virtue. This was the spirit of independence. Remarking upon what had, by then, become the peculiarly patriarchal *English* family, French sociologist Émile Boutmy observed the curious effect of, what he called, 'monarchy by divine right' in early twentieth-century Anglo-Saxon domestic arrangements. This, he believed, had forged a 'virile...race', at once 'accustomed...to discipline' and yet also habituated 'to liberty and responsibility'. That was, in part, because the chastening experience of strict patriarchal authority encouraged young English sons to yearn for liberty in their own right; that is, to become fathers themselves. It was also, and in equal part, because the Puritan marriage bond (which, let it be recalled, tied men to women as surely as it subordinated wives to husbands) ensured that Englishmen learned from the earliest age 'that they did not come before their father in the affection of their mother'.[32] To that degree, they remained, in Harold Nicolson's memorable phrase, 'strangers to their parents'. But such distance neither deprived them of functional role models – *vide* Nicolson himself – nor turned them into Oedipal maniacs. On the contrary, it helped to endow England's younger male population with precisely those 'manly qualities' that enabled them successfully to assume 'the roles of husband and...father'.[33] Quickly, too; for men fortunately spared 'the enervating tendencies' of parental indulgence soon learned that '[they] must count only on themselves'. This furnished them with the confidence 'to take the initiative and command' throughout the rest of [their] lives'.[34] That was true even for one so ambivalently driven as Nicolson himself. It might also go some way to explaining why Somerset Maugham later observed:

> Few misfortunes can befall a boy which bring worse
> consequences than to have a really affectionate mother.[35]

It certainly does point to a powerful contrast with the 'boomerang babies' of contemporary complaint. Whatever its shortcomings, the patriarchal family was never burdened by innumerable young men and (increasingly) women unwilling to abandon the parental nest for fear of relinquishing its infantilising indulgences.[36]

There was another point. Boutmy's analysis very deliberately declined to differentiate between the fate (and characters) of first and subsequent sons. Indeed, he insisted that the eldest's so-called 'testamentary liberty' did not 'move...him any less profoundly' in the desired direction 'than his brothers'.[37] This was, superficially, strange. But it was not an oversight of ignorance. That the 'system of entail', according to which perhaps three-quarters of all land in England was settled by the end of the nineteenth century, invariably guaranteed its fortunate beneficiaries 'revenue exceeding the ordinary limits of individual powers of enjoyment' while leaving their siblings '[in]secure in every part of their inheritance', he understood perfectly well.[38] That the principal purpose of this allocation of property was to protect the fortunes of the historical family against either the ambitions or the imprudence of each inheriting generation, he recognised with similar clarity.[39] However, his observation that, as an unintended corollary, this institution also had the effect of steering landlords towards 'the concept of social mission' – more specifically, to 'power exercised for good' by the 'endow[ment] of useful institutions in perpetuity' – whilst simultaneously pushing otherwise well-born young gentlemen out into the world of 'empire and commerce', provided a new and peculiar insight into the matter. Moreover, he judged its 'overall effect' to be the creation of an 'unusually ample…human personality' in England.[40]

This gift he argued to be the product, in part, of wealth. For it was wealth that allowed people such as the Duke of Bridgewater to undertake 'massive works' of a public character – in his case, canal construction. But, he insisted, it was not only dependent upon wealth. It was also the result of lineage and training. In effect, it was the function of a kind social standing that also habituated its inheritors either to service or to work, and sometimes to both. This combination, he believed, created not simply a peculiar class but, by extension, an entire nation – that is, a body of citizens – willing and able not only to 'supply the deficiencies of state' when and where necessary, but also, and no less importantly 'to resist its pretensions to monopoly power', as such contingent crises arose.[41] Put another way: citizens who were students of Burke for the most part, but followers of Algernon Sidney if need be.[42]

PRIVATE PROPERTY AND POLITICAL FREEDOM

There is no need to accept all – or indeed any – of Boutmy's sweeping psychological generalisations in order to appreciate the force of his altogether more subtle social commentary.[43] The lasting value of his account lies in its precise understanding of the vital historical link forged between the patriarchal family and entailed property. This was true in England especially, but also throughout the civilised world more generally, from the later middle ages onwards.[44] To be sure, it was by no means a simple connection. Indeed, the capacity of English property law to restrict the terms of landed succession in the interests of first sons, living or unborn, often encouraged exactly that *irresponsibility* of youth – of feckless older children beyond the discipline of disinheritance – that shadows the novels of Jane

Austen.[45] For all that, no better system for the preservation of property through the generations was ever invented.[46] It is thus no coincidence that, outside Bohemia and Austria, its provisions were never confined just to the nobility. Indeed, from the end of the fifteenth century, they became the characteristic method by which land especially was legally transferred among the possessing classes of Europe and beyond.[47]

Its broader social implications not only defined families by property, but also domestic relations according to propertied imperatives. In England, anyway, this was so to an extraordinarily far-reaching degree. Following the abolition of the Court of Wards in 1660, the emergence of so-called Strict Family Settlement provisions enabled those in possession to settle their lands on unborn children. There were very good reasons for them to do this. For mere biological survival itself was then far from easy. Indeed, the English landed classes actually failed to reproduce themselves in the century after 1640.[48] Even in the age of the first Sykes fortune, wastage among the gentry was extraordinarily high. As late as 1838, only 22 per cent of peers held titles that dated back beyond 1688. Similarly, of 1,226 baronetcies created between 1611 and 1800, only 295, or 24 per cent, survived to 1928.[49] From that brutal contingency followed one simple truth, and one powerful moral. As a matter of fact, the great English landed aristocracy was as much a collection of parvenus as the product of ancient lineage. Not for nothing did Defoe caustically celebrate 'Lords whose parents were Lord knows who'.[50] But in matters of manners, the origins of the beast never defined the ends of the angel. As Wellington supposedly put it, being 'born in a stable' did not 'make him a horse'.[51] Down to the agricultural depression of the 1880s, the *nouveaux riches* enthusiastically pursued the goal of gentlemanly standing, invariably seeking to acquire all the accoutrements – of birth, title and land – necessary to enable them to do so. Yet, by the same token, the irreducible difficulties of descent continued to emphasise the value – that is, to mark the sense of achievement – implicit in the historic continuity of family and property through heredity succession. Thus, men of substance who 'worshipped' their ancestors were neither fools nor fanatics. They were shrewd chroniclers of estimable effort; minimally, of commendable endurance. Some now smile at Lord Sudeley's hobby; few formerly scoffed at Churchill's *Life of Marlborough*.[52]

For such boasting commonly masked a more serious claim. Certainly, it was seldom merely a celebration of past glory. Rather, it pointed to a declaration of continuing significance. It did not, normally, threaten rebellion. For men of property were usually among the monarch's most loyal subjects. Rather, it was a statement of independence, typically advanced as a polite, but firm, assertion of the priority of family arms over state honours. Indeed, as economic reality (independent wealth) matched feudal pretensions (family colours) so the privileges of first sons broadened out into the representations of related siblings. Thus England's landed elite enjoyed local authority as a class – not just as property owners, but as magistrates and representatives too. In so doing, they also sustained broader social and political freedoms far beyond their own exclusive enjoyment. Under their tutelage, entire localities participated in the reality of liberty through gratuitous self-government. By extension, uncounted individuals were guaranteed the blessings of domestic security in the dispersed multiplicity of private property.[53] Hence the paradox of England after 1660: that a unitary, monarchical regime was effectively governed by a few thousand proudly uncowed – and, at least in that sense, uncorrupted – families. It was this social and political order that was championed by foreign admirers of this country, from de Tocqueville to Namier. Its spirit can still be dimly discovered in our time by the pluck of men such as James Lees-Milne who, in turning down the offer of a CBE in 1988, remarked: 'I may...be a snob...but I am not that kind of snob.'[54]

THE PRIVILEGES AND RESPONSIBILITIES OF STEWARDSHIP

In this understanding of family, the function of property was overwhelmingly preservative. That is, it was understood as the best means of maintaining what already existed. As one famous clan motto put it: 'Let Curzon holde what Curzon held.'[55] To be sure, it could be – and it was – property mightily decorated. From 1660 onwards, few English propertied families did without a beautified country house; certainly not the Curzons.[56] And such beautification often had profound social and psychological consequences. Remember where we started, with Christopher Sykes. Moreover, the possibilities of accumulation implied in entail never ruled out the richer pickings to be had from a more rational exploitation of a valuable natural resource. From eighteenth-century enclosure to Victorian 'high farming', plenty of sound entrepreneurship went into the organisation of British agriculture.[57] But Adam Smith spoke truer than he knew when he condemned the economic consequences of the English landed estate – that is, what he perceived to be the inadequate valorisation of resources.[58] For those who invested in such property prior to 1945 were 'agrarian capitalists' only as a last resort. Their real priorities lay elsewhere.[59]

Ecological, social and even political conservation after this fashion had many purposes. These are perhaps best summarised in the concept of stewardship. This was a sensibility that first arose as an expression of gratitude; of being glad for what one had been bequeathed. That sentiment was entirely compatible with the duty of improvement. From the ancients down, men proudly boasted that they had 'found brick and left...marble'.[60] Yet, by the same logic, they also roundly condemned those 'covetous of others' possessions' and 'prodigal...of [their] own'.[61] Apparent contradiction was rendered coherent in a broader convention that emphasised the piety that lay in visible, indeed demonstrable, continuity. No one expressed these feelings more eloquently than Shakespeare's Kentish squire, Alexander Iden. Consider his reflections in *Henry VI, Part II*:

> Lord, who would live turmoilèd [tormented] in the court,
> And may enjoy such quiet walks as these
> The small inheritance my father left me
> Contenteth me, and worth a monarchy
> I seek not to wax great by others' waning
> Or gather wealth, I care not, with what envy
> Sufficeth that I have what maintains my state
> And send the poor well pleased from my gate.[62]

Note also how he acknowledged that these privileges also presumed responsibilities. Two hundred years later, Thomas Drummond put it more crisply still: 'Property has its duties as well as its rights.'[63] There is no need to be sentimental about the balance of bounty and burdens; merely to comprehend its significance. The attendant chores were seldom selflessly exercised. They could be evaded. Kenneth Clark's unforgettable autobiography outlines the lengths to which his own parents went to avoid theirs.[64] That does not alter the fact that those who were dutiful in this way thereby understood something that was lost on such baleful specimens of the 'idle rich'. For they comprehended the vital connections between their own family and those families dependent upon them; those links specifically mediated through the institution of property itself. They grasped that, just as first sons had an obligation to dowagers (in the form of accommodation) and daughters (in the provision of portions), so they properly bore analogous burdens, as landlords, to tenants and labourers beyond their kin – indeed to anyone who came under their propertied jurisdiction – under the guise of social administration and political leadership.[65]

These relationships are inadequately described as 'paternalistic'. For that – invariably pejorative – designation presupposes an extension of the notion of patriarchy beyond what contemporaries took to be its legitimate boundaries. First sons were not their brothers' keepers; nor were landlords their tenants' fathers. Rather they were men, such as Lord Eustace Percy's father, in whom 'large private responsibilities...tended...to form...a certain talent for public affairs'. Note 'a certain talent'; actually, 'one that is apt to be restricted in range'. This was because that aptitude in a landowner 'tended to be essentially personal, best employed in affairs which he could know and measure by sight and touch'. As such, 'he could manage men with whom he could talk, but was uncertain in judging public opinion or in conducting public debate'.[66] More fundamentally:

> his very vivid moral sense was one of personal duty to a
> personal neighbour, whether his equal or his dependent; what it
> is now called 'a social conscience' seemed to him dangerously
> irresponsible, because impersonal.[67]

BEYOND THE FAMILY: TO WHAT?

That may explain why property so conceived proved so slow to acquire the justification of a social conscience. This failure played a crucial part in its subsequent political downfall. For its supposed selfishness was most effectively exposed in its allegedly inadequate contribution to the public purse.[68] Death duties were designed to put that right.[69] State-sponsored social antagonism in our own time has, ironically, only made this provenance smaller. To be sure, we still have rich, propertied families; in England, as elsewhere. In many ways, they are wealthier and securer – more likely to survive – than they ever were.[70] But – perforce – the scope of their common concern is, and especially in England, narrower than it ever was. At the same time, a decline in the differentiated social obligations of family has inspired a concomitant growth in the affective bonds of family relations; just as de Tocqueville predicted it would.[71] Husbands today do not command their wives' obedience. Children do not fear their father's wrath.[72] Families are as equal as the law can now render them.[73] To observe that they more frequently dissolve is, perhaps, to do no more than describe how prevailing social arrangements now reflect – as they once assuredly suppressed – the imperatives of individual preferences. But perhaps the wisdom of our times can be challenged in an understanding of the family that concentrates not so much upon its supposed equity – which must always be ambiguous – but more upon its historic functions. On purposes that were once clear but manifold, and are today both obscure and diminishing. Is the family now the primary source of infant socialisation? Not in the welfare state. Not perhaps among the self-consciously enlightened, since Hegel elevated the 'right[s] of civil society' over 'the arbitrary…preferences of parents' in 'all those matters of… education bearing upon the child's capacity to become a member of that society'.[74] Is a 'haven in a heartless world' our principal hope of happiness? Not in the age of the Child Support Agency. Not, indeed, for modern liberationists like Edmund Leach, who insists that 'with its narrow primacy and tawdry secrets [it] is [actually] the source of all our discontents'.[75]

In truth, families have always been restrictive – to both good and ill effect. This is true for the ambitions of parents, but also of children. Note Bacon's lament on parenthood:

> He that hath a wife and children hath given hostage to fortune; they are impediments to great enterprises, either of virtue or of mischief.[76]

Then recall Mary Wollstonecraft's rejection of that 'bondage to parents [which] cramps every faculty of the mind'.[77] Let us grant that they were both right; in part anyway. We might still doubt the wisdom of their words. Humane understanding once grasped the plenitude as well as the burden that lay in families. Common sense once taught that society is both necessarily and admirably

> a partnership not only between those who are living, but between those who are living, those who are dead, and those who are to be born.[78]

The loss of those insights is no trivial matter. Its consequences are already visible in the demographic degeneration of western Europe.[79]

1   *Who's Who 2005* (London: A. and C. Black, 2005), p. 2147.
2   Christopher Simon Sykes, *The Big House: The Story of a Country House and its Family* (London: HarperCollins, 2004), p. 5.
3   *ibid.*, p. 375.

4   *ibid.*, See Ch. XV 'Sledmere Reborn', *passim*.

5   Llewellyn Powys, *Earth Memories* (London: Chatto and Windus, 1951), p. 273.

6   John Paul II, *Observer*, 7 December 1986.

7   Cited in James Lees Milne, *A Mingled Measure: Diaries, 1953–1972* (London: John Murray, 1994), at p. 217; entry for 19 March 1972.

8   'Essex Man', a term allegedly invented by journalist Simon Heffer, refers to the aspirational working class of South East England. This body of men (and women) voted disproportionately Conservative during the 1980s, at once reflecting the social values, and constituting the key political constituency, of what became known as 'Thatcherism'.

9   Jane Lewis, *The Pursuit of Happiness: Family and Values in Jefferson's Virginia* (Cambridge: CUP, 1983), pp. 25–30 and 144–55.

10 Cf. George Lefebvre, *The French Revolution: From its Origins to 1793*, trans. Elizabeth Moss Evanson (London: Routledge and Kegan Paul, 1962), pp. 148–63 and Theodore Zeldin, *France, 1848–1945*, Vol. I, *Ambition, Love and Politics* (Oxford: OUP, 1973), Chs 12 and 13.

11 The essential history is H. J. Habakkuk, *Marriage, Death and the Estates System: English Landownership, 1650–1950* (Oxford: OUP, 1994); for post-1914 developments, see pp. 694–704.

12 See the remarks in J. V. Beckett, *The Aristocracy in England, 1660–1914* (Oxford: Basil Blackwell, 1986), pp. 474–81; also G. E. Mingay, *Land and Society in England, 1750–1980* (London: Longman, 1994), Ch. 11.

13 To the extent that it ever did; see the argument in Karl Marx, *Capital*, Vol. 1, Pt 8, 'So-Called Primitive Accommodation', trans. Ben Fowkes (Harmondsworth: Penguin Books, 1972), esp. Chs 26–9, pp. 873–957.

14 F. Scott Fitzgerald: 'Let me tell you about the rich. They are different from you and me.' Ernest Hemingway, 'Yes, they have more money.' Cited in Angela Partington (ed.), *The Oxford Dictionary of Quotations* (Oxford: OUP, 1992), p. 284.

15 Roger Scruton, *The Meaning of Conservatism*, 3rd edition (London: Palgrave Macmillan, 2001), p. 95. I owe the substance of this paragraph to that work.

16 Edward Gibbon, *The History of the Decline and Fall of the Roman Empire*, ed. David Womersley (Harmondsworth: Allen Lane, 1994), Vol. II, Ch. XLIV, esp. pp. 806–19; note its juxtaposition to 'Right of Property', pp. 819ff.

17 Saint Augustine, *The City of God*, trans. Marcus Dods (New York: Modern Library, 1993), pp. 694–5; for a modern commentary, see Jack Goody, *The Development of the Family and Marriage in Europe*

(Cambridge: CUP, 1983), pp. 21–30 and 151–5.

18 Alexis de Tocqueville, *Democracy in America*, trans.
Harvey C. Mansfield and Delba Winthrop (Chicago: University of
Chicago Press, 2000), p. 558.

19 Genesis 3:16; Robert Alter (trans.), *The Five Books of Moses*
(New York: Norton, 2004), p. 26; Jean Bodin, *On Sovereignty:
Four Chapters from the Six Books of the Commonwealth*,
ed. Julian H. Franklin (Cambridge: CUP, 1992), pp. 6–8, 13, 27–34
and 49–50; Gordon Schochet, *Patriarchalism in Political Thought:
The Authoritarian Family and Political Speculation and Attitudes,
Especially in Seventeenth-Century England* (Oxford: Blackwell, 1975),
esp. Chs XII and XIII.

20 John Locke, *The Second Treatise of Government*, Chs 1, 2, 7 and 8,
ed. Peter Laslett (Cambridge: CUP, 1967), pp. 285–96 and 336–67;
cf. Sir Robert Filmer, *Patriarcha and Other Writings*,
ed. Johann P. Somerville (Cambridge: CUP, 1991), Ch. 1;
on the eighteenth-century catalogue of 'contract theory', see esp.
David Hume, 'Of the original contract', in Eugene F. Miller (ed.),
Essays: Moral, Political and Literary (Indianapolis: Liberty Classics,
1985), pp. 465–87. More generally, Adam Ferguson, *An Essay on the
History of Civil Society*, ed. Faria O. Schutzberger (Cambridge: CUP,
1995), Pt 2, Section III, 'Of rude nations prior to the…establishment
of property', pp. 80–94.

21 Richard M. Smith, 'Some issues concerning families and their
property in rural England, 1250–1800', in R. M. Smith (ed.),
Land, Kinship and Life Cycle (Cambridge: CUP, 1984), pp. 1–86;
W. A. Armstrong, 'Social structure from the early census returns',
in Peter Laslett, D. E. C. Eversley, and W. A. Armstrong (eds),
An Introduction to English Historical Demography (New York: Basic
Books, 1966), Ch. 6.

22 See Robert Blake, *Disraeli* (London: Eyre and Spottiswoode, 1966),
pp. 522–4, where this speech is analysed in detail.

23 Thomas Hobbes, *Leviathan*, Pt 2, Ch. 20, 'Of Dominion paternall
and despoticall', ed. Richard Tuck (Cambridge: CUP, 1996), p. 139.

24 M. Doggett, *Marriage, Wife-Beating and the Law in Victorian
England* (London: Harvard University Press, 1992), *passim*; for a
contemporary commentary, see Stephen M. Cretney, Judith M. Masson
and Rebecca Baily-Harris, *Principles of Family Law*, 7th ed. (London:
Sweet and Maxwell, 2003), pp. 231–2. To be fair, Hobbes conceded
that very point in the same paragraph, above; see Hobbes, *Leviathan*,
pp. 139–40.

25 William Shakespeare, *King Lear*, Act I, Scene 1, lines 107–119;
Arden Shakespeare, ed. Kenneth Muir (London: Eyre Methuen, 1952),
p. 10.

26 Lady Gwendolen Cecil, *Life of Robert, Marquess of Salisbury*, Vol. 1, *1830–1868* (London: Hodder and Stoughton, 1921), Chs 2 and 3; Andrew Roberts, *Salisbury: Victorian Titan* (London: Weidenfeld and Nicolson, 1999), Chs 2–4; cf. Michael Benthay, *Lord Salisbury's World: Conservative Environments in Late Victorian Britain* (Cambridge: Cambridge University Press, 2001), Ch. 5.

27 Sykes, *The Big House*, pp. 219ff.

28 Michel de Montaigne, 'On solitude', in *The Complete Essays*, ed. and trans. Michael Screech (Harmondsworth: Allen Lane, 1991), Bk. 1, Ch. 39, pp. 266–78, at p. 267.

29 Scruton, *Meaning of Conservatism*, p. 23.

30 Edmund Burke, *Reflections on the Revolution in France*, ed. J. C. D. Clark (Stanford, CA: Stanford University Press, 2001), p. 366.

31 Norman St John-Stevas, *Walter Bagehot: A Study of His Life and Thought* (London: Eyre and Spottiswoode, 1959), p. 2.

32 Emile Boutmy, *The English: A Study in their Political Psychology*, trans. E. English (London: John Murray, 1904), p. 217.

33 Harold Nicolson, *Diaries and Letters*, Vol. 1, *1930–9*, ed. Nigel Nicolson (London: Collins, 1966), p. 113, entry for 30 March 1932; Boutmy, *The English*, pp. 217–18.

34 Boutmy, *The English*, p. 219.

35 W. Somerset Maugham, *A Writer's Notebook* (London: William Heinemann, 1949), p. 87; the entry was originally written in 1896.

36 'Boomerang Babies'; a journalistic term, invented during the 1990s in order to describe the peculiarly English (?) phenomenon of young men and women, who, having left the family home aged 18 or 19 to attend university, return (usually unmarried) in their twenties and thirties. This phenomenon is also ascribed to the, previously unprecedented, willingness of parents to permit their offspring to engage in sexual relations under the family roof.

37 Boutmy, *The English*, p. 220.

38 *ibid.*

39 *ibid.*, p. 220.

40 *ibid.*, p. 220.

41 *ibid.*, p. 222.

42 Cf. Burke, *Reflections*, p. 202; and Algernon Sidney, *Discourses Concerning Government*, ed. Thomas G. West (Indianapolis: Liberty Classics, 1990), see esp. Ch. 3.

43 For a historical context, and a very different account, see Lawrence Stone, *The Family, Sex and Marriage in England, 1500–1800* (London: Weidenfeld and Nicolson, 1977), Ch. 9.

44 Beckett, *Aristocracy in England*, pp. 58ff; Habakkuk, *Marriage*, pp. 1–26.

45 Above all, *Mansfield Park*, ed. Kathryn Sutherland

(Harmondsworth: Penguin Books, 1996); see esp. Vol. 1, Ch. 4, pp. 33–42 and Vol. 1, Ch. 9, pp. 79–90; for a historical account, see Habakkuk, *Marriage*, pp. 89–97.

46 Beckett, *Aristocracy in England*, p. 59; more generally, Habakkuk, *Marriage*, Ch. 1.

47 Beckett, *Aristocracy in England*, pp. 58ff; J. P. Cooper, 'Patterns of inheritance and settlement by great landowners from the fifteenth to the eighteenth centuries', in Jack Goody *et al.*, *Family and Inheritance: Rural Society in Western Europe, 1200–1800* (Cambridge: Cambridge University Press, 1976), pp. 192–305.

48 H. J. Habakkuk, 'English landownership, 1680–1740', *Economic History Review*, Vol. X, No. 1 (February 1940), pp. 2–17, remains the classic account: for the evolution of extended settlements, see his 'Marriage settlements in the eighteenth century', *Transactions of the Royal Historical Society*, 4th series, Vol. XXXII (1950), 15–30.

49 Beckett, *Aristocracy in England*, p. 96.

50 Daniel Defoe, *The True-Born Englishman*, Pt 1, line 428; *The True-Born Englishman and other Writings*, ed. P. N. Furbank and W. R. Owens (Harmondsworth: Penguin Books, 1997), p. 37.

51 Probably apocryphal; the fullest account of Wellington's undeniably curious pedigree is found in Elizabeth Longford, *Wellington: The Years of the Sword* (London: Weidenfeld and Nicolson, 1969), pp. 4–12.

52 Winston S. Churchill, *Marlborough: His Life and Times*, 4 vols (London: George Harrap Ltd, 1933–8); see esp. 'Preface', Vol. 1.

53 L. B. Namier, *England in the Age of the American Revolution*, 2nd edition (London: Macmillan, 1961), Chs 10 and 11. For the argument, see F. A. Hayek, *The Road to Serfdom* (Chicago: University of Chicago Press, 1944), pp. 103–5.

54 James Lees-Milne, *Ceaseless Turmoil: Diaries, 1988–1992*, ed. Michael Bloch (London: John Murray, 2004), p. 334; entry for 30 November 2002; Namier, 'Social foundations' in *England in the Age of the American Revolution*; Tocqueville, *The Old Régime and the Revolution*, ed. François Furet and Françoise Mélonio (Chicago: University of Chicago Press, 1998), Bk 2, Chs 7–10, pp. 145–71.

55 'Scarsdale', *Burke's Peerage: Baronetage and Knightage*, 107th edition, Vol. III (London: Boydell and Brewer Ltd, 2003), p. 3538. Actually the first motto; the second being '*recto et suaviter*'; 'justly and mildly'.

56 Richard Wilson and Alan Mackley, *Creating Paradise: The Building of the English Country House, 1660–1880* (London: Hambledon, 2000), pp. 89–97; David Gilmour, *Curzon* (London: John Murray, 1994), Ch. 1.

57 B. A. Holderness, 'Prices, productivity and output', in G. E. Mingay (ed.), *The Agrarian History of England and Wales*, Vol. VI, *1750–1850*

(Cambridge: CUP, 1989), Ch. 2; M. E. Turner, 'Agricultural output, income and productivity', in E. J. T. Collins, *The Agrarian History of England and Wales*, Vol. VII, Pt 1, *1850–1914* (Cambridge: CUP, 2000), Ch. 3.

58 Adam Smith, *An Enquiry into the Nature and Causes of the Wealth of Nations*, ed. R. H. Campbell and A. S. Skinner (Oxford: Oxford University Press, 1976), Vol. 1, pp. 382–4 and 423. By contrast, see Nigel Everett, *The Tory View of Landscape* (New Haven: Yale University Press, 1994), Chs 2 and 9.

59 J. P. Cooper, 'In search of agrarian capitalism', *Past and Present*, No. 80 (August 1976), pp. 20–65; see esp. his remarks at the bottom of p. 65; more broadly, Alan Howkins, ed., 'Rural society and community', Part V of Collins, *The Agrarian History of England and Wales*, Vol. VII, Pt I, pp. 1229–1513.

60 Suetonius, 'The deified Augustus', in *Lives of the Caesars*, Bk 2, Section 28, trans. J. C. Rolfe (Cambridge, MA: Harvard University Press, 1913), p. 193.

61 Sallust, *The War with Catalina*, Ch. 5, trans. J. C. Rolfe (Cambridge, MA: Harvard University Press, 1921), p. 9; spoken of Lucius Catalina.

62 William Shakespeare, *Henry VI, Pt II*, Act IV, Scene 10, lines 17–24; *Arden Shakespeare*, ed. Donald Knowles (London: Eyre Methuen, 1999), pp. 336–7.

63 Drummond to Earl of Donoughmore, 22 May 1838; reprinted E. R. Barry O'Brien, *Thomas Drummond: Life and Letters* (London, 1889), p. 237.

64 Kenneth Clark, *Another Part of the Wood: A Self-Portrait* (London: John Murray, 1974), p. 1.

65 For a non-idealised account, see Beckett, *Aristocracy in England*, Ch. 10.

66 Eustace Percy, *Some Memories* (London: Eyre and Spottiswoode, 1958), p. 15.

67 *ibid.*, pp. 15–16.

68 See, above all, Lloyd George's, 'Limehouse Speech', of 30 July 1909; crisply analysed in John Grigg, *Lloyd George: The People's Champion, 1902–1911*, 2nd ed. (London: Methuen, 1997), pp. 203–8.

69 Habakkuk, *Marriage*, pp. 660–2.

70 W. D. Rubenstein, *Men of Property: The Very Wealthy in Britain Since the Industrial Revolution* (London: Croom Helm, 1981), Ch. 8; and for some of the reasons, *Elites and the Wealthy in Modern British History* (Brighton: Harvester Press, 1987), Ch. 7.

71 de Tocqueville, *Democracy in America*, pp. 562–3 and, for the evidence, in a British context anyway, Cretney *et al.*, *Principles of Family Law*, pp. 2–3; and Ch. 7; also Christie Davies, *The Strange*

Death of Moral Britain, 2 vols (New Brunswick: Transaction Publishers, 2004), Ch. 2.

72 Cretney *et al.*, *Principles of Family Law*, Ch. 17.

73 *ibid.*, Ch. 3. For a historical background, see Stephen Cretney, '"What will women want next": The struggle for power without the family, 1925–1975', in S. Cretney, *Law, Law Reform and the Family* (Oxford: OUP, 1998), Ch. 7.

74 G. W. F. Hegel, *Philosophy of Right*, trans. and ed. T. M. Knox (Oxford: OUP, 1967), Para. 239, p. 148.

75 Edmund Leach, 'Ourselves and others', *The Listener*, 30 November 1967, pp. 693–5, at p. 695.

76 Francis Bacon, 'Of marriage and single life', in *The Essayes or Counsels, Civill and Morall*, ed. Michael Kiernan (Oxford: Clarendon Press, 1985), pp. 24–5.

77 Mary Wollstonecraft, *A Vindication of the Rights of Women*, ed. Sylvia Tomaselli (Cambridge: Cambridge University Press, 1995), p. 247.

78 Burke, *Reflections*, pp. 260–1.

79 Ben J. Wattenberg, *Fewer: How the New Demography of Depopulation Will Shape our Future* (Chicago: Dee, 2004), Ch. 2.

PART 2

THE NEW VIRTUES

CHAPTER 7

DISTRIBUTIVE JUSTICE OR SOCIAL JUSTICE

NICHOLAS CAPALDI

In the United States today, there are many people who consider former president Bill Clinton a moral hero. This may, at first sight, seem very strange, given that the former president lied under oath, committed adultery, pardoned people who contributed money to his library, and was largely ineffective in implementing the domestic programme favoured by the very people who lionise him. According to the long-established conventional virtues, Clinton is not a moral hero. He fails at least on the grounds of infidelity and dishonesty. Another widely admired person, Jesse Jackson, also has well-known personal failings. Both, however, are regarded as moral heroes under the new standards, which judge a man virtuous if he allies himself with the correct causes, opinions and institutions. Today it is not what a man is, but the causes he associates with that matter. I say 'ally with' and 'associate with' because, to be a hero today, one does not even have to sacrifice oneself – sacrifice might have counted under the old virtues – for such causes. Neither man has noticeably suffered, and certainly not impoverished himself for the causes. Chief among these fashionable causes is social or distributive justice.

DEFINITION
A concept of distributive justice[1] goes back as far as Aristotle, but it is only since the Second World War that it has become a major contemporary virtue. Needless to say, the meaning of 'distributive justice' has been completely transformed in the modern context.[2] For Aristotle, distributive justice was the assigning of responsibilities and rewards to individuals, based upon merit. For the contemporary world, the notion of merit[3] (desert) has completely disappeared. The contemporary virtue of distributive justice is an attempt to reconfigure society in such a way that all social goods are distributed on the basis of fairness.

Before offering a formal definition, let me say at the outset that the contemporary idea of 'distributive justice' is not a coherent and well defined concept, even in the minds of those who espouse it. Nor can it become such without losing its vitality. It cannot become clear because the notion of distributive justice is a reaction against some-thing else – a something else we shall describe below. Moreover, the vitality and effectiveness of the idea of 'distributive justice' in its contemporary sense is, in large part, dependent upon its vacuity. It is precisely this vacuity that gives it its great appeal, because it permits a wide variety of advocates to employ it in endless, and even con-flicting, ways.

Contemporary distributive justice adheres to the following pre-sumptions:

Liberalism[4] Each individual is an end in himself.

Scientism Each individual has a life-project.[5]

Social environmental determinism Whether each individual has an opportunity to pursue a life-project depends *totally* upon external circumstances, over which the individual has no control.

Justice as positive rights In order to respect and protect that life-project, government recognises certain rights.
For the government to recognise and protect rights under these circumstances, rights must be welfare rights, i.e. they must be such that others have a positive obligation to provide such goods, benefits or means to accomplish the life-project.

Distributive justice as public policy Government should distribute and redistribute goods so as to maximise each individual's life-project. This is what fairness is.

EXAMINING THE PRESUPPOSITIONS OF DISTRIBUTIVE JUSTICE

Let us examine each of these presumptions. The first presumption, namely that each individual is an end in himself, is a presumption formally found in all forms of liberalism, from Hobbes to the pres-ent. No doubt it owes something to the Judaeo-Christian heritage. In any case, distributive justice is not to be confused with classical notions of a common good, or with modern notions of a collective good, either authoritarian or totalitarian. We may, therefore, conclude that distributive justice is, or pretends to be, a version of liberalism.

The second presumption, namely that each individual has a life-project, can be either a tautology, or a trivial and incontestable empirical truth, or a highly controversial notion. Specifically, advo-cates of distributive justice maintain (a) that a scientific[6] account of human nature will allow us to identify fundamental human drives (wants, needs, etc.) shared by all human beings, and (b) that these drives form a homeostatic system, so that, if properly understood, they do not conflict. Science has not actually to date established either (a) or (b).[7] The beauty of this, however, is that, as an advocate of distributive justice, you are free to plug in whatever you want here.[8]

The third presumption, namely that individuals are shaped by their social environment (i.e. a form of social environmental determinism), is a denial of the existence of the freedom of will (something one would expect if you adhere to scientism), and a denial of the existence of serious differences among human beings. That is why, by this account, there cannot be either inherent merit or earned merit. This is the fundamental presumption of distributive justice, and it leads to a radical break with other versions of liberalism. It eventually entails a positive conception of rights.

The fourth presumption, namely the recognition of positive rights, is a radical departure from the classical liberal conception of rights. In its original Lockean formulation, 'rights'[9] (qualified as 'natural', 'human', etc.) are absolute, do not conflict, and are possessed only by individual human beings. Rights are morally absolute or fundamental because they are derived from human nature and God (or the categorical imperative), and as such cannot be overridden; the role of these rights is to protect the human capacity to choose. Finally, such rights impose only duties of non-interference. In its distributive-justice form, rights are only *prima facie*, may be overridden, and may be possessed by any entity, not just individual human beings. Such rights can be welfare rights, i.e. they may be such that others have a positive obligation to provide such goods, benefits or means. What distinguishes one liberal social philosopher from another is (a) whether rights are understood to be absolute or *prima facie*, (b) the content of the rights, and (c) the lexical ordering of those rights.

The fifth presumption, namely that government can and should exercise distributive power, raises, at the very least, the question of whether it is possible to formulate an algorithm that can do this coherently. Certainly Hayek has claimed that this is conceptually impossible. Distributivists, as we shall see, have an answer for this.

THE HISTORY OF DISTRIBUTIVE JUSTICE

In order to explain the emergence of distributive justice as the major contemporary virtue, we need to review a few historical develop-

ments. From Aristotle to the eighteenth century a concept of distributive justice, or a surrogate, was necessitated by the widespread
existence of (a_1) the poverty of resources and (b_1) the perceived differences in character (virtues and vices) among human beings. Both
(a_1) and (b_1) served as the reference points to define fairness. From
the eighteenth century[10] to the present a new definition of fairness
emerged. We have (a_2) come to believe in greatly expanded, or possibly unlimited, economic growth (according to many, the so-called
production problem has been solved) and we have (b_2) seen a significant change in explanations about differences in human character.
Whereas wealth was the scandal of the medieval world, poverty is
the scandal of the contemporary world. Whereas poverty and
human vice were once viewed as regrettable but inevitable, society is
now called upon to eliminate both.

Both Plato and Aristotle believed that there were inherent
differences in intelligence among human beings, and that these differences created a serious divide between those who could be truly
virtuous and all the rest. In addition, Aristotle asserted the existence
of 'natural slaves', that is, people who were inherently incapable of
running their own lives. Following St Paul and St Augustine,
medieval Christian thinkers promulgated the notions of free will,
sin, and grace to explain the existence of intractable evil recidivism.
Even as late as the nineteenth century it was widely held that there
was an important difference between the 'deserving poor' (poor
because of misfortune) and the 'undeserving poor' (poor because of
vicious character). From the eighteenth century on, all of these
notions came to be challenged and then swept aside, and in their
place we get *the political agenda of the Enlightenment Project*,[11]
which amounted to the following:

- Human beings are basically good, not sinful, and the
ultimate goal of human existence is happiness in this life
(secularisation).
- Human beings are to be understood mechanistically;
hence evil behaviour is exclusively the result of external[12]
forces (scientisation).
- Social technology can create a utopia[13] by the control
of external forces.
- Society is best served by a powerful state supervised
by a new clerisy.

THE VANISHING OF VICE

There have been six major accounts of human character:

- Rationality model (Plato);
- Aristotelian–Stoic self-mastery (rationality + habitual training);
- Ascetic self-mastery (religion);
- Divine predestination;
- Free will (+ possibility of sin);
- *Environmental determinism.*[14]

The first five accounts all allow for the possibility of wide-spread failure. That is, they all make possible the existence of irremovable vice. Moreover, any combination of these six allows for the possibility of the failure to achieve virtuous status. It is only when the sixth account is held by itself that it is possible to envisage the elimination of vice.

The most prominent advocate of distributive justice is John Rawls. He has explicitly endorsed environmental determinism.[15] Rawls famously claimed that the social world will always 'affect the wants and preferences that persons come to have'.[16] Moreover, 'even the willingness to make an effort, to try, and to be deserving in the ordinary sense is...dependent on fortunate family and social circumstances'.[17] Distributivists[18] are sometimes vague about this doctrine. They tend to fudge the difference between the following propositions: (a) we are sometimes *influenced* by social circumstances (something no one would deny); (b) we are sometimes *determined* by social circumstances (controversial[19] but not implausible); and (c) we are *always determined* by social circumstances. It is (c) that has to be held in order to deny human freedom and justify distributive justice.

Strictly speaking, if environmental determinism is true, there is, in one sense, no such thing as vice (or evil for that matter). That is, if vice is a character defect, and if we are not responsible for our characters, then it is not clear that there is either character or vice *per se*. 'Vice' is perhaps best understood as environmentally induced *dysfunctional behaviour*. The latter notion would have to mean that the behaviour inhibits the pursuit of the life-plan. Given different conceptions of the life-plan, there will inevitably be different conceptions of what is and what is not dysfunctional behaviour.

Many forms of human behaviour traditionally characterised as vices (rape, murder, incest, homosexuality, etc.) are either not vices

137

at all (homosexuality, euthanasia, having sexual relations with animals, etc.), or are better described as dysfunctional forms of behaviour caused by external circumstances. It is difficult to be precise here, because, since there is no consensus yet on what a strictly scientific account of human action comprises, no two lists will be the same. Again, this is an excellent opportunity for advocates of distributive justice to put anything they choose on the list. If some lists gain prominence, it is largely because of the influence of their advocates, rather than any definitive science.

Vice (or, more precisely, environmentally induced dysfunctional behaviour) is to be eliminated in two ways. First, the human condition is to be reconceptualised, so that the sources of human character are given a new account. Second, virtues and vices are to be redefined and regrouped. The new account of the human condition is not available at this time. Certainly there is no definitive science or consensus even among Distributivists. We shall discuss this when we look at virtue. This further reinforces the notion that distributive justice is a largely negative idea.

The redefinition of virtue and vice, however, proceeds apace. Some traditional virtues are no longer virtues, but actually vices. For example, charity, mercy, generosity, and beneficence are no longer virtues. If human beings deserve to have resources, services, etc. as a matter of right, and therefore of justice, it should not be left to private initiative. Moreover, charity and related traditional virtues are bad because they establish a hierarchical relationship between giver and receiver. The giver usually expects the receiver to exhibit the traditional virtues of humility and gratitude. Those traditional receiver-virtues can now be reclassified as acts of (demeaning) servility. Finally, there is no longer any such thing as the undeserving poor; this whole category can be eliminated by giving them the resources (including genetic engineering) they deserve as of right. If human beings are totally a product of their social environment, and if vice is the result of a lack of resources (political, social, and material), and if there is greatly expanded wealth or resources, and if those resources are wisely distributed (or redistributed), then vice will be eliminated.

DISTRIBUTIVE JUSTICE AS THE SUPREME
CONTEMPORARY VIRTUE

Distributive justice is the virtue of promoting virtue in others. It is, in this sense, the supreme virtue. All other virtues are virtues only insofar as they contribute to this end. Distributive justice has thus become the basis for all other forms of justice; it is now identical with what was previously called universal justice.

Distributive justice is enshrined in the 1948 United Nations Declaration of Human Rights:

> *Article 22.* Everyone, as a member of society, has the right to social security and is entitled to realization, through national effort and international co-operation and in accordance with the organization and resources of each State, of the economic, social and cultural rights indispensable for his dignity and the free development of his personality; *Article 23.* (1) Everyone has the right to work, to free choice of employment, to just and favourable conditions of work and to protection against unemployment. (2) Everyone, without any discrimination, has the right to equal pay for equal work. (3) Everyone who works has the right to just and favourable remuneration ensuring for himself and his family an existence worthy of human dignity, and supplemented, if necessary, by other means of social protection. (4) Everyone has the right to form and to join trade unions for the protection of his interests; *Article 24.* Everyone has the right to rest and leisure, including reasonable limitation of working hours and periodic holidays with pay; *Article 25* (1) Everyone has the right to a standard of living adequate for the health and well-being of himself and of his family, including food, clothing, housing and medical care and necessary social services, and the right to security in the event of unemployment, sickness, disability, widowhood, old age or other lack of livelihood in circumstances beyond his control. (2) Motherhood and childhood are entitled to special care and assistance. All children, whether born in or out of wedlock, shall enjoy the same social protection.

Virtue can be newly understood on two levels: the individual and the public. On the individual level, we need some positive conception of human nature in order to delineate the presence of virtue. In the absence of a scientific determination or of a public consensus, it is difficult to see initially how this can be done. It will turn out, as we shall see, that the positive conception emerges when we see what exactly is to be distributed. Old-fashioned distributivists were content not to challenge older conceptions of virtue and vice, but merely to argue that such vice could be eliminated through the redistribution of material resources such as property. Among material resources we must now count healthcare. Norman Daniels, for one, has argued that healthcare needs to be redistributed.[20] In Canada this has taken the form of not permitting private health insurance, for such insurance allows the wealthy to get better healthcare.[21] Part of healthcare now includes genetic engineering healthcare and plastic surgery.

However, once environmental determinism is taken seriously, the whole issue has to be rethought. There is now a wide range of views on personal virtue, and this is best seen by noting what it is that distributivists want to see distributed. New categories of what is to be distributed appear all the time. Among the latest and most fashionable is what we shall call 'ideal goods' to distinguish them from material goods. James Tully calls this 'recognition capital', that is, 'status, respect, and esteem', and claims that granting it will lead to economic and political well-being.[22] This reverses the usual distributivist scheme, by which economic and political well-being were thought to be means to individual well-being.

What this means in practice is that if one identifies oneself by membership in a group such as a race, a culture, sexual orientation, or physical disability, then it is incumbent upon government to guarantee and uphold the legitimacy of these self-perceptions. Identification with a group might suggest that liberalism is here being surrendered, but what makes this a form of liberalism is that individuals get to decide what group they belong to.

Will Kymlicka, for example, claims that governments must preserve disadvantaged minority cultures.[23] Therefore, some cultures or subcultures are to be protected or immunised against criticism. That is, they have a protected identity. Negatively, it means punishing those who make statements deemed to be detrimental to those who identify with these groups. For example, the famous American football player and minister Reggie White had his contract to become a game analyst on TV revoked when, following his religious beliefs, he spoke out against homosexuality. Apparently being a member of certain religious groups is not a protected identity.[24] At the very least, a speech code needs to be enforced to forbid statements about other identities. This becomes difficult, if not impossible, to enforce if making such statements is itself part of the identity. So, not all identities will be protected. There is no principled basis available at present for resolving this issue.

Complexities begin to abound. By one interpretation, the

physically disabled, or handicapped, are to be given special help, perhaps even genetic engineering. On the other hand, being disabled has become, for some, a form of identity (virtue). For example, a deaf couple with a normal newborn child recently asked the courts for permission to raise the child in a deaf environment.

Recognising the importance of 'ideal goods' or 'recognition capital' helps to resolve another paradox. Old-fashioned distributivists were frequently criticised – and worried about the criticism – that various forms of redistribution of material goods were inefficient. That is, the way goods were distributed vitally impacted on production. If we distribute or redistribute goods in the wrong way, then we are brought to the impoverishment of all. But, on the new view, the inefficiency, corruption, and counter-productivity of some welfare programmes is irrelevant: one of the programmes might work, and in the meantime it is necessary to show symbolically that we are trying – this gesture itself shows respect for the deprived. It is an example of recognition.

VIRTUE ON THE SOCIAL LEVEL

Virtue is a form of human excellence; vice is a fault or imperfection. What constitutes a virtue or vice depends upon your conception of humanity or human agency. This conception is to be determined purely by scientific investigation. Distributivists disagree among themselves as to what the correct conception of humanity is. It is thus an open question as to what constitutes individual virtue or vice.[25] What distributivists do tend to agree on are public (i.e. social or political) virtues and vices. Public policies that favour the distribution of whatever is needed are good. All principles that facilitate the distribution so that individuals may achieve virtue are social virtues.

Equality (synonymous with fairness) is such a virtue because it means providing the same[26] circumstances (resources, etc.) that permit the elimination of vice and the development of virtue. Equality means that each individual's life-project is just as valuable as everyone else's.

Diversity is a virtue because each individual[27] chooses for himself/herself. However, diversity has to be understood to mean diversity of things that subscribe to the presuppositions of distributive justice. Individuals, programmes, or advocacy of policies inconsistent with the basic presuppositions (e.g. denial of the truth of social environmental determinism) cannot be tolerated. Hence, the faculties of US universities are overwhelmingly Democratic, because Republicans are generally out of sync with distributive justice. Among that Democratic faculty, there is, or should be, a wide diversity of race, sexual orientation, etc.

Public virtue begins with endorsement of *socialism*,[28] that is, economic planning designed to 'enhance' production, distribution, and consumption. Distribution takes priority over production (hence the irrelevance of inefficiency critiques) in order to avoid inequality. Certain forms of consumption (e.g. private non-government controlled education, private healthcare plans, private retirement plans, etc.) are ruled out because they lead to inequality.

The virtue of socialism means that capitalism is a vice. Globalisation in its present form is also a vice, for it simply extends capitalism throughout the world. Moreover, the redistribution is not confined to one's own country. Traditional nation-states reflect historical accident and inequality. Goods and recognition are to be transferred from wealthier countries to poorer countries, and again, it should be done through the UN, otherwise we re-enact the relationship of giver and receiver and demean the receiver. Martha Nussbaum,[29] for one, denies the Ciceronian distinction between justice and beneficence; she claims that there is no distinction between doing harm and failing to provide benefits.

With regard to globalisation, let me call attention to one website called, in fact, 'Distributive Justice'. This is what one finds there:

> Distributive justice is not only a central issue of moral and political philosophy, but also an object of common-sense moral reasoning. Everyone is sensitive to the question of his/her share of the common good. Even those who get the best piece of the social pie are in need to justify the actual model of distribution. It has become a truism that most people (especially in the transition countries) experience their own social position as 'unjust', relying on certain intuitive principles of distributive justice.
>
> Multidisciplinary project 'Distributive Justice' is a work in progress designed by people with different backgrounds (art, philosophy, sociology, photography, design, programing). The project deals with the topic of distribution of goods in a society. It consists of two parts: (1) the part of the project in the virtual space, URL: www.distributive-justice.com – an Internet game in which participants in the project freely distribute

> material and nonmaterial goods building a 'society' that
> undergoes dynamical changes; several types of societies
> emerge as result of the distribution game.

Public virtue requires social planning as well: that is, the regulation, if not redesign, of all institutions. Families may have to be redefined so as to avoid (a) invidious comparison and (b) unequal tax benefits. Homosexual couples demand the 'right' to be recognised as legally married. Children may be exempt from performing chores on the grounds that assigning chores reflects an outmoded notion of human agency (a misguided belief in the importance of asceticism, stoicism, or self-discipline).

Nor is the government limited to economic planning. True to its Marxist origins, the government is called upon to address and resolve every conceivable problem. Each and every problem is diagnosed as the result of 'massive inequalities in the distribution of resources'. Both domestically and internationally this is alleged to be the case. International warfare, it is alleged, will not come to an end with the spread of a market economy and democracy, but only with a massive redistribution of wealth in the form of a world government structured as democratic socialism under the aegis of the UN.

Legal institutions will have to be reconfigured, so that everyone, including illegal immigrants and terrorists, receives the same legal protections. Keep in mind that the distributivist notion of globalisation means the end of nation-states. International law is now to be understood not as anything resembling the Anglo-Saxon rule of law, but as the use of the legal machinery to achieve specific political objectives. Judges who fail to understand the correct political objectives will be replaced. The glare of international tribunals will be focused on anyone who does not subscribe to world government and democratic socialism. A new definition of a rogue state will be instituted, namely any society that fails to subscribe to or that defies world government and democratic socialism. The US emerges as the primary example of a rogue state.

Certain hypotheses about the root causes of social problems may be barred from consideration on the grounds that they are both (a) false and (b) demeaning to some groups (e.g. differences in IQ by race or gender, etc.). Speech codes may have to be introduced into the internal functioning of all social institutions.

Merit or desert is no longer a virtue because of environmental (social) determinism. Charity is no longer a virtue because it

(a) reflects an unfair initial distribution of resources, (b) is voluntary not obligatory, and (c) reflects a hierarchical relationship between the giver and the receiver. Philanthropy is no longer a virtue for the same reasons. Magnanimity is no longer a virtue because it reflects historical accident.

THE MODERN MORAL HERO THAT DISTRIBUTIVE JUSTICE CREATES

'A' Moral Hero is anyone engaged in promoting this distribution (politician, teacher, journalist, or pop-psychologist). 'The' Moral Hero is the architect or organiser of the distribution. 'The' Moral Hero may exhibit behaviour that reflects traditional and outmoded notions of vice (philandering, lying, stealing, etc.), but this is irrelevant to his/her status as a distributivist moral hero. We can now understand the status of such a figure as Bill Clinton.

What distinguishes the contemporary virtues from the classical virtues is that the former deny individual responsibility and substitute social planning. The contemporary conception of distributive justice can be criticised on the following grounds. First, there was no agreement on what things should be redistributed or equalised, i.e. there was no consensus on which universal facts about human nature entailed normative social arrangements. Second, given that lack of agreement, demands for redistribution or equality would remain nothing more than rhetorical masks for private political agendas. Third, even if it were possible to redistribute everything, so that we all started out equal, differences in ability and circumstances (e.g. luck) would soon lead to inequalities. Fourth, and last, in order to overcome the non-egalitarian recidivism, it would be necessary to maintain the most all-encompassing social tyranny. Finally, I want to offer an explanation about why anyone would hold such an embarrassingly simplistic position.[30]

Distributive justice is not a positive position – it implies no agreement on what is fair, only agreement on what is unfair. The advocacy of distributive justice is a reaction. It is a reaction against the rise of the autonomous individual. What is also crucial for us to remember is that, even within our own liberal culture that goes back as far as the Renaissance and the Reformation, many people have not made the transition to individuality. There is a whole complicated history behind this, but what is important is to recognise that the most serious problem within modern liberal societies is the presence of the failed or *incomplete* individual. What in the eighteenth century was identified as the 'mob', and what even Hegel was to call the 'rabble', became in the nineteenth century the working class. By the end of the twentieth century it had become the movement for distributive justice.

Being an incomplete individual is a state of mind. It is not directly correlated with income, intelligence, or how articulate one is – some incomplete individuals are highly intelligent. Either unaware of, or lacking faith in, his ability to exercise self-discipline, the incomplete individual seeks escape into the collective identity of communities insulated from the challenge of opportunity. These are people focused on avoiding failure, rather than on achieving success. Phenomenologically speaking, the incomplete individual is identified by feelings of envy, resentment, self-distrust, victimisation, and self-pity: in short, an inferiority complex.

What really inhibits these people is *not* a lack of opportunity, *not* a lack of political rights, and *not* a lack of resources, but a character defect, a *moral inadequacy*. Having little or no sense of individuality, they are incapable of loving what is best in themselves; unable to love themselves, they are incapable of loving others; incapable of loving others, they cannot sustain life within the family; in fact, they find family life stultifying. What they substitute for love of self, others, and family is loyalty to a mythical community. Instead of an umpire they want a leader, and they conceive of such leaders as protectors who relieve them of all responsibility. This is what makes their sense of community pathological. What they end up with are leaders who are their mirror image: leaders who are themselves incomplete individuals and who seek to control others because they cannot control themselves; who seek the emasculation of autonomous individuals; who prize equality and not competition. In place of a market economy and limited government, we get economic and political tyranny.

SELF-TEST: ARE YOU A MORAL HERO ACCORDING TO DISTRIBUTIVE JUSTICE?

Are you sympathetic to distributive justice? Here is a list of the basic eleven commandments[31] of distributive justice. If you agree with any or all of this, you qualify as an advocate:

- Thou shalt not be loyal to nation-states.
- Thou shalt not advocate the use of military force.
- Thou shalt believe that social dysfunction, such as crime,

145

can only be affected by greater social and economic equality.

• Thou shalt believe that the major institutions of society, such as religion, the firm, the school, the family, should be eliminated or replaced.

• Thou shalt believe that traditional values, such as private property, decentralisation, checks and balances, are obstacles to real reform.

• Thou shalt believe that environments are threatened only by free market economies.

• Thou shalt believe that the pursuit of excellence and efficiency are masks for discrimination.

• Thou shalt labour to remove all hierarchies.

• Thou shalt believe that the state is to be preferred to private agencies.

• Thou shalt believe that equality before the law and equality of opportunity should be replaced by equality of result.

• Thou shalt believe that bourgeois morality needs to be replaced by…[fill in the blank].

1 'Social justice' is a synonym for distributive justice. We are not here concerned with strictly semantic issues. Hence, we are less concerned with who used the expression 'distributive justice' and how, than we are with a certain set of ideas. What set of ideas is that? Every society we know of makes some provision for dealing with those who are not capable of caring for themselves. Insofar as this involves either distributing to the unfortunate assets that are publicly owned and controlled, or redistributing privately owned assets, the society has a conception of 'distributive justice' or some principled basis on which the distribution or redistribution takes place. It makes perfectly good and obvious sense to talk this way. Unfortunately, Aristotle was the first to use the expression 'distributive justice', and he did not mean it in this way. Hence, when we talk about 'distributive justice', we are anachronistically projecting a contemporary notion onto previous historical periods.

2 Given the obvious disparity between Aristotle's usage and contemporary usage, we are led to ask why contemporary authors use the same expression. Part of the answer is simple historical ignorance; another part of the answer is that presenting one's own position as a development of previous positions adds to it an air of legitimacy (appeal to authority); a final part of the answer is that to acknowledge the disparity would require offering a defence that advocates are either unwilling or unable to provide.

3   According to Rawls, '...need is emphasized' and 'moral worth is ignored'; *Theory of Justice* (Cambridge, MA: Harvard University Press, 1971), p. 312.

4   Ken Minogue has pointed out that, strictly speaking, distributive justice is a form of socialism, rather than liberalism, and, of course, he is correct. Advocates of distributive justice use liberal language as a rhetorical way of getting a sympathetic audience in what is still a largely liberal culture. They either do not see the inconsistency of their position, or they do not care. Keep in mind that I shall claim that the advocacy of distributive justice is inconsistent, incoherent, and a reaction, rather than a carefully thought out position.

5   I use the expression 'life-project' to mean that an individual pursues a good or goods, and, in the case of the latter, those goods form a coherent system. I am not endorsing such a view. Distributivists need some sort of norm to be the basis of their system, and they need to believe that it is uniform.

6   Briefly stated, the Enlightenment Project asserts the truth of scientism, the fundamental role of physical science, the usefulness of physical science in developing technology and mastering the physical universe, and the promise of social science in developing a social technology that will solve all social problems. It is no accident that these views are widely prevalent in the social sciences (sociology, some versions of economics, political science, anthropology, psychology, etc.) because it is precisely practitioners in these disciplines who claim to have discovered (or are in the process of discovering) such information. Different disciplines tend to have their favourite external source of corruption, and even these favourites change with fads. So, for example, Marx and Freud became icons because of their reductive explanations of dysfunction at one time or another. The list of icons varies and is somewhat difficult to keep up with. *The Enlightenment Project is an attempt to define and explain the human predicament through science, as well as to achieve mastery over it through the use of a social technology.* This project originated in France in the eighteenth century with the *philosophes*. The most influential among them were Diderot, d'Alembert, La Mettrie, Condillac, Helvétius, d'Holbach, Turgot, Condorcet, Cabanis, and Voltaire. See N. Capaldi, *The Enlightenment Project in the Analytic Conversation* (Dordrecht: Kluwer Academic Publishers, 1998), Chapter 1. Isaiah Berlin, *The Magus of the North: J.G. Hamann and the Origins of Modern Irrationalism* (London: John Murray, 1993), pages 27–8, characterises the Project as follows: '...there were certain beliefs that were more or less common to the entire party of progress and civilization, and this is what makes it proper to speak of it as a single movement. These were, in effect, the conviction that the world, or nature, was a single whole, subject to a single set of laws, in

principle discoverable by the intelligence of man; that the laws which governed inanimate nature were in principle the same as those which governed plants, animals and sentient beings; that man was capable of improvement; that there existed certain objectively recognizable human goals which all men, rightly so described, sought after, namely, happiness, knowledge, justice, liberty, and what was somewhat vaguely described but well understood as virtue; that these goals were common to all men as such, were not unattainable, nor incompatible, and that human misery, vice and folly were mainly due to ignorance either of what these goals consisted in or of the means of attaining them – ignorance due in turn to insufficient knowledge of the laws of nature...Consequently, the discovery of general laws that governed human behaviour, their clear and logical integration into scientific systems – of psychology, sociology, economics, political science and the like (though they did not use these names) – and the determination of their proper place in the great corpus of knowledge that covered all discoverable facts, would, by replacing the chaotic amalgam of guesswork, tradition, superstition, prejudice, dogma, fantasy and "interested error" that hitherto did service as human knowledge and human wisdom (and of which by far the chief protector and instigator was the Church), create a new, sane, rational, happy, just and self-perpetuating human society, which, having arrived at the peak of attainable perfection, would preserve itself against all hostile influences, save perhaps those of nature.'

7   Advocates of distributive justice sometimes claim that progress in making these discoveries is retarded by the presence of members in their respective professions who do not subscribe to this view. Hence, otherwise competent and even brilliant individuals are to be excluded from such positions. Further, it is important to subscribe to speech codes for the same reason. See below.

8   It is even possible for some redistributivists to maintain that presumption one, namely liberal individualism, is itself a cultural by-product and not a fundamental truth. Here we begin to face self-referential obstacles. For example, if the scientific evidence is not yet in, perhaps redistributivism itself is a cultural product, and perhaps human nature will turn out to be something despicable.

9   I am indebted here to J. Hasnas, 'From cannibalism to caesareans: two conceptions of fundamental rights', *Northwestern University Law Review*, lxxxix, 1995.

10   It is no accident that the first place where this appears (as well as the central focus on how poverty harms the poor) is in Adam Smith's *Wealth of Nations*. By 1890 Alfred Marshall declared in his *Principles of Economics* that the purpose of the study of economics is to eliminate poverty.

11 See Capaldi, *The Enlightenment Project*, Chapter 10. Liberalism, socialism, and Marxism, are all variants of this project.

12 'External' may be taken either narrowly to mean outside the body, or widely to include the body as long as it denotes something not capable of direct control by the will.

13 The classic discussion of utopias as forms of Gnosticism is to be found in Eric Voegelin, *The New Science of Politics* (Chicago: University of Chicago Press, 1952 and 1987). Voegelin provides (in Chapter 4) a historical progression that begins with medieval immanentism, then progresses to humanism, and then to the Enlightenment, to progressivism, to liberalism, to positivism, and finally to Marxism.

14 This is what distinguishes Kant from contemporary distributivists. Kant insisted that sin is wholly rooted in human freedom. He maintains that freedom makes possible a radical evil in human nature.

15 We leave aside philosophical issues about the intelligibility of determinism and whether any norm (including being rational) would make sense or can be generated if determinism were true. My suspicion is that distributivists would have to subscribe to miraculous dualism, namely the view that everything is determined but there is an epi-phenomenal level that is teleological and is perfectly co-ordinated with the deterministic level. See Rawls, *Theory of Justice*.

16 John Rawls, 'Distributive Justice', in *Collected Papers*, ed. S. Freeman (Cambridge MA: Harvard University Press, 1999), p. 157.

17 *Theory of Justice*, pp. 311–12.

18 When I use the term 'distributivist', and unless otherwise qualified, it will mean adherence to the notion of distributive justice as here defined. Many writers have advocated some form of redistribution without necessarily subscribing to all the premises here defined.

19 What we have to avoid is claiming that we are partly determined and partly free; this can no more be true than being 'partly pregnant'.

20 Norman Daniels, *Just Health Care* (New York: Cambridge University Press, 1985).

21 A recent Canadian film exhibits this and identifies one of the characters as a new type of moral hero because he accepts the limitations of the system.

22 James Tully, 'Struggles over recognition and distribution', *Constellations*, 7:4, 2000, pp. 469–82.

23 Will Kymlicka, *Liberalism, Community, and Culture* (New York: Oxford University Press, 1989), Chapters 8 and 9.

24 I presume that 'legitimate' religious communities are ones that subscribe to, or are compatible with, the world view of distributivists.

25 It is not clear, for example, if there are vicious forms of sexual practice or even if there can be any notion of a purely individual vice, as opposed to supporting or endorsing the 'wrong' public policies.

26 Distributivists disagree on what exactly this entails.

27 Distributivists disagree on whether this unit is the individual person, a culture, a race, a polity, etc. One argument for denying that it is the individual is that the notion of choosing for oneself makes no sense if environmental determinism is true.

28 It need not be democratic; orthodox Marxists can claim that democracy only works when everyone is properly informed, but that prior mis-education makes the populace unfit to make such decisions by popular vote. Distributivists are usually democratic socialists for reasons that we shall explain later.

29 Martha Nussbaum, 'Duties of justice, duties of material aid', *Journal of Political Philosophy*, 8:2, 2000, pp. 176–206.

30 Following Michael Oakeshott's discussion of anti-individualism in 'The Masses in Representative Democracy', Distributivism will be explained as a negative reaction against the notion of autonomy in classical liberalism; in *Rationalism in Politics and Other Essays*, ed. T. Fuller (Indianapolis: Liberty Press, 1991), pp. 363–83.

31 Adapted from Richard E. Morgan, *Disabling America* (New York: Basic Books, 1984), pp. 194–5.

CHAPTER 8

THE ENVIRONMENTAL VIRTUES

CHRISTIE DAVIES

ENVIRONMENTALISM IS NOT A VIRTUE; RATHER THE ENVIRONMENT IS A NEW ARENA WHERE VIRTUE MAY BE PRACTISED

Virtues are praiseworthy qualities that we perceive in other human beings when we describe someone as, say, honest, generous, courageous, reliable, diligent or fair. They are the basis on which we assess an individual's character.

The environment is an aspect of the human world about which it is necessary to take decisions that have beneficial, rather than harmful consequences. Concern for the environment has increased as our power to control, but also to damage, the natural world has grown, and as our knowledge of how our activities may affect the environment has become more accurate. Our present concern for the environment must be placed in a particular historical context; one in which increased scientific knowledge is a crucial factor.

The key question is how to link these together. It is doubtful whether there are any new environmental virtues. Rather, there is a new arena in which virtue can be exercised, and we should ask, rather, which *existing* virtues are most important when we are faced with environmental questions, as well as where they are to be found. Different eras call for – and emphasise – different virtues because they face different problems and have available different opportunities. It is worth asking how this has happened in the case of the environment, and also to place these changes in the more general context of the development of modern societies, which are distinguished from their predecessors by their scale, wealth, technical capacities and scientific knowledge. We must also not lose sight of the fact that human beings have always damaged their environments; what has changed is our increased capacity to create such damage, and our greater concern to limit and even reverse it.

A HISTORICAL INTRODUCTION

Under conditions of severe scarcity, people do not give much

thought to the environment. Our ancestors killed off a large proportion of the large mammals and birds in Europe, as did their
Amerindian and Polynesian counterparts in other parts of the
world.[1] We were all hard-killing noble savages. The deserts of the
Middle East and North Africa advanced, in part, because of the
wanton destruction of trees for firewood or as a raw material.[2] The
Turks even placed a tax per tree on those who owned trees – with
predictable consequences. Entire civilisations, such as the Maya, col-
lapsed because they overused the tropical soil uncovered by cutting
down the jungle.[3] Overpopulation caused by high birth rates was
regularly succeeded by population collapse due to famine, malnutri-
tion and disease.[4] Collapse was a product of a lack of concern for
the environment, and yet it was collapse that saved what remained
of that environment. It was a Malthusian[5] world, in which human
beings were forced to attack nature, but soon after suffered the consequences of doing so. It was not consideration for the environment
that prevented destruction of the environment; rather, it was that
levels of population density and population growth were far lower
than today and were accompanied by a sheer inability to subordi-
nate the natural environment to human ends.

As population grew in the nineteenth century and as very large
cities grew up, we saw the emergence of the first stage of a modern
concern with the environment: a realisation that pollution of the
water supplies and the local atmosphere is damaging to the health of
the public. Yet such problems cannot easily be solved through the
exercise of individual virtue. The pollution caused by any one individual is trivial. A theft, a murder, a rape, a fraud – all have victims
in each and every case, and these acts are thus unambiguously
wicked. But pollution is cumulative. If one person deposits ordure in
a lake, or has a coal fire, it does not matter very much. If a million
people do likewise it ruins the environment and puts public health at
risk. Similarly, the problem cannot be solved by calling upon the
virtues of individual purity and cleanliness – indeed they may even
make matters worse by transferring dirt from private to public
spaces.

When I visited Bombay University in 1973 an earnest young
Scandinavian, who was writing a guidebook to the city, picked me
up at the airport and gave me a lift to the town centre. On the way
he stopped to photograph some handsome *dhows* that had sailed in
from Oman. He peered through his well-zoomed viewfinder and
swore. Spoiling his photograph was a line of pious, high-caste

Hindus squatting in their immaculate white *dhotis* and crapping on the beach; afterwards they would left-handedly clean their hind-quarters with water from the Indian Ocean. For them it meant personal purity; for the beach it meant something else. Their very virtue had befouled their environment.[6]

THE RISE OF A NEW MORALITY: UTILITARIANISM

Personal cleanliness and individual prudence cannot create modern sanitation.[7] When we speak of sanitation and, by extension, of pollution in general, we do not use the language of virtue, but that of utilitarianism, a 'new' moral system developed at the end of the eighteenth century, at the same time as a modern society shaped by market forces, impersonal organisations and technical change was emerging. As a guide to individual conduct, utilitarianism may be inadequate, but it is a moral system and one with particular application to pollution and public health.[8]

Utilitarianism was a new moral system, but not one that created new kinds of virtue – or indeed one that concerned itself with virtue. A concern for the environment is not even a new morality, for it cannot be extended to other aspects of human conduct. It is merely a particular set of preferences expressed within a limited sphere.

To take a further example, it is difficult to see how individual virtue could have rid London of the fogs recorded by Conan Doyle and James McNeill Whistler which – right up to the early 1950s and the great smog of December 1952 – literally choked tens of thousands of Londoners to death with smoke particles and sulphur dioxide. It would have done little good for lone individuals to set an example by giving up their coal fires and denying themselves the pleasure of setting light to yesterday's newspaper to fire the kindling, of fanning a mass of coal and fuel lumps into a blaze, and later of poking it back down into cinders. After the bronchitis epidemics of the 1940s and early 1950s the citizenry was compelled to switch to cleaner gas and electricity. One coal fire can mean individual pleasure, but several million mean air pollution. To light an old-fashioned coal fire is no crime, but it has to be prevented lest others do the same. When we speak of the Clean Air Act of 1956 we do not use the language of virtue, but of externalities, of organisation, of epidemiology, of aggregates, of liability, of cause and effect.[9]

For the thoroughgoing utilitarian, virtues are of value as a set of useful habits, rather than as something admirable in themselves.

So long as the consequences for public health or other aspects of the environment are good, the motives and character of those who make decisions and put them into practice are irrelevant.

UTILITARIANISM AND VIRTUE

Yet surely this takes too much for granted. To build a modern sewage plant or to enforce pollution controls demands an exercise of personal virtue by all those involved, notably honesty, disinterestedness, reliability, prudence, sobriety and a sense of duty. The scientists, engineers, skilled workers and administrators need these virtues as much as they need technical qualifications, if any large project in which they are involved is going to succeed. Indeed, even if those carrying out more routine tasks were to be light-fingered, unreliable, untruthful, neglectful, reckless or drunken, it could cause an environmental disaster, as could a willingness by administrators or clerks to take bribes or to set the rules aside for a cousin. What we have here are the Victorian virtues, derived not from utilitarianism but from the 'Protestant Ethic'. They may well indeed be derived from an earlier Protestant morality and ethos.[10]

One strength of utilitarianism in this context is that it undermines rhetorical greenism, a rhetoric that can lead to a policy being judged by the image and supposed motives of its proponents. Utilitarianism always forces a return to the basic questions: What alternatives are there? Which will cause least overall harm? Faced with the possibility that the release of carbon dioxide and methane into the atmosphere does lead to global warming, or at least adds to it,[11] as Svante August Arrhenius had already predicted in 1896, utilitarians ask, 'How big a change in our climate is it likely to cause, and over what time scale?' 'What is the cheapest, most effective and least disruptive way either of reducing emissions or of extracting the gases from the atmosphere?'[12] The answers may well lie in a switch to nuclear energy, accompanied by a high carbon tax and coupled with a general reduction in taxes on incomes and profits; in the purchase of large areas of rainforest for non-development; in seeding the oceans with nutrients so that a more abundant plant life can, by photosynthesis, remove carbon dioxide faster; in the planting of forests of genetically modified fast-growing trees in semi-desert or salty areas, which, after rapidly reaching maturity, would keel over and enrich the soil or would be used for construction to replace lime, cement, concrete and bricks, all of which release CO_2 in their manufacture; in the design of more efficient engines and of super-storage batteries and fuel cells burning hydrogen, of better insulated houses, cheaper, stronger, more efficient solar panels, or offshore windmills; indeed a mixture of all of these, for they can all be justified on other grounds.

I cite this long and ungainly list because it enables us, from a utilitarian point of view, to see that we have to decide the marginal cost of an increment of change in the use of, or investment in, each of these projects, and the marginal value of the improvement produced. An optimum position can be sought and, in order to achieve it, we also need faster economic growth and technical progress. Sensible people who are worried about the environment accept that this is the best procedure to follow. In this area, at least, instrumental rationality must prevail, not the vain pursuit of absolute ends[13] which give a semblance, but only a semblance, of virtue.

GREENISM AND ITS VICES

Yet this approach is bitterly opposed by 'true', green-dyed in the wool greenists, who see themselves as exercising distinctive virtues (in fact, preferences). Theirs is a new, secular way of being against the world and worldliness, against mass affluence and consumption, and against high technology. In the service of nature they are willing to accept for themselves, and to impose on others, the virtues of simplicity and asceticism, and possibly even the disciplines of poverty and obedience to a rationing state.[14] These are not new virtues, but rather versions of old ones, which others have pursued for a variety of different reasons, both religious and secular – hermits, monks and nuns in strict orders, devotees in an *ashram*, Gandhi's ideal self-supporting Indian villages, or Thoreau or Knut Hamsun in their lonely cabins.[15] Yet few greenists choose to live such simple or arduous or uncomfortable lives. Refusing to own a car or energy-using gadgets or central heating is hardly asceticism, particularly if much of the rest of such a person's life is filled with other pleasures, whether sexual or drawn from nature's illicit pharmacy. Also, their modest lives are often subsidised by affluent families or state benefits.

They remind one of the heretic Girolamo Savonarola, who, in 1497, induced and forced the citizens of Florence to burn their luxuries and works of art (Botticelli even burned his own pictures) in a bonfire of vanities. Greenists would not have a bonfire (because bonfires create carbon dioxide) but we may be sure that they would like to see dishwashers beaten into ploughshares and sports cars dismantled to produce bicycles.

One indication of their perverted sense of what virtue is lies in their hatred of capitalism, mass consumption, and the advertising of consumer products. In the days of the old Soviet empire they had little to say about – and did little to protest against – the grotesque environmental damage directly caused by the pursuit of socialism: the pollution of Lake Baikal, the Danube or the Baltic; the damage to the 'virgin lands'; the repulsive consequences of socialist industrialisation in Katowice or Northern Moravia; or the carelessness in dealing with nuclear materials that was finally exposed at Chernobyl.[16] There were never savage demonstrations outside the relevant embassies or massive boycotts of East European products, and nor was personal abuse directed against Soviet apologists in Britain. There was outrage in Germany at the thought that 'acid rain' from Britain or France might be harming German forests, but not at the fact that pollution alarms in West Berlin were only set off when the wind came from the East.

The Swedes quietly sought extra safety measures on East German nuclear reactors, which would otherwise not have survived a large airliner crashing into them, and in 1974 uncovered the fact that a secret KGB plant was, contrary to international agreements signed by the Russians, dumping polychlorinated biphenyls (PCBs) in the river Neman that runs into the Baltic.[17] Needless to say, they did not hector the communist countries, nor did a mob in Stockholm burn Soviet flags. It was a case of take a big stick to the capitalists and speak softly to the Reds.

No one was willing to point out that the grossly enhanced danger, the pollution and environmental damage in Eastern Europe were all a direct product of socialism. Without market capitalism and prices there is no incentive to innovate and to save on resources. Without bases of power independent of the state and its central planners there can be no constraints on those who seek to maximise economic production for its own sake, or to enhance military power. The polluters have all the power and the polluted have none. The greenists could not see this because they were fixated on what they saw as the vices of capitalists and consumers – the drive for profits and the drive for possessions. The workers and peasants, commissars and apparatchiks, in theory selflessly toiling for the public good under socialism, were clearly the world's worst polluters;[18] but this was as unacceptable to the greenists as being told that synthetic food preservatives prolong human life (they contain antioxidants). As far as they were concerned, it could not possibly be true. It seems likely that the greenists were not so much mistaken, as acting and agitating in bad faith. They lacked one of the most basic of the virtues: honesty. They still do. They use imagined calamities not to seek ways of finding policies to deal with problems, but to scare us into radical social change.[19]

UTILITARIAN MORALITY AND ITS LIMITS

We can now see why there are no environmental virtues. Even the virtues that underpin a reasonable concern for the environment cannot stand on their own. Virtue is not enough: it has to be supplemented by a utilitarian, or at least a consequentialist, morality. The antithesis between the two is a false one. In practice, all decisions have to be measured against both.

A strong, and even sincere, commitment to greenism may actually get in the way of preserving and improving the environment, because it leads to an obsession with symbolically acceptable means, rather than to selection of the most effective way of achieving environmental ends. A further problem with what the greenists themselves regard as green virtues is that they are so embedded in ideologies, such as anti-capitalism, anti-modernity, anti-science or *Blut und Boden* nationalism, that they cannot be extracted and analysed. The nature of the environment is such that the starting point for protecting it has to be instrumental rationalism. Good impulses are no substitute; even if they were called virtues, they would have to be set aside.

However, an ethic of consequences cannot tell us why we should concern ourselves with the environment in the first place, except in so far as it impinges on our other activities, as, say, severe pollution does, or sudden climate change, or a rise in the sea level would. It is necessary to seek and identify the virtues that lie behind a disinterested concern for the environment. Yet even here a utilitarian morality cannot be entirely set to one side. It still provides both the framework within which to exercise virtue and a way of differentiating between virtue and excess, in the same sense that we distinguish between courage and recklessness, thrift and stinginess, or kindness and indulgence; in each case we decide the boundary between them by considering the probable consequences.

EXISTING VIRTUES AND VALUING THE ENVIRONMENT

What are the true 'environmental virtues' and how do they relate to, indeed grow out of, earlier, more traditional ones? If we ask these

157

questions, we find that there exist two worthwhile sources of the 'environmental virtues', old virtues that already exist in other contexts, but are particularly applicable to the environment. Studying them will enable us to go beyond the virtuous 'church' of the environment and reveal the sectarian vices of the greenists, and also to uncover a distorted form of secular spirituality that leads to a profitless fanaticism.

The first and key source of 'environmental virtue' is discrimination: the ability to appreciate and, where necessary, to conserve that which is beautiful or of scientific interest. One of the most important aspects of the environment for the person of discrimination is the landscape. Whether it is a wilderness or has been created over time by human skill, whether it is a coral reef, Cadair Idris, a garden designed by Capability Brown, a coppiced woodland or maintained meadow or wetland, the Painted Desert of California, a savannah full of wildebeest being eaten by lions, or a jungle loaded with monkeys, it has an aesthetic value to be recognised and preserved from molestation by those seeking other human objectives. Of course, this argument does not apply to the deep sea bed below the point where light cannot penetrate. However, even a landscape that few get to see, or that few can appreciate, is still worth preserving at great cost; that is the meaning of discrimination.

Only the discriminating, those who possess the virtues of cultivation and discrimination and who by nature, training and choice have aesthetic judgement, will want to make that choice, and indeed they will – and should – wish to force that choice upon others at the expense of the latter's indulgence in coarser tastes. Sometimes we can see this happening by accident, as on the coasts of Dorset or Pembrokeshire in Britain, where the landscape has been preserved by intermittent military activity, or on the British coast near the Sizewell, Dungeness or Hinckley Point nuclear power plants, or on Porton Down, close to Britain's chemical weapons research facility. A sense of danger has repelled those who prefer trips a shilling with their funfairs, sticks of rock, dirty postcards and ukuleles, and has led to the preservation of nature.

There is nothing wrong with liking funfairs; indeed I confess to a liking for bumping cars and attempting to win a woolly gorilla, and I enjoy the cacophony of a steam-powered organ. It is merely that those who know landscapes know both, and know how to discriminate.[20] It is right and proper that those who do not know both should be discriminated against. It is the duty of a minority with higher aesthetic sensibilities to defend the landscape on these grounds alone, against those who would profit from destroying it – not because there is anything wrong with profit, but in order to frustrate the external consequences of consumer choices freely made by the coarse-fibred. It is not the arrogance of the greenists who want to destroy the 'others" very way of life and make them lead a 'higher' existence, but merely an insistence that, within certain limited geographical areas, beauty comes first. No caravans, no windmills. It has gone democratic, in that so many people have been converted to the finer aesthetic sensibilities that we are now faced with a new problem in both America and Britain: that we may love the landscape to death.

Love of beauty is a virtue that has to be adhered to even in the face of pressure from those who purport to defend the environment, such as the planters of windmills or conifers. Today the hills above Avila in Spain are disfigured by windmills, and they have, no doubt, spread to La Mancha. They march around and just outside the boundaries of national parks. Come back, Don Quixote; all is forgiven! Why can they not put the things offshore and out of sight? If, at present, this is too expensive, then put the money into cost-reducing research, not proliferation! Windmills are the greatest single enemy of the landscape since the British Forestry Commission's lurch into larch. They are repulsive in the same way as an oil spill on the coast, and potentially as destructive of birds. There is no reason why ugly, empty plains should not be filled with conifers and windmills, but to ruin a coastline or a hilltop in this way is to betray the main virtue that underlies our concern for the environment.

A second virtue is revealed when a concern for the environment leads us to seek to preserve species, not just handsome, appealing species such as gorillas, tigers, whales, pandas, orchids or sequoia, but also ugly and obscure plants and animals. With today's slow but progressive elimination of species, we do not know which ones are being wiped out or what their characteristics are. Knowledge is being lost, in the same way as it is when a jerry-builder in Greece or Egypt secretly bulldozes and drowns in cement an unknown and unrecorded archaeological site. There is no way of ever salvaging the material reality thus destroyed, or obtaining the knowledge embodied in it. There is, of course, nothing new about the extinction of species. The fossil record largely consists of plants and animals that no longer exist. Who weeps for the trilobites or the giant tree ferns? Today the world's peasants and fishermen regularly eliminate species by destroying the habitats of animals and plants and by over-fishing. Why should this concern us, apart, of course, from the practical reason that they might have been useful to us in the long run?

The answer lies in our very nature as a curious, knowledge-driven and ultimately scientific species, completely different from all others. To know and to name the creatures and plants of the earth is an imperative on a par with the desire and pursuit of beauty. They are defining characteristics of what human beings are. There are two overlapping sets of reasons why we should not wish to see species wantonly eliminated. One is that we do not know what use the species might have been to us. A plant that has irrevocably vanished might have contained a vital ingredient for the pharmaceutical industry or, when genetically modified, a new source of food or raw materials. The disappearance of a particular living creature may upset the entire balance of nature in a particular area. Prudence tells us that we should be careful. But prudence also tells us that, while conserving beetles is a good thing, the cost of protecting the marginal beetle *in situ* may be prohibitive.[21] A zoo for endangered beetles or a Jain *pinjrapol* for rare insects where they can feed on human visitors may be better and cheaper.[22]

The second, and for the discussion of virtue more important, reason is that both our feel for beauty and our scientific curiosity are combined in a sense of wonder that is offended by a shrinking of the span of creatures that exist. There is no virtue in survival of the fittest; fitness does not incorporate any worthwhile human value. Fitness is an utterly circular concept. Why admire the rat? It is for this reason that it is ethical to cull successful species in order to protect endangered ones. The controversies in Britain about whether to shoot Ruddy Ducks to preserve Turkish Ducks, whether to kill grey squirrels to protect red ones, or to cull the fast-breeding magpie to save scarce songbirds should really only be about whether it would be effective. If it is effective, then not to do so is to be complicit in the elimination of a species, albeit in some cases only locally.

There is a virtue that lies behind our species seeking the conservation of other species. These ends are what the scholarly and cultivated person would seek. To describe someone as cultivated, learned, scholarly or possessed of aesthetic sensibility is to praise him or her and to speak of virtue. We respect such people. In the context of this discussion, their real virtues beget 'environmental virtues'. Yet the cultivated person, unlike the greenist, can see the limits to what he or she can achieve, because their outlook is shaped by virtue, by qualities gained by effort and self-restraint in the pursuit of knowledge, refinement and subtlety. If the construction of a beautiful building disturbs the rabbits, well so be it. Greenism, by contrast, is merely a set of ideological preferences that say nothing about a person's character or virtues. What admirable personal qualities do you need to be a greenist? What virtues do you have to cultivate? In and of themselves, preferences are not virtues. Virtues are praiseworthy qualities that we perceive in another person's character.[23]

In the absence of the exercise of the virtues outlined in detail above, it is difficult to see why the environment should matter at all. If, for example, someone were to dump pieces of old iron in the middle of a flat, arid, lifeless stony desert, whether on Earth or another planet, it would not matter. A dead truck or the ruins of an old shed might even bring interest or sentiment to an otherwise unbearably ugly and monotonous vista. Rust to rust. Some pristine landscapes are utterly without merit of any kind, for they neither support life nor exhibit beauty. To call something a wilderness is not necessarily to praise it.

BRENT SPAR: A STUDY IN ENVIRONMENTAL VICE

These general points may be illustrated by looking at a particular European case: that of the Brent Spar controversy of the 1990s. It is both close to being an ideal type of environmental vice masquerading as virtue, and a turning point which enables us to understand many other subsequent environmental controversies in North America, as well as Europe and much of the rest of the world. In 1991 the Brent Spar, a floating oil storage and loading construction owned by Shell Petroleum, ceased operating. The question now arose as to what was the best practicable way to dispose of it with least damage to the environment. Independent experts advised that it should be sunk in deep water in the Atlantic Ocean.[24] There it would do no harm, and possibly some good as a new home for any creatures that might hide in it or even colonise it. In February 1995 the British government gave its approval and the decision was made public.

In April, Greenpeace falsely claimed that the Brent Spar contained over 100 tonnes of toxic sludge and over 5,000 tonnes of oil.[25] The real figure was less than 2 per cent of the estimates given to the press by Greenpeace.[26] Then Greenpeace activists occupied the Brent Spar. They claimed that deep water disposal would set a bad precedent, that another 400 oil rigs would be disposed of in the same way, and that this would cause major damage to the marine environment.[27] This illegal occupation triggered off violence in Germany, where 'heroic' green stormtroopers firebombed Shell petrol stations during *Tankstellenacht*, the Night of the Filling Stations. Rather than dealing firmly with these acts of terrorism, the German Chancellor Helmut Kohl begged John Major, the British Prime Minister, to force Shell to dispose of the Brent Spar in some other way, even though, according to Major's own experts, it would cause more damage to the environment.[28]

Greenpeace took out a full-page advertisement in a national newspaper attacking Shell, saying: 'If you let Shell have its way it'll soon be the only shell left in the North Sea.'[29] A further false claim was made that poisonous chemicals from the rig were a major threat to marine and human life. Shell capitulated, and the Brent Spar was dumped to rot in a Norwegian fjord. Subsequently, in September 1995, Greenpeace apologised to Shell for the false allegations it had made against the company. The Advertising Standards Authority has also forced the withdrawal of Greenpeace's anti-nuclear advertisements.[30] During the Brent Spar farce David Gee, formerly the director of Friends of the Earth UK, said in June 1995 that 'The incident has established the moral principle of "not dumping at sea" over the narrow technical "best practicable environmental option".'[31]

It is striking that he should see this as a *moral* principle, at the same time as recognising that the consequences were worse. Why should it be wrong to dump an object into an ocean trench where no one can see it and where it will do no harm to human beings or to marine life? It may be crushed by the weight of water above it, sit there like a natural nodule, or provide a haven for the creatures of the deep, but why should its presence at that depth matter in the least?[32]

The Brent Spar episode also revealed the nature of environmental vice, though the vices concerned are also to be found in other quite unrelated areas of human life. One key environmental vice is the view that because we feel good about our own cause, we need not worry about truth or accuracy or the adverse consequences of our agitation. It is the vice of the reckless crusader. It is the vice of the sentimentalist who places feeling above precision. It is the vice of fanatics who demonise their opponents. However convinced of his or her virtue someone is, he or she is still necessarily constrained, as a matter of moral principle, both by a requirement to seek and

respect the truth and by a requirement to consider the relative consequences of alternative modes of action. These principles apply to
and constrain environmental virtue and activism as they do any
other type of human action. They were not followed in the agitation
over Brent Spar. Were the greenists to claim in retrospect that the
long-run consequences of their mendacious, illegal and violent activities justified them, this would not only be unjustified on the facts
but would establish not only their lack of virtue but their inability to
comprehend what virtue is.

THE VIRTUE OF TRUTHFULNESS

To tell lies – either deliberately or recklessly – to assist a cause you
believe in is not a virtue. You can try to justify such an act, before or
after the event, on short-term, utilitarian grounds, but you have still
been untruthful, and that can hardly be described as a virtue. Even
in utilitarian terms you cannot justify deliberate, systematic and
reckless lying in an environmental context, for even if you were to
achieve something worthwhile it would be by accident. What is
more, you would have undermined trust and respect for truth. Does
that sound like a virtue?

This kind of disregard for the truth is very widespread among
environmental activists, who produce scare stories that can easily be
shown to be false and to have caused considerable harm, as we can
see from the numerous examples given by Aaron Wildavsky, who
tellingly entitled his book *But is it True?*[33] What is far worse is that
such activists have produced doctrines that justify their habitual
disregard for truth and accuracy. To exaggerate, to go for closure
when the evidence is uncertain, to eliminate inconvenient data by
questioning its reliability because you are convinced you are right, to
be partisan, to float the uncertain as a good story are ordinary
human weaknesses that we take for granted; we can, perhaps
should, be indulgent towards them. Indeed, in everyday life we
assume that people will do this and we make allowances for it. 'We
are all guilty', though some are more guilty than others. What is
wicked is to produce and adhere to a set of conventions, such as the
precautionary principle[34] or the Lalonde doctrine,[35] that justify the
deriving of 'loud, clear and unequivocal'[36] statements from evidence
that is uncertain and ambiguous. Such doctrines are the father and
mother of lies. We know what conclusions to draw about the lack of
the virtue of honesty among those who espouse them.

VIRTUE AS COURAGE AND SACRIFICE

It is worth asking what, if any, virtues are displayed by greenist activists. If what is at stake is a disagreement over the allocation of resources, which other disinterested people prefer to see going into educational or health expenditure, defence, relieving hardship or raising the standard of living of the ordinary citizen by bringing down prices, or allowing money to fructify in the taxpayers' pockets, rather than being used in furtherance of green ends, then it is difficult to see why the greenist activists should be seen as virtuous. They merely have different priorities, or perhaps they merely favour different ways of achieving a similar set of priorities. To be adjudged virtuous, the greenists would have to show that they had displayed an exemplary degree of courage or self-sacrifice. Yet what degree of courage does a demonstrator or activist in a safely democratic country need to display? To stand out against the government on an environmental issue in the old Soviet Union or in Saddam's Iraq or in Zimbabwe would take courage. You might end up dead, or beaten up, or in a labour camp or in prison.[37] To travel to Amazonia and obstruct someone clearing the forest, or to block a road in Borneo would likewise show guts and stamina. However, to trash a field of genetically modified crops in Britain, or to hurl stones at scientists in the Federal Republic of Germany trying to protect an experimental plot[38] is risk free, because you know in advance that you will not be harshly dealt with. In Europe it would take rather more courage to see the invaders and stone-throwers off with a shotgun, to overturn windmills strung along the boundary of a National Park, or secretly to sow and harvest genetically modified seed imported from North America because, given the appalling biases of the Attorneys General and the Courts, you would then be given a long custodial sentence. You would have been unjustly felled by the message-sending powerful.

You can call yourself Feral or Skunky and climb a tree about to be felled for a new road, knowing that the police or security guards will be called upon to show far more courage in getting you out of it safely than you showed in getting up it in the first place. You can chain yourself to a railway line to prevent the passage of a freight train carrying flasks of nuclear gunk, knowing full well that the authorities will cut you free before it arrives. Where is the courage and self-sacrifice here? Given that demonstrators enjoy the carnival atmosphere, the combination of collective feeling and anonymity, and the freedom to behave offensively with impunity that demonstrations provide, it is difficult to see how virtue comes into it. Even demonstrations at sea are no more hazardous than most adventure holidays. It was noticeable how very cautious greenist demonstrators were against the highly destructive Soviet trawlers and whaling ships. Soviet vessels were always addressed politely, indeed deferentially, in English from a safe distance through loudhailers; no use was ever made of the kind of obscene political abuse for which the Russian language is so celebrated. It was pain-free glory in front of television cameras, the modern equivalent of Carrie Nation chopping down a bar with an axe.[39] Occasionally, there has been an accident and one single case of the criminal manslaughter of a Greenpeacer consequent on the orders of the French President François Mitterand,[40] but in general the risks taken, and the hardships experienced, have been unremarkable. Over time, environmental activism has become big business and provides profitable careers spiced with media appearances and little excitements.[41] There is no more virtue in doing well out of a green cause than in performing the routine tasks that keep the societies going, within which such causes are pursued. Greenist claims to virtue are false.

WORSHIPPING FALSE GODS

Another false claim to virtue made, or at least implied, by the greenists is rooted in their assertion that they are pursuing pure and absolute ends not subject to qualifications and compromises, or indeed the claims of truth or reasonableness. They have found a kind of perverse spirituality in the material world that, in their view, renders their claims about that material world immune from criticism. They have returned to the old pagan nature deities. Thus, in the case of the Brent Spar, what offended the objectors most was its being dumped in what they saw as a secular sacred spot, the pure, pristine sea bed that must remain for ever free from the presence of human beings. They seem to have an unrealistic view of nature as benign until disturbed by human intervention.

We can see this in the agitation in Germany over the *Waldsterben*, the supposed death of the forests due to acid rain. It never happened.[42] Forests always contain a proportion of trees that will die because they become overshadowed by their neighbours and cannot compete for their necessary share of sunlight. The stunted ones succumb to insects, fungi and viruses, if they are not thinned out by human beings, until a new equilibrium is reached, in which there are fewer trees than originally sprouted.[43] Forests are places of death. The tree-worshippers could not see this. Forests, for them, were kindly places, sacred groves where human free-birds, the *Wandervögel*, could flutter and sing and wander freely in their leather shorts and goat-skin rucksacks and play guitars next to particulate and carbon dioxide-producing camp fires; a place of life and peace far from the jostling, competing crowds of the city. The idea that forests could be overcrowded and places of competition between trees could not even be contemplated; the acids of distant, dark satanic power stations must be to blame. Forests and lakes may well be damaged by sulphur and nitrogen oxides emitted by distant high-chimneyed power plants that cause acid rain (though it should be noted that lightning also produces nitric oxide, which has always been described as a source of nitrate fertilisers, not acidity) but that is beside the point. The point is that a large proportion of the trees that died had been killed by other trees and not by acid rain, yet the greenists' ideology insisted, without evidence, that the opposite was the case.

In the American National Parks it was, at one time, park policy to extinguish all forest fires to 'save' the forest. Then it was realised that many of the fires were caused by lightning and were part of a natural cycle by which old growth burned away and new shoots replaced them. Now it was the cycle itself that had to be treated as eternal, not the trees; a step forward from hysteria at the death of a forest, but still problematic. Accordingly, every time there was a fire a decision had to be reached as to whether it was due to natural causes and, therefore, was to be allowed to burn on, or was the result of some careless, guitar-playing, happy wanderer throwing away a smouldering marijuana-laden cigarette end. The latter, and only the latter, were to be extinguished by the park authorities. It would have been simpler to decide from a computer programme how many natural fires there were likely to be, and extinguish fires at random until this target had been met; or, even better, to calculate what the optimum number and size of fires would be for the kind of forest it was desirable to encourage and preserve from an aesthetic and scientific point of view. Yet, at the time, this would have been seen as environmental heresy and as subjecting eternal autonomous nature to human decision making. However, nature is not eternal, nor is it, in any meaningful sense, autonomous.

Accordingly we cannot seek wisdom and meaning in a nature independent of ourselves. Nothing in the material world is eternal: neither the living creatures of the Earth, nor the mountains, nor the

Earth itself. It will all pass away, just as we do as individuals. Human beings, and most other species, will one day probably be wiped out by an asteroid or comet hitting the earth. Such a catastrophe, the 'elimination of species' has happened at least twice before in geological history. In the very long run the sun, that source of green goodness, will swell up and swallow us all. Attempts to find in nature a secular substitute for religion are vain, and, by extension, nature cannot provide us with any moral principles. There are no, and can be no, specifically environmental virtues.

CONCLUSION

What we have rather is an arena in which to exercise well-known human virtues that have long had applications elsewhere. We need to exercise prudence, charity, care and thrift, making use of institutions governed by a utilitarian moral framework, which in turn requires the virtues of honesty, disinterestedness, concern for the truth, duty and reliability. Perhaps most important we must give precedence to the virtues of the cultivated and the discriminating, the scientist, scholar and artist. Such precedence does not mean that those who exemplify these virtues have a licence to disregard such other virtues as honesty, self-restraint, and human decency,[44] which both characterise the good person and are the very basis of social life.

1   Daniel R. Botkin and Edward A. Keller, *Environmental Science: Earth is a Living Planet* (New York: John Wiley, 1998).
2   W. M. S. Russell, *Man, Nature and History* (London: Aldus, 1967), pp. 135–6, 139.
3   See Russell, *Man, Nature and History*, pp. 87–8 on the fatal dilemmas of swidden farming.
4   Russell, *Man, Nature and History*, pp. 223–4. Claire Russell and W. M. S. Russell, *Population Crises and Population Cycles* (London: Galton, 1999).
5   Thomas Robert Malthus, *An Essay on the Principle of Population* (London: John Murray, 1826); Jack Parsons, *The Reverend Thomas Robert Malthus AM. FRS* (Llantrisant: Population Policy Press, 2002).
6   It is doubtful whether public spaces in India can be clean until the sweeper throws away his brush and the Brahmin dispenses with his ritual bath.
7   The British minister Benjamin Disraeli, who was responsible for the Enabling Act of 1858 that allowed the Metropolitan Board and Bazalgette to put sewers under someone's land whether the owner

consented or not, and for the Public Health Act of 1875, saw this point quite clearly. As he said, in a witty twist on the Latin translation of the words of King Solomon, 'Sanitas sanitatum, omnia sanitas.' When Joseph Chamberlain cleaned up Birmingham, England, with 'sagacious audacity' and made it the best-governed and best-sewered city in the world, he called upon municipal pride, not individual virtue or cleanliness to achieve this utilitarian end.

8   Christie Davies, *The Strange Death of Moral Britain* (New Brunswick, NJ: Transaction, 2004), pp. 100–104.

9   I am not saying that regulation by the central government as such was the crucial factor. Indeed the rate of decline of air pollution before and after the 1956 Clean Air Act was much the same. I am merely saying that, in this particular case, it was quicker and more effective to use local and central government regulation than to create new kinds of property rights and leave it to private litigation. Whether you do it the former way or the latter is not a question of personal virtue but of choice of means.

10 See Max Weber, *The Protestant Ethic and the Spirit of Capitalism* (London: Unwin, 1930). My argument does not depend on the accuracy of Weber's account, but on more recent historical evidence about nineteenth and early twentieth-century Britain; see Davies, *The Strange Death of Moral Britain*, pp. 1–61.

11 Even if much of the warming were due to changes in the sun or in the Earth's orbit, it would still make sense to consider what to do in response to this. Ironically, it may also be the case that reducing particulate pollution has led to less of the sun's radiant energy being bounced back into space by the filth in the atmosphere, i.e. cleaner air has unleashed global warming caused by other factors.

12 See discussions in Bjørn Lomborg, *The Skeptical Environmentalist* (Cambridge: CUP, 2001), pp. 258–324, and in Robert C. Balling, Jr, *The Heated Debate* (San Francisco: Pacific Research Institute, 1992), pp. 133–51.

13 See Max Weber, *Economy and Society: An Outline of Interpretive Sociology*, eds. Guenther Roth and Claus Wittich (Berkeley: University of California Press, 1978), Volume 1, pp. 24–5; see also H. H. Gerth and C. W. Mills, *From Max Weber, Essays in Sociology* (London: Routledge and Kegan Paul, 1991), p. 9. For a variety of reasons, I think that instrumental rationalism is an inappropriate and indeed failing way of organising many institutions, i.e. to use it as a basis for action is irrational. Likewise, to advocate 'modernity' is often destructive, or just a deceitful way of legitimating harmful changes that its proponents want for other reasons. However, these arguments do not apply here. The main effect of obsessive greenist, healthist or 'it must be proved to be safe' regulations is to imprison us in a second iron cage, in addition

to the one manufactured by the demand not just for efficiency, but, more dubiously, for best practice or excellence. It is tilted at an angle to our other cage, so that our space for autonomy is doubly restricted. See Weber, *The Protestant Ethic*.

14 Robert Heilbroner, 'The human prospect', *New York Review of Books*, 14 January 1974, pp. 30, 31, 34.

15 Knut Hamsun, *Pan* (Harmondsworth: Penguin Books, 1998); Henry David Thoreau, *Walden* (London: Walter Scott, 1886), pp. 88–9; www.gandhiserve.org/information/writings_online.html

16 Boris Komarov (pseudonym of Ze'ev Wolfson), *The Destruction of Nature in the Soviet Union* (White Plains, NY: M. E. Sharpe, 1980); Andrew Csepel, 'Czechs and the ecological balance', *New Scientist*, 27 September 1984; Anna Ahaffy-Bathar, 'Need for scientific and political co-operation in the Danube Basin' (pp. 47–58) and M. G. Khublaryan, 'Water pollution and its consequences in the former USSR' (pp. 151–71) both in Klaus Schleicher (ed.), *Pollution Knows No Frontiers* (New York: Paragon, 1992).

17 Komarov, *Destruction of Nature*, pp. 32–3.

18 Andrzej Werner, 'Marxism and pollution – some East European experiences before the Revolution' in Schleicher *Pollution Knows No Frontiers*, pp. 291–303. Werner originally wrote this in 1988, at considerable personal danger to himself, before the overthrow of socialism.

19 See Lomborg, *The Skeptical Environmentalist*, pp. 318–22.

20 See John Stuart Mill, *Utilitarianism, On Liberty, and Essay on Bentham*, ed. Mary Warnock (Oxford: Blackwell, 2003), pp. 129, 259.

21 See discussion in Lomborg, *The Skeptical Environmentalist*, pp. 249–57.

22 A *pinjrapol* is a Jain institution for the welfare of animals, particularly those that are old and sick. It is said that travellers can stay in one such *pinjrapol* in Gujarat if they allow the insects who dwell there to feed on them. This may be a myth derived from others' perceptions of the Jains' very strong commitment to *ahimsa*, the religious principle of causing no harm to any living creature, not even an insect. Jains will even feed grains of sugar to the ants that live in the cracks between paving stones.

23 We infer character from observing a person's behaviour in a variety of situations and noting his or her display of virtue (or its opposite or absence). Their patterns of preference are part of this assessment, but only part and a problematic part. To hold conforming opinions about matters distant or ideological is not a virtue.

24 Aberdeen University Research and Industrial Services, *Removal and Disposal of Brent Spar – a Safety and Environmental Assessment of the Options* (1994); Shell, *Brent Spar Abandonment Impact Hypotheses*,

prepared for Shell UK Exploration and Production by Rudall Blanchard Associates Limited 15/12/94; Smit Engineering BV, *Feasibility Study – Report for Scrapping of the Brent Spar* (1992).
25 'Brent Spar – a strange affair', *Financial Times Energy Economist*, July 1995.
26 'Greenpeace fiasco', *Daily Telegraph*, 7 September 1995; 'Greenpeace loses some of its veneer doing double blast', *Wall Street Journal*, 7 September 1995.
27 'Greenpeace loses some of its veneer doing double blast', *Wall Street Journal*.
28 'Green for danger', *Daily Telegraph*, 21 June 1995.
29 John Davidson, 'A platform for punchy propaganda', *Sunday Times*, 25 June 1995.
30 Minette Marrin, 'Fight the bad hype', *Sunday Telegraph*, 11 September 1994.
31 *Independent*, 22 June 1995.
32 There *are* reasons for being concerned about the sea bed, for example in relation to fishermen who dredge the surfaces of high under-sea 'mountains', destroy the wildlife that thrives there and reduce them to deserts. There is a strong case for banning such activities. However, none of this applied in the Brent Spar case.
33 Aaron Wildavsky, *But is it True? A Citizen's Guide to Environmental, Health and Safety Issues* (Cambridge, MA: Harvard UP, 1995). For further examples of a particularly flagrant disregard for truth and accuracy, even involving the deliberate falsification of experimental evidence by the 'concerned' and 'committed', see Mark Neal and Christie Davies, *The Corporation Under Siege* (London: Social Affairs Unit, 1998) and John O'Neill, 'The foundation and the fall', *Sydney Morning Herald*, 19 December 1988.
34 See Wildavsky, *But is it True?* pp. 427–47 on 'rejecting the Precautionary Principle'.
35 John C. Luik, *Pandora's Box* (Boston: University of Boston, 1994).
36 *ibid.*
37 See note 18 and Andrew Csepel, 'Czech authorities round up outspoken scientists', *New Scientist*, 26 November 1987, p. 26.
38 Henry Miller, *Biotechnology Regulation: The Unacceptable Costs of Excessive Caution* (London: Social Affairs Unit, 1997), pp. 9–10.
39 Carrie Nation was a very successful late nineteenth and early twentieth-century American advocate of Prohibition. Her cause was a righteous one, but today she is not seen in America as a model of virtue and good sense.
40 The death of Fernando Pereira on the *Rainbow Warrior* was not a case of greenist heroic self-sacrifice, but merely of French villainy. The Greenpeace ship *Rainbow Warrior* was safely in harbour in Auckland,

New Zealand when it was blown up in July 1985 on the personal orders of the French President François Mitterand to *liquider* the ship. Major Alain Mafart and Captain Dominique Prieur, two of the many French terrorists involved, were caught by the New Zealand police masquerading as a honeymoon couple called Turenge, pleaded guilty to arson and manslaughter, and were sentenced to 10 years' imprisonment by the New Zealand courts. While they were in prison, the French Foreign Minister, Roland Dumas, tried to send them a crate of wine from his own vineyard as a Christmas present. Later the French government agreed to compel the EU to permit the United Kingdom to import New Zealand butter during 1987 and 1988, and the New Zealanders allowed the two prisoners to be transferred to the French atoll of Hao in the Pacific in July 1986. Mafart, travelling on a false passport, was returned to France, allegedly suffering from 'stress' or neurasthenia in 1987, and was promoted to colonel in 1994.

Mme Prieur's husband Joël, a fireman, was sent to join her in Hao in August 1986 and she was returned to France on the grounds of pregnancy in May 1988. She had often been seen shopping in Tahiti in dark glasses and a wig. Before the bombing, a lesbian lieutenant in the French military was used to infiltrate green organisations in New Zealand. See Alex W. du Prel , 'La VRAIE histoire d'attentat contre le "Rainbow Warrior"', *Tahiti-Pacifique*, 49, May 1995, pp. 15–25. It was just an everyday story of French political folk. As M du Prel writes, '*Lisez. Ce n'est pas triste.*' The crew of the ill-named and ill-fated *Rainbow Warrior* were not courageous, merely foolish. It would take courage to try and stop the testing of a North Korean bomb in the atmosphere because it is known in advance that the Korean response will be savage. The Greenpeacers merely made the political error of thinking that France behaves with the kind of considered and sometimes naïve restraint that characterises much of the rest of western Europe, and indeed New Zealand. Anyone with any sense and with a knowledge of French history adopts an attitude of caution and mistrust in dealing with the rulers of France.

41 Reiner Luyken, 'Die Protest-Maschine', *Die Zeit*, 37, 9, 6 September 1996.

42 Lomborg, *Skeptical Environmentalist*, pp. 178–81; Wildavsky, *But is it True?*, pp. 274–303.

43 Wildavsky, *But is it True?*, p. 296.

44 Another greenist vice is to make personal attacks on particular individual opponents whose human dignity and feelings they ignore. To use strident rhetoric against opposing groups is a normal and acceptable part of the way controversies are conducted in mature democratic countries, and indeed that is as it should be. What is quite wrong is to behave in the way greenists have done to particular

171

individuals who have sought to expose them, as in the case, say, of the noted Danish environmental sceptic Bjørn Lomborg. In my view he is seriously mistaken on some points, notably on population and aspects of development that stem from this, and I can see why the tone of his language might irritate the more olivine greenists, but that is no excuse for the underhand attacks that have been made on him, from accusing him of scientific fraud before the Orwellian-titled Danish Committees on Scientific Dishonesty (whose findings were quashed by the Danish Ministry of Science; in particular, the committees were criticised for using the circular, slippery and tendentious term 'good scientific practice'), to putting up details of his personal life and of his family on the web, to throwing a custard pie at him at a book launch, to misuse of copyright law to prevent him from defending himself. What really hurt the full-fathom-five greenists was that he had shown, to a very wide reading public through a reputable publisher employing a proper reviewing procedure, that there is no scientific consensus on many questions which the greenists treat as articles of faith, but rather there are disagreements and uncertainty among experts. Even if you are totally convinced you are right, as the greenists are, not only is such behaviour wrong (it is the equivalent of a vested interest trying to dig up dirt on a whistle-blower), but it is also going to diminish the chances of your views being taken seriously. See, for March 2005, www.lomborg.com; www.lomborg-errors.dk (run by K. Fog); www.lomborg-errors.dk/lomborgstory1.htm; www.greenspirit.com/lomborg; www.techcentralstation.com/051104C.html

CHAPTER 9

THE CARING VIRTUES

PETER MULLEN

THE NEW MEANING OF 'CARING'

What does 'in care' mean? It refers to the holding of a person – usually a child – in an institutional establishment because the people who might be supposed to care for him are unable to, or will not, do so: perhaps they are dead, or merely incapable of fulfilling their duty of care. Sometimes the child is removed from the family home into care because the parents have been sexually abusing or otherwise ill-treating him. There is another misnomer: a person in care is usually described as being in 'a care home'. These places are not homes, they are institutions provided by the government at the taxpayers' expense. This fact by itself adds to the euphemistic and darkly misleading use of the expression *care* – for, as everybody who reads the papers knows, there have been numerous cases in which these institutionalised children (or old people) have been exploited and abused by their professional carers. So 'in care' often means that people don't care.

In the old days, before society was 'modernised' and former aspects of life that were always private were nationalised and socialised, the word 'care' had specific and familiar meanings. Romantic black and white Hollywood films featured heroic lovers who courted their beloved with the words, 'You know how I care for you.' More prosaically, husbands and wives cared for one another, and mothers and fathers cared for their children. More frequently these days mothers and fathers desert one another – if ever they were together in the first place for any longer than it takes to procreate; so they are not there to care for their children. It is paradoxical, then, that the children are said to be 'taken into care'.

The phenomenon of institutional caring is of great and widespread interest to children. For example, one of the most popular children's television programmes is called *Tracy Beaker* – a long-running series about a ten-year-old girl in a care home, constantly looking forward to being imminently reclaimed by her mother.

Once in care, individuals – young or old – are looked after by professional carers. The notion of the professional carer is an unusual one, suggesting as it inevitably does that a human activity – caring – which is traditionally associated with personal affection, is something that people can do to earn a living. In fact, jobs in caring have a promotions ladder and a recognised hierarchical structure. And, inevitably, there are professional courses and qualifications, and a whole apparatus of bureaucratised public service operated according to a particular jargon or code of caring.

A recent report, *Children in Care: Now and Then*[1] typically describes the new mode of caring as *holistic*, where children are educated in 'life skills' and 'given the confidence to discuss problems with those in authority'. (The presupposition that life is defined by its problems is fundamental to the caring industry, and I shall return to this issue many times.) There are 'targets' and inevitably there is 'a current package'. And obviously there must be 'a culture of listening'. There is always a frequently updated slogan of the minute, and two of the latest are 'Quality Protects' (for England) and 'Children First in Wales' (for that principality). The result of this descent into jargon is the submersion of the primary job of care and protection under the mulch of management-speak – 'managing the caring process' – and the demands of public relations.

The language of professional carers is at once anodyne and sinister:

> Jan Stacey, Director of Children's Services, said, 'We cannot be complacent. There is still a lot of learning to do. We must recognise that children in foster homes are potentially very vulnerable.'

Why 'vulnerable' if they are 'in care'? Because, as already noted, children in care are, as the authorities themselves say, 'at risk' of abuse by their carers. Notorious examples of abuse – such as the so-called 'Pin Down Inquiry' in Staffordshire, the 'Frank Beck Case' in Leicester and the 'Waterhouse Inquiry' in North Wales – have encouraged the authorities to close down many institutional homes and attempt to find foster care for children in individual families. Though the danger of abuse persists here too:

> The NSPCC says that home fostering is generally an improvement, but these children are more isolated. Families are notoriously difficult to inspect and children in small foster families are less likely to complain than they are in homes.

It is also harder to ensure that their voices are being heard.

The structural bureaucratese of the language of *caring* sits awkwardly alongside much sentimentality and sloganising about 'children first' and 'families together' (when actually they are apart) and there is no shortage of tear-jerking pictures and posters: I have before me, as I write, a particularly unpleasant one of a little boy clutching a fluffy rabbit as he cowers in a corner of a 'care home'.

Even caring for one's own children hides a self-referential motive, as an anecdote from a *parenting manual* demonstrates:

'You'll feel like a nicer mummy', whispers the tutor encouragingly. 'Mmmmm!'

And as I write, there is a new report in the newspaper – from OFSTED, which is meant to be concerned for standards in education:

Young children should spend less time reading and being read to and more time getting in touch with their inner selves.

It has long been useless to point out that one does not have a 'self' to get in touch with until one has at least begun to fashion such a self out of one's experience – and that is partly the outcome of reading.

Institutionalised or professional caring is a depressing affair – almost an oxymoron or contradiction in terms – and a bitter example of Eliot's warning against '…men dreaming of systems so perfect that no one will need to be good'.

In short, caring in the modern, institutional, sense is not a virtue, but a paid job. And the truth is that care is not something that people can do for a wage. A carer is described as a 'professional friend', but to whom does the professional friend turn when he needs a friend?

CARING FOR ANIMALS

W. C. Fields once said, 'A man who hates children and dogs can't be all bad.' The comedian was disgusted by the lavish care that was given to pets back in the 1930s. He should see us now. An alien might be excused for coming away with the impression that the British are animal worshippers. A recent survey shows that £3.5 billion are spent each year on 'pet foods, vets' fees, grooming and other luxuries'. This represents a three per cent year-on-year increase since the 1930s, despite the fact that the number of cats and dogs in the country has decreased from 14.2 million to 13.6 million. A fifth of those interviewed for this survey said that they bought Christmas and birthday presents for their pets. Some 22 per cent take out health insurance for them.

Websites dedicated to animal lovers are filled with testimonies as to the amount of care bestowed upon domestic pets:

> My Staffordshire terrier gets only the best organic meat and he wears a coat and collar from Burberry…

> We have six cats and they are our friends. We talk to them. They have a great sense of humour but they won't make a sound. They sit and watch while we give them lessons in purring and miaowing…

You do not have to be a consultant psychiatrist to feel that there might be a degree of attention-seeking in that last example, and indeed it does look as if the extremely anthropomorphic attitude that devotees display towards pets is an attempt to create surrogate love relationships:

> Why not pamper our dogs? After all, they give us unconditional love – which is more than humans do…

Whether 'love' can be ascribed to animals is a matter for linguistic philosophers, but pets do have a lot to offer their owners. A general practitioner writing in *The Times*, says,

> Nearly all pet owners would rather share the bed with their four-legged friend than with their partner. And, given the health benefits of keeping an animal, maybe that's not such a bad thing.

Apart from the emotional support that may be derived from sleeping with the dog, there is evidence that many dogs are cleaner than their owners, and that they spread fewer germs. So self-interest on the part of humans may be the barely concealed motive for the extravagant care that so many lavish on their pets. Certainly the tendency to anthropomorphise is widespread, and nowadays animals are adjudged to suffer the same sorts of emotional and psychological disorders as their owners:

> Cats are liable to be as stressed as their owners by the arrival of a new baby or a sudden upheaval in their lives…A study of family pets suffering from bladder problems revealed that in

most cases their illness was stress related. Those most affected by anxiety were pedigree, middle aged and overweight males...

Exactly like their owners, in fact!

And then there is the saga concerning the banning of hunting with hounds. What might one conclude about the caring priorities in the population at large that so many express such distaste for fox-hunting, yet remain untroubled by the 180,000 foetuses that are aborted every year as a means of birth control?

CARING: DEATH AND GRIEF

The new caring society is not a community of faith – at least not in the traditional sense. But, since even the modern euphemistic and sentimental society has not yet developed a way of abolishing death, something has to be offered to those who mourn. What they, in fact, get offered is a kind of ersatz religion without God or any definite credal statements, or hope of life in the world to come. It is as if doctrinal orthodoxy and the traditional Christian teaching about death were too precise, to the point of being 'offensive' to those who do not share the Christian hope. Those who now care for the bereaved – the grief counsellors and related therapists – would not for a moment think of reading to the grief-stricken client Christ's reassuring words in St John's gospel:

> Let not your heart be troubled: ye believe in God, believe also
> in me. In my Father's house are many mansions: if it were not
> so, I would have told you. I go to prepare a place for you...
> I will come again, and receive you unto myself; that where
> I am, there ye may be also.

Still less would they turn to St Paul:

> For since by man came death, by man came also the
> resurrection of the dead. For as in Adam all die, even so
> in Christ shall all be made alive.

Instead, the materials on offer are such as this:

> It is the dimension of care for the dying which energises
> and brings meaning to the days of journeying to the eventual
> farewell and allows us to become a touching place and
> permission to find a truth which dignifies and heals.[2]

The first thing to notice about this is that it is almost completely meaningless. Almost, but not quite; for it contains shades and echoes of meaning and reference. First, 'the days of journeying' echoes the old notion of pilgrimage – only without saying exactly where the journey is leading. Similarly, 'a touching place' – despite obviously belonging in the touchy-feely world of emotional counselling that has replaced pastoral care – may be a fond and vacuous hint of the dim recollection that once there were such things as sacred places and spaces; and it may even carry a faint remembrance of the idea – 'touching' – of anointing with holy oil. By these means, the modern carer in the grief-counselling business is able to conjure up a vaguely religious feeling, while carefully avoiding the issue of religious truth. The entire production is sham antique.

A few words are added from the vocabulary of New Age 'spirituality' – words such as 'energises' (suggesting powerful but non-specific influences, brought to bear, perhaps, by magic) and 'a truth which dignifies' (which manages to mention the strong word 'truth', but without – unlike St Paul – pointing to any particular truth). The carer's psychobabble can become very pretentious and intrusive: 'The first task of a spiritual carer is to affirm the patient's personhood and identity.' It is tempting to write a satire: SUCKERING THE GRIEVING: EMPOWERING THE DEAD. But perhaps not, for the grief counsellor's manual is a satire already. Notice now that the bereaved person has become 'a patient'. So grief is no longer a natural response, but a sickness requiring therapy. But if grief is a sickness, then we are all patients. I hesitated before I wrote that last sentence for fear that a member of the Grief Counsellors' Union might seize upon it for a slogan with which to advertise their sentimental and euphemistic ministrations: GRIEF: WE ARE ALL PATIENTS NOW.

The religious echo is very useful for the grief counsellor, so we are offered 'Our helplessness is a gift to the helpless', which just might remind a religious person of the glorious words in Philippians about Christ's emptying himself – but which again neither commits the speaker to any doctrine, nor prescribes for the bereaved any specific remedy.

There is sometimes a pretension to philosophical expertise and psychological insight: 'Whatever else a god is, it is the personification of our ideal.' What, any ideal? – heaven, hell, reincarnation as a turnip, becoming a god oneself, or rotting in the earth? 'Any' will do – for, of course, all 'personifications' are equal in the grief counsellor's non-judgemental ontology.

There is an orthodoxy in the grief-counselling industry nonetheless – as there is in 'death preparation, the science of leave-taking', and it takes the form of a sequence of mechanistic responses. This is succinctly explained for us by Elisabeth Kubler-Ross, who informs us that the 'terminally ill' (why not 'dying'?) person proceeds through the following mental states: 'denial and isolation; anger; bargaining; depression; acceptance'.[3] And it is the carer's job to pilot the dying person through these varieties of psychological determinism.

As a priest with thirty-five years' parish experience, I can confirm that grief-counselling is pretentious bunkum and designed as much to answer the attention-seeking lust of the counsellor, as for any good it might do to the bereaved. It is also dangerous and damaging, for it inculcates notions and feelings far removed from the true care required. Unfortunately, it sometimes partly succeeds – because the dying will reach out for any consolation available. But there is no real comfort here. New Age froth instead of the promises of the gospel. Psychobabble in place of pastoral care. And which of you with a son who asks for a fish would give him a serpent?

PUBLIC DEATH AND SHOWBIZ GRIEVING

The mass hysteria that followed the death of Princess Diana might encourage a stranger to conclude that the favourite pastime of the British is to watch expensive funerals on television and relieve the excitement occasionally by rushing out into the street to throw teddy bears at passing hearses. For not only must we expect to be cared for – or cared *over* – when we are dying or bereaved, we, in turn, must show ourselves to be *caring*. And, according to the new touchy-feely orthodoxy, we are to care not only for our parents and grandparents whom we know, but for television and movie celebrities whom we have not even seen. (A useful definition of 'celebrity': someone you've never heard of.)

So, we are to care for those who perished in wars long since past. This is not to be confused with what goes on at the Cenotaph on Remembrance Sunday, when there is a respectful recollection of the fallen and even formal prayers. Instead, we are meant to 'take responsibility' for the wars of the distant past and ideally to 'apologise' to the French for having defeated them in so many conflicts, and to the Muslims for the Crusades. In other words, we are commanded to emote: that is, to show our 'caring' by working up in ourselves feelings which no one in his right mind could possibly have. A classic of the genre is a report in *The Times* from the Holocaust Memorial in Jerusalem:

I won't try to describe it... [But the reporter nevertheless does!]
Enough to say that we empty-headed Englishers arrived at 9am
and didn't feel able to leave until 1pm. Our unimpeachable
Israeli guide, the beautiful and brilliant Ms Ora Schlesinger,
spoke to us softly after about three hours: Julie, Nadia, I hate
to have to say this, but we must go soon. We were uncontrol-
lable in our grief: every time we thought we could move on,
one of us would utter a cry of anguish and dart back into the
darkness of the halls. When we emerged though, we felt calm
and ready for anything. Come on Israel – let's do it...[4]

There is a feast of hysterical pathology here for the *aficionado*.
And that reporter and her companion are more than half in love
with death – but it's far from easeful. There is something unwhole-
some about the reference to the *beautiful* Ms Ora. One recollects the
maudlin sexuality of Victorian verse commemorating the death of
children – the fetid gardens of Swinburne's luscious *Proserpine*.
Whatever else their 'caring' might be, it is certainly a display.

Every road death is now marked by bunches of flowers placed
by the wayside. When pop stars and characters in soap operas die –
as even they, like chimneysweeps, must – schoolchildren are offered
counselling. It happened to the young daughter of one of my parishioners. And the result was that – although she had previously known
nothing of the dead celebrity – the educational grief-counselling so
upset her that she could not sleep for weeks afterwards. And certainly the mass media knows its own – and how it cares for them, sharing this caring with millions of listeners and viewers, whether or not
they want to join the *Schmaltzfest*. When the disc jockey John Peel
died last year at the respectable age of 65 – nearly twice as old as
Mozart – the BBC filled the first eleven minutes of the main evening
news broadcast with 'tributes'. He was one of their own trade, and
the broadcasters' response to his death was an opportunity for self-
advertisement, for a parade.

In 2004, when there was a huge commemoration on the 60th
anniversary of the D-day landings, some of the journalists who
accompanied the entourage and took the guided tour laid on for
them were later offered counselling. When one of these reporters
later mentioned this at a dinner for the Guild of Air Pilots, one of
the old fliers said to him: 'I was there over the beaches in '44 in my
Spitfire – but nobody offered me counselling.'

Television producers are hugely talented in being able to combine the modern virtue of sublime caring with the most complete self-interest. After the Indian Ocean disaster, for example, when the BBC had chided western leaders mercilessly for their allegedly tardy response, the *Indian Times* newspaper filled its front page with a complaint from the editor: WHEN WILL THE BBC END THIS CORPSE SHOW? The editor said that the BBC had respected calls for restraint and had agreed not to broadcast suicides jumping from the top of the Twin Towers on 9/11, but the Corporation was persisting in showing close-ups of rows of corpses on the beaches of the east coast of India. This may be evidence for all who suspect that the sentimental caring attitude is inseparable from psychopathy: for both alike are perversions of genuine feeling. Through the familiar accounts of the criminal sadism of Al Capone and the London East End's Kray twins, we know that vicious madness goes hand in hand with protestations of the deepest affection.

There are, of course, the many Dead Icons, the mere mention of whom never fails to kick-start the caring reflex: John Lennon, JFK, Martin Luther King, Jimi Hendrix, Princess Diana – though, interestingly, not Winston Churchill or Queen Elizabeth the Queen Mother.

We are coerced into caring – or at least to pretend we care. But we may be left wondering whether it is possible, or desirable, to try to have feelings for those whose distant disasters are communicated to us via the BBC. Evelyn Waugh said, 'To worry about Argentina when you live in Tunbridge Wells is the first sign of madness.' His words might be an adaptation of the First Epistle of St John to read,

> He who careth not for his near neighbour whom he hath seen, how can he care for the stranger whom he hath not seen?

Of course, in the modern age there is nothing left unseen, for television is always with us, allowing us to participate in – the gurus in the caring industry usually say 'empathise with' – the suffering of all and sundry, whether they be unfortunates killed in traffic accidents whose memory needs to be marked with roadside bouquets and Disneyfied messages of mourning, or nameless victims of distant earthquakes. We are especially invited to enter the sufferings of sportspeople:

> Paula Radcliffe was a broken woman and her grief became
> as much a spectator sport as the rest of the Athens Olympics,
> causing heartbreak and disappointment nationwide.[5]

181

If someone is described as 'a broken woman' because she failed to finish in a sporting event, what words are left to describe her mood if she were to witness the deaths of her children in a house fire? What sort of nation are we supposed to be if we are heart-broken when a favourite runner fails to win the marathon? Not the sort of nation that could endure a Blitz. *Caring* always cheapens emotional response by exaggerating and misapplying it.

SPIRITUALITY AND THE NEW NARCISSISM

The old commandment said that we should love our neighbour as ourselves, and this was meant to be a practical instruction about what it means to try to care for others: care for them, take care of them, in the same way you take care of yourself. Or, more bluntly: don't just care for yourself – think about others. The new virtue of caring is defined as a duty to care for oneself. The old religious idea that you tried to act virtuously for virtue's own sake, or for God's sake, has been replaced by the new psychotherapeutic notion of virtue for well-being's sake – your own well-being. Indeed, not to look after your own health according to the current medical, dietary and lifestyle fads is regarded as irresponsible. The religious concept of self-respect has been supplanted by the egocentric notion of self-esteem. But, whereas self-respect involved the peace that comes from attempting to lead a virtuous life (and its consequential blessing of a clear conscience), self-esteem means merely feeling good about your-self. Like the rest of the caring industry, it is devoid of moral content.

The milieu of self-caring is mediated by 'lifestyle' which is supposed to make us feel good about ourselves and at home among our contemporaries. It does this by informing us as to our choice of clothes, food, holidays, motor cars, domestic appliances – and especially our choices in the matters of sexuality ('Discover your feminine/gay/dominating side'), partners and religion. It came as a surprise to me to learn that I might decide to be homosexual 'for a spell', in much the same way as one might be tempted to take up Morris Dancing. Sexual relations in the new therapeutic community have been removed from the traditional realm of commitment, faithfulness and what is sacred, and deposited in the world of consumerism: 'Try this sensation and see if you like it. If not, don't worry – here's a different one you can try.'

It is all expressed in the language of the advertising slogan, so demonstrating the indissoluble union between caring and the commercial interest.

'Startling new research', reported *The Times* – though we are not startled, for we see this sort of thing every day...

> ...people are increasingly losing their faith in the church and the Bible and turning instead to mysticism, astrology, reiki, feng shui, crystals, t'ai chi classes on the NHS and other forms of spirituality to improve their physical and mental well-being.[6]

One regular advertisement for a particular chain of 'holistic therapy centres' claims that, among the many desirable results of the cluster of therapies on offer, one treatment 'increases capability for clearer thinking'. Could there be a clearer example of self-refuting propaganda?

This 'research' is supported by a number of authoritative quotations:

> A one-hour service on Sunday isn't enough to address your self-esteem issues...

> Christianity now is very verbose. You don't get a chance to be your silent self...

> Many gain increased self-awareness and feel better about themselves through attendance at places like the spiritual meditation centre in Dent, Cumbria – formerly the United Reform Church – where Chris from the centre practises yoga on the nearby hills...

How refreshing it would be instead to visit that Dales country chapel and come across the URF minister reading Luther's Bible!

> We are seeing a shift away from the church and towards the social empowerment of individuals in modern times. It is part of a general flight from deference...

The people who go in for this rubbish – they are not empowered, but rather enslaved.

> Self-observation methods increase awareness of your mind–body connection and promote enhanced self-image.

That could be rewritten as: 'Try narcissism: it helps you become obsessed with yourself and promotes your personal smugness.'

The suppressed premise supporting the ideals of the new caring, therapeutic community is that there is no such thing as truth. Whereas once one might have been received into the Catholic

Church because one believed that its teachings were true, no such epistemological or fideistic strictures attend the new world of caring self-esteem, where the only justification for any 'spiritual' activity is how good it makes you feel.

A presupposition of traditional religion was that we all fall short in some way or another, and that we stand in need of spiritual repair: in the old language this realisation was cast in terms of sin and forgiveness. But a client of the new caring therapies would be outraged to be told that he was deficient in virtue or the moral aspect. Why, it would damage his self-esteem to be told he is a sinner! The new Gospel of self-realisation is that, inasmuch as we fail to achieve the perfection of life and mood latent in us all, we do so only because we are falling short in our application of the correct technique, which, for an appropriate fee, the purveyor of the new spirituality will happily supply: it may be 'a misalignment of Yin and Yang', an unaccountable neglect of a new massage and exercise programme, or ignorance of the correct feng shui procedures when setting up your new home. So the caring therapies not only de-intellectualise traditional faith, but they de-moralise it as well. There is no truth and falsity, and there is no right or wrong. When it comes to the new caring virtues, what *is* true and good is simply anything that makes you feel good – anything at all. In the absence of any other philosophical, theological or ethical criteria, what else could it be?

Perhaps it could be something 'scientific'? Robert Matthews, science editor of the *Sunday Telegraph*, wrote an article commending religion for its therapeutic benefits, while disclaiming any convictions as to its truth:

> A host of troubled celebs have turned to religion and put their lives back on track. A comprehensive review covering more than 600 studies of links between religion and mental health concluded that overall the mainstream religions make a net positive contribution to individual human happiness.

It turns out that Dr Matthews is not talking about what most religious people would recognise as religion, but about something akin to:

> ...mindfulness, which involves developing moment-to-moment awareness of one's own mental and physical states.[7]

As an example of a technique to achieve perfect self-absorption and chronic hypochondria this could hardly be bettered. But it has nothing to do with religion as traditionally understood. It is what passes for religious response in the caring therapeutic community. Eventually, Dr Matthews does get round to discussing something recognisably religious – prayer:

> Among Christians, the act of prayer does appear to bring genuine benefits – not necessarily for those being prayed for, as those who are doing the praying.

But prayer in that spirit and for those reasons is not religious devotion at all. It is part of the medicalised, touchy-feely modern culture that makes the individual's personal wishes and desires the sole criterion for action. By contrast, according to traditional religious teaching, prayer is not something that the worshipper perceives as an activity with a good track record of bringing him benefit, but as a duty offered to God. The personalised utilitarianism of affect is bound to be at odds with the self-sacrificing obligations of religious devotion. But it would be difficult to think of any concepts more inimical to the spirit of 'caring' than those of sacrifice and devotion – unless 'sacrifice' is what you make when you pay all that money for your dog's luxury foodstuffs and grooming appointments, and 'devotion' is what he returns to you in the form of 'unconditional love'.

And if there is a new scientific version of virtue, can art be far behind? C. H. Sisson, writing about T. S. Eliot, said that great poetry usually emerges out of a deep sense of anxiety, but under the new scheme of virtues the products of musical, literary and artistic creativity themselves become a part of the therapeutic narcissism of the culture of caring:

> The television presenter Daisy Goodwin is the leader of a new literary trend: poetry as self-help.

All these theological and ethical comparisons have practical results for the conduct of life in the public realm. The old virtues were meant to act as working parables and paradigms: through them, goodness created more goodness as beneficent habits were set in place. So, for example, how one behaved in public was important. There were manners: 'please' and 'thank you', men opening doors for ladies and walking on the outside of the pavement, raising their hats, people conducting themselves with restraint and decorum. That world of public decency – the word used by all classes of society to describe it was 'respectable' – has now been overturned and replaced by a voracious self-indulgence. The so-called 'yob culture' has been created and encouraged by the care-for-yourself therapeutic culture of self-esteem and self-expression. Here is one example – a report in *The Times* – which comes so close to parody that satire becomes impossible:

> To help regenerate Old Street, Islington Council will put in place benches customised for the drinking community, complete with ashtrays and a privacy-guarding low wall. The benches will lean inward to encourage a free-flowing conversation between the Special Brew aficionados. The architects behind this scheme say, 'We want them to feel good in a place that is right for them.'[8]

CONCLUSION

Contemporary notions of caring are sentimental and destructive of genuine care and concern. This is partly because they make impossible demands: no one can possibly care about the multifarious examples of suffering which we are asked to care about. So any attempt to do so is bound to be unrealistic and highly inflationary of the meaning of 'caring'.

And the idea of professional care is far removed from the old commitment to service. To illustrate this, we need look no further than the changed nature of the institutions that provide care. Doctoring, nursing and teaching were formerly regarded as vocations. Nowadays these are unionised professional services, governed according to bureaucratic structures, whose moral ground comprises the modern values of universal rights, equal opportunities, monitoring and testing, and political correctness.

The modern virtue of caring is intrinsically corrupted because it is a vast industry with the requirement that all industries share – to make a profit. It must, therefore, offer its palliatives in a style, and with a content, that is agreeable to the consumer. Hair shirts are bound to prove less acceptable than techniques for enhancing self-esteem and the feel-good factor.

The old virtue of love or charity had as its goal something, or someone, that was not itself. That is to say, it was religious. The new virtue of caring is self-referential and narcissistic, and thus a devaluation of the original meaning and purpose of the commandment to love God and your neighbour as yourself.

1   *Children in Care: Now and Then*, BBC One, 15 February 2001.

2   Penelope Wilcock, *Spiritual Care of the Dying and Bereaved People*
(London: SPCK, 1996), p. 2.

3   Elisabeth Kubler-Ross, 'Introduction' in *On Death and Dying*
(New York: Simon and Schuster, 1997), p. 5.

4   Julie Burchill in *The Times*, 27 November 2004.

5   *The Times*, 28 August 2004.

6   *The Times*, Body & Soul Supplement, 15 January 2005.

7   *Sunday Telegraph*, 23 January 2005.

8   *The Times*, 20 January 2005.

CHAPTER 10

HELP-SEEKING AND THE THERAPEUTIC VIRTUES

FRANK FUREDI

VIRTUES TREATED AS A MEDICAL PROBLEM

Human action can be interpreted as an act of sinning or of virtue through a wider web of moral meaning. Once that web of meaning is lost, society finds it difficult to criticise behaviour as either sinful or virtuous.

A secular society always feels uncomfortable with the moral imagination that makes sense of human behaviour through the categories of sin and virtue. Nevertheless, until recently, secular rationalism shared with religion the belief that individuals were responsible for wrongdoing, as well as for exemplary virtuous acts. These days, however, it is not simply that we feel estranged from a moral universe; we find it difficult to imagine that individuals are capable of genuine virtuous behaviour.

Classically, religion sought to make sense of the subjective inner experience of the individual through a vocabulary shared with others in the community. In this way it helped make sense of life, and helped temper the impact of harsh reality. In recent decades, society has been continuously confronted with a quest for meaning. Without a socially accepted moral compass to help people negotiate the problems they face, ambiguity and confusion surround the question of how to make sense of existence. The weakening of shared values fragments this quest for meaning. This fragmentation of the search for meaning privatises it and lends it an individualised character. Therapeutics promises to provide answers to the individual's quest for the meaning of life. That is why the confusions that surround important life events can create a demand for psychological answers.

In a pioneering study of the rise of therapeutic culture, Philip Rieff observed that 'each culture is its own order of therapy'.[1] What distinguishes circumstances today from past therapeutic regimes is that the system of therapy is not confined to a distinct and functionally specific role; it has merged with wider cultural institutions and has an impact on all institutions of society.[2] The therapeutic ethos has a significant impact on education, the system of justice, provision of welfare services, political life, and medicine. It appears to have colonised all the professions and institutions of society. The invasion by the therapeutic ethos of other professions and forms of authority is particularly striking in relation to its former competitor – religious institutions. Religion has not only declined in influence, but it has also been forced to internalise important elements of therapeutic culture. One former Archbishop of Canterbury claims that therapy is replacing Christianity in western countries. According to Archbishop Carey, 'Christ the saviour' has become 'Christ the counsellor'.[3] Priests are increasingly encouraged to adopt counselling skills. Gradually, the theologian has assumed the role of a therapist. Organisations that have sought to harness therapeutic expertise in the work of the Church have inevitably assumed a secular orientation. For example, the Westminster Pastoral Foundation, which was established by a Methodist minister in the early 1970s in order to combine the insights offered by counselling, psychotherapy and Christianity, has weakened its religious connection. Its director, Dr Tim Woolmer, states that, nevertheless, they are still interested in 'wider religious questions such as: why are we here and what's it all about'.[4] This subordination of religious doctrine to concern with people's existential quest reflects a wider shift in orientation towards preoccupation with the self. A study of 'seeker churches' in the US argues that their ability to attract new recruits is based on their ability to tap into the therapeutic understandings of Americans.[5] In the US, the therapeutic approach has been self-consciously adopted by different faith communities and organisations; the American Association of Pastoral Counsellors, for example, promotes itself as a Mental Health Service.

One of the most curious features of contemporary therapy culture – with its acclamation of 'emotional intelligence', 'emotional literacy', 'emotional openness', 'getting in touch with yourself' or 'expressing yourself' – is its suspicion of the human capacity to do good. It feels more at ease with people who *feel* good. Feelings associated with classical virtues are often targets of suspicion and medicalisation.

In the Middle Ages, practising the seven contrary virtues – humility, kindness, abstinence, chastity, patience, liberality, diligence – was believed to protect one against the temptation of the seven deadly sins. Today, people who practise some of these virtues are just as liable to be offered counselling as those who are tempted by the sins. Kindness? Too much kindness may lead to 'compassion fatigue'. Diligence is sometimes dismissed as the act of someone suffering from a 'perfectionist complex'. Humble people lack self-esteem, and chastity is just another sexual dysfunction. Virtue is not so much its own reward, as a condition requiring therapeutic intervention.

These days, literally any manifestation of the classical virtues of love, friendship and loyalty can be medicalised as a form of addictive behaviour. Kindness and altruistic behaviour towards friends and the elderly are sometimes diagnosed as the addiction of 'compulsive helping'. It appears that compulsive helpers disregard their own needs and focus far too much on helping another person. According to this definition, individuals who make great sacrifices to care for elderly parents or relatives, or who devote their energy to helping others, may well suffer from compulsive helping.

Responsibility and loyalty are still upheld as public virtues, but in practice these ideals are compromised by the exhortation to put the self before the other. Consequently, the ideal of responsibility to another, and the sentiment of sociability and loyalty, can now be characterised as symptoms of relationship addiction. The very idea that a relationship of dependency can be a root cause of emotional addiction represents a deeply pessimistic statement about the informal world of private life. Even love has lost its association with virtuous behaviour. Increasingly, love is treated as a form of compulsive behaviour. Take the following press release issued recently:

> Psychologists say that 'lovesickness' is a genuine disease that needs more awareness and diagnosis. Those little actions that are normally seen as symptoms of the first flush of love – buying presents, waiting by the phone for a call or making a bit of an effort before a date – may actually be signs of deep-rooted problems to come.

> Many people who suffer from lovesickness 'cannot cope with the intensity of love', and have been 'destabilized by falling in love, or suffer on account of their love being unrequited', according to Dr Frank Tallis, a clinical psychologist from London. Symptoms can include mania, such as an elevated mood and inflated self-esteem, or depression, revealing itself as tearfulness and insomnia. In most serious case [sic],

lovesickness could result in suicide, Tallis warned. Tallis called for greater awareness of lovesickness in a report published in *The Psychologist* magazine, the official publication of the British Psychological Society.[6]

The message is clear: people cannot be trusted to understand their self-interest when confronted with powerful feelings. The therapeutic culture demands that, in such circumstances, people seek help.

THE VIRTUE OF HELP-SEEKING

Today's open and relatively uninhibited display of emotion in Anglo-American societies is frequently applauded by the cultural elites. The ability to display spontaneous and natural feelings is frequently cited with approval.

We are exhorted to 'get in touch with our emotions' on the grounds that it will help us to know ourselves. However, the act of self-discovery requires that strong feeling should be managed by competent professionals. Acknowledging emotions is a prelude to managing them. This process of 'cultural cooling' invites individuals to moderate their feelings in line with today's emotional script. The voyage of self-discovery, with its promise of open and authentic experience, sits uncomfortably alongside the exigencies of therapeutic management. Nor is the management of emotion a project that can be left to the individual. Individuals get in touch with their emotions not simply through their own efforts, but by accessing therapeutic support. Despite the orientation of therapeutic culture towards the self, the management of emotions is seen as far too important to be left to the efforts of normal human beings. That is why the appeal to 'attend to your emotional needs' often masks a call for therapeutic intervention, and in practice indicates that you should be prepared to seek therapeutic support. In fact, therapeutic professionals frequently use terms like 'exploring your emotion' as a euphemism for seeking help. One British university counselling service describes its role in the following terms: 'counselling is about exploring our feelings and learning to accept their reality'.[7] Increasingly, emotional well-being is associated with the willingness to seek help.

Many professionals warn vociferously against people trying to deal with their conditions themselves. Some therapists dismiss individual attempts to overcome addiction and other problems as futile expressions of a 'perfectionist complex'. 'Admit that you're sick and you're welcome to the recovering person's fold; dispute it and you're

"in denial"', is how Kaminer describes the attitude of many therapists.[8] Avoiding professional treatment serves as proof of the gravity
of the problem facing the victim. Therapeutic professionals describe
denial as avoidance of the pain of acknowledging a problem and of
taking action to seek help.[9] Help-seeking has become the principal
therapeutic virtue, because it acknowledges the authority of the only
agent of recovery – the therapist. Recovery has become a caricature
of salvation. Once in recovery, the patient is saved.

Forms of behaviour that run counter to help-seeking are often
castigated as symptoms of emotional illiteracy. Despite its celebration of the self, therapeutic culture is hostile to behaviour patterns
that manifest the virtue of self-reliance and self-control. One expression of this hostility is the stigmatisation of stereotypical masculine
behaviour. It is frequently claimed that the masculine aspiration for
self-control represents a ludicrous attempt to deny genuine emotion.
'We have learned to go it alone and to do without the help of others',
complains a New-Man academic. He also objects to an ethos by
which men 'learn in diverse ways to minimize hurt and pain and to
take pride in this as a sign of our strength', since it 'makes it very
difficult for us to accept our vulnerability, as an integral part of our
male identity'. The apparent inability of masculinity to acquiesce to
weakness is presented as a fatal flaw in the male psyche.[10] Self-
control and the aspiration for individual autonomy are invariably
represented as psychologically destructive impulses. The therapeutic
profession continually decries the tendency of young boys to aspire
to autonomy. According to two British psychologists – Dan Kindlon
and Michael Thompson – 'stereotypical ideas about masculine
toughness deny a boy his emotions and rob him of the chance to
develop the full range of emotional resources'.[11]

The aspiration for control is often interpreted as especially
damaging to the emotional well-being of men. One ethnographic
study of skydivers concludes that men tend to develop a distorted
sense of their ability to control 'fateful circumstances'. Critics of
what cultural feminist (female and male) academics call 'hegemonic
masculinity' go a step further and claim that risk-taking men who
value control are not only deluding themselves, but are, in reality,
also losing control over their lives by not attending to their emotional needs. They contend that the failure to disclose vulnerability
ensures that men become incapable of handling emotional problems
maturely.[12] Invariably, the aspiration for control is portrayed in
pathological terms as a delusion with damaging consequences. This

pathologisation of masculinity has become a *fait accompli* in the field of health promotion. One study condemns 'high masculinity' for its refusal to ask for help, and claims that it is a 'significant predictor of poor health practices'.[13] Health professionals continually insist that men are incapable of expressing emotion and find it difficult to talk about anything other than sport and beer. From this perspective, men are forever portrayed as suicidal, self-destructive and psychologically out of control.

Criticism of the 'male desire for control' represents an attitude towards emotional life in general. That is why ultimately this debate is not really about men. Women who display such 'masculine' characteristics as self-control, rationality and strong ambition have also come under intense suspicion.

Men who act like women are clearly preferred to women who act like men. According to the emotionally correct hierarchy of virtuous behaviour, feminine women come out on top. Feminine men beat masculine women for second place. And, of course, masculine, 'macho' men come last. This hierarchy informs the attitude of many health professionals. According to the study mentioned above, masculinity signals poor health practices. In contrast, 'feminine characteristics' are linked with 'health promoting behaviour'. The emphasis here is not on gender but on behaviour. The study argues that 'highly feminine men' exhibit the greatest concern about their health, and that, irrespective of sex, those with a feminine orientation are more likely to 'maintain good health habits'. From the perspective of therapeutic culture, the preoccupation with personal health and the willingness to seek help represent the foundation for emotional maturity.

A CRUSADE TO FORCE PEOPLE TO SEEK HELP

Individuals who are not inclined to adopt help-seeking behaviour face considerable pressure to fall into line with the prevailing cultural expectations. After the tragic bombing in Oklahoma in 1995, the 'grief industry' invaded the city. Within a short space of time, this tragic event was 'translated into an official or authoritative language of suffering by "trauma" experts'. And although some family members of the victims 'resented the overwhelming presence of the grief industry', the psychological interpretation of the experience came to define the event.[14] The relentless pressure to experience a tragic event according to a pre-given emotional script ensures that the public internalises help-seeking behaviour.

The promotion of help-seeking behaviour was systematically promoted in the British countryside during the BSE crisis in the late nineties. This campaign reached its climax during the outbreak of the epidemic of foot-and-mouth disease in 2001. As a result, the hardy, self-sufficient British farmer of lore was gradually transformed into a figure overwhelmed by the trauma of grief. It all began back in the 1990s, when mental health campaigners began to publicise the claim that farmers could not handle the pressure they faced without professional support. It was frequently argued that farmers were twice as likely to kill themselves as men of the same age in other occupations. The focus on suicide in the farming community swiftly gained nation-wide publicity. Commentators in the media were quick to point out that British farmers were particularly prone to suicide because of their reserved, stoic and self-sufficient outlook. Unlike their urban cousins, farmers found it 'difficult' to ask for help and lacked the 'emotional skills' to handle difficult circumstances. The mental health charity Rural Minds explained that 'farmers don't like asking for help' since by the nature of their work, they are a 'pretty solitary bunch'. The issue of rural suicide continued to be publicised, and in October 2000 a government-backed scheme to stop farmers killing themselves was launched. The Rural Stress Information Network (RSIN), promoted as the 'listening ear for stressed farmers', was set up in partnership with the Ministry of Agriculture, Fisheries and Food. By the time the recent epidemic of foot-and-mouth disease broke out, the counselling industry was well prepared to deal with the therapeutic needs of the countryside. Within weeks of the outbreak of this disease, mental health experts were predicting a rise in suicide and an outbreak of post-traumatic stress disorder in rural Britain.

Mental health campaigners perceived the farming community as a challenge to be conquered, and regarded the outbreak of foot-and-mouth as an opportunity to re-educate the emotionally illiterate farmer. Campaigners took a barely concealed delight in highlighting the psychological problems of farmers. 'We are talking about basically self-sufficient people who have to rely on their own resources for much of their life and work', noted Sue Barker of Mind, before adding that sometimes 'their own resources are not enough'.

CULTURE CLASH – THE STOIC FARMER VERSUS THE MENTAL HEALTH ACTIVIST

As the recent experience of rural Britain demonstrates, the virtue of help-seeking is zealously promoted by the therapeutic lobby. It regards the ideals of self-help, stoicism and self-sufficiency not as cultural norms, but as values that have to be stigmatised. The ideals of rural Britain ran counter to the therapeutic virtue of help-seeking, and for that reason those ideals had to be undermined and destroyed. That is why the professional mental health response to the crisis in rural Britain took the form of a cultural crusade that sought to weaken farmers' resistance to the therapeutic world view.

Mental health campaigners and advocacy groups frequently took the view that farmers did not know what was in their best interests. Rural culture, with its apparent emphasis on individual resilience and self-help, was dismissed as outdated, if not downright ridiculous. The ideal of resilience, which maintained some influence in rural Britain, was tackled as an obstacle that had to be overcome. The self-conscious hostility of rural stress campaigners to the ethos of self-help indicates that promotion of therapeutic values also assumed the form of a culture clash with what were perceived as outdated rural values.

From the standpoint of the therapeutic world view, rural communities were presented as inadequate and unreliable networks for farmers to air their problems. Their intervention sought to bypass communities, to forge a relationship between individual farmers and service providers. The former director of the Rural Stress Information Network, Rev. Nick Read, exhorted farmers to seek help from his organisation: 'We would urge anyone in rural occupations suffering from stress or depression to get in touch with the Samaritans or phone our helpline for advice.'[15] The cultivation of the ethos of help-seeking attempted to legitimate the construction of a relationship of dependency between the farmer and the professional.

It is worth noting that church activists were in the forefront of constructing the problem of rural stress. For example, most of the early campaigners involved with the Farm Crisis Network were also involved with the Church. It appears that at least some church activists embraced counselling in order to find a role for themselves and their institution. In effect, they were substituting the therapeutic virtue of help-seeking for the traditional Christian virtues.

The ethos of help-seeking and dependency on professional agencies was advanced through a campaign targeted at the traditional, culturally independent attitudes of farmers. A spokeswoman for the Samaritans in Northern Ireland outlined the problem in a way that questioned the posture of resilience. 'Farmers are very proud and don't like sharing their feelings', she observed. '[T]hey tend to keep things to themselves.'[16] Dr John Wynn-Jones, director of the Institute of Rural Health, further elaborated this perspective:

> Significantly, the institute chides farmers themselves. They can be too self-reliant and too ready to say they are 'coping'.
> They may know a great deal about falling livestock prices, but they are not accustomed to discussing their emotional needs.
> In some cases, they may even, mistakenly, believe the available services are simply not appropriate for them.[17]

The notion that farmers lacked the capacity to know what was in their best interests and possessed mistaken beliefs about mental health services served as an argument for giving others, including professional outsiders, the authority to monitor the state of mind of rural people. Thus, the *Scotsman* even counselled farmers' loved ones to inspect them for symptoms of stress: 'friends and families are urged to be on the lookout for telltale signs such as broodiness, increased alcohol consumption and irritability, and to offer support'.[18] It appears that this approach had some resonance. Annemarie Wells, the co-ordinator of RSIN recounted that 'many of the reports we get of potential problems are from third parties, such as friends and neighbours or even the Ministry of Agriculture'.[19] Farmers faced considerable pressure to experience their plight according to a pre-given emotional script that valorised help-seeking behaviour.

Advocates of the virtue of help-seeking tend to express their cause as something of a crusade against outdated cultural attitudes. In line with wider cultural norms, forms of behaviour that run counter to help-seeking are often castigated as symptoms of emotional illiteracy. One expression of this hostility is the stigmatisation of self-control and privacy.

As far back as March 1994, at a conference on rural stress, the farmer was depicted as not only prone to emotional difficulties, but also as suffering from an inability to communicate problems. It was widely noted 'by those trying to open up communication' that 'families in trouble are extremely reluctant to talk about their problems' since 'many farming people feel that it is humiliating to discuss difficulties of any kind with strangers'.[20] Rhian Thomas of the Samaritans observed that the 'farming community is notoriously insular and farmers don't want to ask for help'.[21] One reason why advocates regarded the poor communication skills of farmers as a problem was that it prevented them from gaining access to their internal life. 'All farmers I know are very stalwart', commented Bob Davies, a country doctor, who went on to note that they keep problems to themselves: 'That can be damaging, because it means those of us with the tools can't get in and effect repairs.'[22] Davies and other professionals regarded the attachment of farmers to their private world as directly contradicting prevailing cultural norms that affirm the public display of emotion. The need to convince the rural community of the advantages of openness to the therapeutic management of their emotions informed the publicity campaign of rural stress activists.

The traditional ideal of the robust, independent and resilient farmer, once considered a positive virtue by the prevailing culture, was increasingly presented as a chronic flaw. Such former virtues were now depicted as a false façade, assumed by emotionally primitive people, and the indirect cause of the problem of rural stress. According to vicar Alex Welby from Devon, 'the people whom you thought strong and robust prove the worst affected'.[23]

From the perspective of mental health activists, the farming community was perceived to be a problem because of its reluctance to seek help and professional support. It was an obstacle they sought to overcome by altering the attitudes and behaviour of the country folk. This outlook was clearly expressed during the foot-and-mouth crisis by Dr John Wynn-Jones again, who claimed that 'farmers find it difficult to seek help because of the presence of a culture of self-reliance and exaggerated expectations of coping facilities'. Wynn-Jones argued that farmers are 'unused to expressing emotional needs or have no language of emotional expression'. From this perspective, the emotionally illiterate farming community was perceived as its own worst enemy. 'We need to start working on those kids at an early stage when they are at school', argued Wynn-Jones, adding 'we need to make sure that another generation does not grow up like that'.[24]

Wynn-Jones' objective of ensuring that rural children do not adopt the behaviour and attitudes of their parents is testimony to the arrogance that pervades the outlook of rural stress campaigners. They have benefited from the wider affirmation of their outlook provided by contemporary culture, and their version of events has helped shape public discourse on the subject. More importantly, the fact that this emotional script was adopted by the entire constituency of rural claims makers has ensured that it has also become

197

influential in the farming community. By the end of the foot-and-mouth crisis the virtue of therapeutic help-seeking was well on its way to becoming institutionalised in rural Britain.

Campaigners adopted something of a missionary zeal in using every opportunity to highlight the emotional plight of farmers. In February 2001, the Rural Stress Information Network reported a ten-fold increase in the number of calls made to its help-line. According to Caroline Davis, director of this organisation, many farmers were 'breaking down in tears on the telephone'. 'Part of what motivates them to call is the publicity about high suicide rates', gloated Davis. Unable to resist the temptation of conquering the countryside, other campaigns also jumped on the bandwagon. A few months later, the Depression Alliance announced that it was offering counselling and support to farmers facing pressure due to the foot-and-mouth crisis. By April 2001, the image of the grieving farmer had come to dominate media representations of the crisis in the countryside. The virtue of therapeutic help-seeking had become a fact of life in rural Britain.

PROFESSIONALISING VIRTUOUS BEHAVIOUR

The act of acknowledging one's feelings, and the implicit openness to seeking help, are culturally represented as acts of virtue. By contrast, the reluctance to acknowledge the problem of the emotions, and refusal to seek help, are regarded as something that is responsible both for individual distress and for many of the problems facing society. Help-seeking has acquired positive moral connotations akin to the act of acknowledging guilt in more traditional cultural settings. Within the criminal justice system, offenders who accept help and undertake some form of therapy are frequently rewarded for their positive behaviour. Increasingly, the true act of contrition is not the admission of guilt, but a willingness to submit oneself to the authority of the therapist. Kathleen Lowney's study of American TV talk shows indicates how the virtue of help-seeking is refracted in popular culture. She notes that 'guests are chided until they agree to enter therapy or go to a 12-step program or some other support group'.[25]

Openness to the therapeutic management of one's emotions encourages the public display of feeling. The recent growth in the phenomenon of public emotionalism has been widely commented upon. It is often misinterpreted as being a celebration of the display of intense raw emotion. In fact, the public display of emotion has become a ritual of collective help-seeking that creates a supportive environment for its management. Through the display of emotionalism, therapeutic culture transmits clear signals about the conduct of everyday life.

The virtue of help-seeking is associated with the belief that people lack the inner resources necessary to help themselves. From the standpoint of the therapeutic imagination, the defining feature of humanity is its vulnerability. That is why responsible behaviour is always oriented towards being open to seeking help. Seeking help has the status of a quasi-religious obligation for the vulnerable self. Today's unprecedented cultural sensitivity to people's vulnerability to emotional injury is underwritten by a distinct outlook about the workings of human subjectivity and personhood. Prevailing attitudes about the state of people's emotions can be understood through the concept of ethnopsychology. 'Every culture contains a set of ideas and beliefs about the nature of human beings, what motivates them to act, the way they perceive the world, how their minds work, and the emotions that are natural to them', writes John Hewitt in his description of the concept of ethnopsychology.[26] Ideas about emotion, individual behaviour and vulnerability are underpinned by the particular account that a culture offers about personhood and the human potential. As Derek Summerfield asserts, these accounts embody such questions as 'how much or what kind of adversity a person can face and still be "normal"; what is a reasonable risk; when fatalism is appropriate and when a sense of grievance is; what is acceptable behaviour at a time of crisis, including how distress should be expressed, how help should be sought, and whether restitution should be made'.[27]

People's perception of their ability to cope with the problems of life is shaped by the particular account that their culture offers about the nature of the human potential. Individuals make sense of their experiences by reflecting on their specific circumstances, and in taking account of the expectations transmitted through prevailing cultural norms. The consciousness of their self is the negotiation of individual experience and cultural norms. People have no inner desire to perceive themselves as vulnerable. However, powerful cultural signals provide the public with a ready-made therapeutic explanation for their troubles. And once the diagnosis of existential vulnerability is systematically offered as an interpretative guide for making sense of distress, people are far more likely to perceive themselves to be in need of help.

For the vulnerable self, distress is not something to be lived, but a condition that requires treatment. The rendering of inner pain into a mental disorder alters the relationship between the individual and the experience of misfortune. According to this version of person-hood, the individual lacks the power to deal with the trials of life. The state of vulnerability has become the defining feature of person-hood, entitling the individual to demand help and support from professional experts. According to Lasch, the 'dominant conception of personality sees the self as a helpless victim of external circumstances'.[28]

Paradoxically, the tendency to inflate the problem of emotional vulnerability, and to minimise the ability of the person to cope with distressful episodes, runs counter to the therapeutic idealisation of the self-determining individual. However, in reality the rhetoric of therapeutic self-determination never granted individuals the right to determine their lives. Self-discovery through a professional interme-diary is justified by the assumption that individuals are helpless to confront problems on their own. According to the therapeutic version of personhood, people are not so much the authors, but the victims of their circumstance.

The therapeutic virtue of help-seeking represents the negation of any form of genuine feeling or behaviour that can lead to a virtu-ous act. The problem with the professional management of people's feelings is not that it is always misguided, but that it short-circuits the process through which people can learn how to deal with prob-lems through their own experience. Intuition and insight gained from personal experience are continually compromised by profes-sional expertise. This has the unintentional consequence of estrang-ing people from their own feelings and instincts, since such reactions require the affirmation of the expert. Worse still, this professionali-sation of people's lives sends out the signal that we do not expect human beings to possess any distinct virtues.

1　Philip Rieff, *The Triumph of the Therapeutic: Uses of Faith After Freud* (London: Chatto and Windus, 1966), p. 15.
2　For a discussion of the impact of the therapeutic sensibility on contemporary society, see Frank Furedi, *Therapy Culture; Cultivating Vulnerability in an Uncertain Age* (London: Routledge, 2004).
3　'Therapy is new religion says Carey', *Daily Telegraph*, 1 August 2000.

4   See *Guardian*, 6 January 1996.

5   Ken Sargeant, *Seeker Churches: Promoting Religion in a Nontraditional Way* (New Brunswick, NJ: Rutgers University Press, 2000), p. 45.

6   PA News, 7 February 2005.

7   See 'Profile: University Counselling Service', University of Dundee Press Office, 2000:
www.dundee.ac.uk/pressoffice/contact/2000/decjan/counselling.htm

8   Wendy Kaminer, *I'm Dysfunctional, You're Dysfunctional: the Recovery Movement and Other Self-Help Fashions* (Reading, MA: Addison-Wesley, 1993), p. 36.

9   David Overton 'Why counselling is not sought in deteriorating relationships: the effect of denial', *British Journal of Guidance and Counselling*, 1994, Vol. 22, No. 3.

10 Vic Seidler 'Men, sex and relationships' and 'Postscript: men, therapy and politics' in Vic Seidler (ed.), *Men, Sex and Relationships* (London: Routledge, 1992), pp. 1, 2, 245.

11 D. Kindlon and M. Thompson, 'Fighting inner turmoil', *The Times*, 15 June 1999.

12 See S. Lyng, 'Edgework: a social psychology of risk taking', *American Journal of Sociology*, 95 (4), 1990, p. 872; and Elizabeth Stanko and Kay Hobdell, 'Assault on men: masculinity and male victimisation', *British Journal of Criminology*, 33 (3), 1993.

13 M. Kaplan and G. Marks, 'Appraisal of health risks: the roles of masculinity, femininity and sex', *Sociology of Health and Illness*, 17 (2), 1995, p. 207.

14 See Edward Linenthal, *The Unfinished Bombing; Oklahoma City in American Memory* (New York: Oxford University Press, 2001), pp. 89–96.

15 'Farmers in crisis get a helpline', *Leicester Mercury*, 20 October 1998.

16 'Farmers "are at the end of their tether"', *Belfast News Letter*, 4 March 1997.

17 M. Simmons, 'Mental health: idyll threats', *Guardian*, 3 February 1999.

18 V. Robertson, 'Help network fights on in the season of despair', *Scotsman*, 3 January 1998.

19 V. Robertson, 'Counsellors brace for busy festive period', *Scotsman*, 24 December 1998.

20 Duff Hart-Davis, 'Country matters: everyday story of stressed-out folk', *Independent*, 26 March 1994.

21 Vanora Bennett, 'Surrounded by death', *The Times*, 24 March 2001.

22 Cited in Chris Rundle, 'Stress factor builds as farmers sense despair', *Western Daily Press*, 24 March 2001.

23 'Everything normal here has stopped. It is as quiet as the grave', *Western Morning News*, 9 March 2001.

24 Speech delivered at the Conference of the Rural Stress Information Network, 2002.

25 Kathleen Lowney, *Baring Our Souls; TV Talk Shows and the Religion of Recovery* (New York: Aldine de Gruyter, 1999), p. 18.

26 See John Hewitt, *The Myth of Self-Esteem; Finding Happiness and Solving Problems in America* (New York: St Martin's Press, 1998).

27 Derek Summerfield, 'The invention of post-traumatic disorder and the social usefulness of a psychiatric category', *British Medical Journal*, No. 322, 13 January 2001.

28 Christopher Lasch, *The Culture of Narcissism: American Life in an Age of Diminishing Expectations* (New York: Warner Books, 1984), p. 59.

CHAPTER 11

THE BUSINESS VIRTUES:
TRANSPARENCY AND ACCOUNTABILITY

ELAINE STERNBERG

Contrary to the assertions of the 'new morality', transparency and accountability are not prime business virtues. At best, transparency and accountability are means of detecting and assessing the genuine virtues that business both presupposes and promotes. At worst, transparency and accountability have been advanced as means of undermining the genuine business virtues, by campaigners who actively seek to subvert both the activity of business and accountability itself.

When business is properly understood, the virtues proper to it include most of the 'old' moral and intellectual virtues. Business is therefore an auspicious arena for displaying *megalopsychia*, the greatness of soul that is the crown of the Aristotelian virtues. The entrepreneur who embodies those virtues is a plausible model of the modern moral hero.

DEMANDS FOR TRANSPARENCY AND ACCOUNTABILITY ARE WIDESPREAD

It is undeniable that transparency and accountability have come to be lauded as virtues for business[1]...and many other sorts of organisation. Transparency and accountability are now being demanded in everything from financial markets, to educational standards, to exercises of 'social responsibility' by all and sundry.

It is indeed an official UK government objective to encourage transparency and accountability.[2] Initiating the Company Law Review, Mrs Margaret Beckett (then the President of the Board of Trade) stated:

> I would like companies to think more deeply about how they can be transparent and accountable to *all* those with an interest in their business.[3]

Implementing that intention, the government now requires all

UK public companies annually to produce and publish an Operating and Financial Review; its stated objective is to improve transparency and accountability,[4] as though these were ends in themselves. Transparency and accountability have also been recommended in the government-endorsed *Report on the Corporate Governance of Life Mutuals*,[5] and will 'be at the heart' of the government-financed (Trades) Union Modernisation Fund.[6] Improving accountability and transparency in the Financial Services Authority's own enforcement processes and in the fund management market are amongst the priorities indicated in the FSA's 2004/05 *Business Plan*.

Nor is the focus on transparency and accountability restricted to Britain. They are at the core of the more than 3,000 pages of International Financial Reporting Standards (IFRS) that came into effect on 1 January 2005 in more than 90 countries.[7] Transparency is the subject of a European Union Directive.[8] The US Sarbanes–Oxley Act, passed in response to a series of misunderstood company failures, is aimed at improving corporate governance standards, largely through increasing transparency and accountability in financial reporting. The chairman of the Australian Competition and Consumer Commission considers that 'transparency and accountability are fundamental to any workable regime'.[9] And according to a former president of the World Bank, transparency and accountability are central both to good corporate governance and to healthy democracy.[10]

But what exactly are transparency and accountability, and in what way are they virtues?

Following Aristotle, 'virtue' will be used here to designate a characteristic excellence, that which enables its possessor to perform its definitive function well.[11] The virtue of a knife is its sharp cutting edge; the virtue of a sponge is its absorbency. Similarly, the virtues of an organisation or an activity consist of the qualities that enable it to achieve its definitive objective well. On the assumption that the purpose of a university is to extend and transmit knowledge, the virtues of a university would include, for example, intelligent, expert faculty and a well-stocked library.

THE MEANING OF TRANSPARENCY

'Transparency' denotes the ability of a medium to transmit light rays without diffusion, so that objects can be seen clearly through it. When applied to systems or processes, 'transparency' refers to the extent to which their elements are either directly visible, or are available for inspection and scrutiny. Understood in this way, it is clear that transparency is a virtue...of those things that have 'being seen through' as part of their definitive function or objective. Accordingly, transparency is a virtue of window glass and of optical lenses. It may also be a virtue of some storage containers and wrappings, and those systems of justice in which it is essential that justice not only be done, but be seen to be done.

For the majority of objects, organisations and activities, however, those that do not have 'being seen through' as part of their functions or definitive objectives, transparency is not itself a virtue. Neither does transparency provide any assurance that their objectives are good. Individuals can be transparent liars, and organisations can be transparently wicked or corrupt: consider Murder, Incorporated.

Nor does transparency necessarily aid in the performance of an organisation's functions. Sometimes it contributes to their achievement, as it did for Roy Brooks, the estate agent who famously eschewed use of the standard industry code. A typical Brooks' real estate ad read:

> FILTHY OLD HOUSE – FASHIONABLE CHELSEA.
> Preserved as of architectural interest – God knows why...
> The horrible patch of weed, refuse-infected earth behind
> wld [sic] make a lovely garden.[12]

His honest advertisements not only sold houses but, more than 30 years after Brooks' death,[13] are now selling books.[14]

But transparency can equally have the reverse effect. Consider Gerald Ratner's candid admissions. He publicly joked[15] that the sherry decanters sold by his eponymous company were 'total crap', and that the earrings were cheaper and probably shorter-lived than a Marks and Spencer prawn sandwich. Such disclosure certainly increased transparency. But it was roundly condemned by the media as an insult to Ratner's customers.[16] Ratner's candour cost the company an estimated £500 million, and led to the collapse of what was previously the world's largest jewellery business.[17] So transparency can be seriously counterproductive. And in some contexts, notably diplomacy and other sensitive negotiations, it usually is.

At best, transparency is a quality that facilitates the detection and assessment of virtue...or its opposite. Historically, demands for transparency have prominently been associated with attempts to combat bribery. The organisation Transparency International has famously existed since 1993 to eliminate corruption, and particularly

bribery, by highlighting its occurrence and its damaging consequences. Transparency may, accordingly, sometimes aid in the
promotion of virtue. But it is rarely a virtue itself.

THE MEANING OF ACCOUNTABILITY

Accountability is also seldom an organisational virtue. Accountability simply means that individuals and institutions are answerable
for what they do: they must account to others for their conduct and
for their use of resources. Accountability typically involves three
elements: one person or set of persons – usually called the 'agent' or
'agents' – is accountable to another person or set of persons –
normally the 'principal(s)' – for the performance of some act or acts,
the 'outcome'.[18] The purpose of accountability is to help ensure that
the stipulated outcomes are brought about...whatever those outcomes may be.

Like transparency, accountability is compatible with both good
and bad organisations and activities. The agents of an organisation
with wicked objectives can be fully accountable to their wicked principals and wicked principles: the Mafia is notorious for holding its
members to their vows. Conversely, to the extent that the outcomes
sought either are or involve the exercise of virtues, accountability
may encourage those virtues. If, for example, a witness is held
accountable for 'telling the truth, the whole truth, and nothing but
the truth', honesty may be encouraged, and perjury deterred. The
extent to which accountability will actually promote achievement of
the desired virtues, however, will vary. It will depend on how carefully the objectives have been framed, on what mechanisms exist for
holding people to account for achieving them, and on what penalties
may apply for unsatisfactory performance. In every case, however,
accountability is at best a promoter of virtue; it is not a virtue itself.

For accountability itself to be a virtue, 'being held to account'
would have to be essential for the function in question, or for
achievement of the objective being sought. It is unclear, however,
what such functions or objectives might be.

One possible candidate might be the role of a personal assistant, or a servant. But as consideration of Jeeves[19] should remind us,
the best servants do not simply follow orders; they anticipate their
employers' wishes. Even if, counterfactually, the functions of a personal servant did essentially involve 'doing the employer's bidding',
the corresponding virtues would be something like obedience or
'biddability',[20] plus the skills enabling the assistant actually to

perform the tasks assigned. Even with respect to a servant, account-ability would at best be only a means of assessing and encouraging the associated virtues.

The same would seem true of representative institutions. Whether it is more appropriate for legislators to represent their con-stituents' interests, or 'virtually' to represent the common good of all the nation's citizens, the corresponding virtues are those qualities that enable the legislator to be representative in the required ways: attentiveness, intelligence, imagination, persuasiveness, shrewdness, etc. Once again, accountability is something that enables one to identify and encourage those virtues; it is not itself a virtue.

But what about the relationship of agency itself? Isn't it a locus in which accountability is essential? Though agency is the most plausible candidate, even here what is most important is achieve-ment of the stipulated outcomes. The central virtues will therefore be those necessary for bringing them about, whatever they may be. Accountability is at best an adjunct, which comes into play mostly when deviation from the stipulated ends is likely. Accordingly, accountability becomes most important when the powers that are delegated are likely to be abused; accountability is essential, for example, to prevent governments from using their coercive powers tyrannically. Accountability can help to ensure that the right ends are pursued, and in the right ways; it acts as an antidote to teleopathy.[21] Accountability does, therefore, have an important role to play. But it is not the one commonly ascribed to it.

Though neither accountability nor transparency is ordinarily a virtue, they are often related. When the outcomes for which agents are accountable include transparency, transparency can be promoted by accountability. Conversely, by making evidence of both compli-ance and transgression more visible, transparency can make it easier to hold agents to account. Accountability is easier to achieve when organisational processes are transparent. Accountability and trans-parency can be mutually reinforcing.

BUSINESS ACCOUNTABILITY IS LIMITED

Nevertheless, accountability is not necessary for the proper conduct of business. Indeed, external accountability is not a feature of many excellent businesses. To achieve its objective, business must be functionally responsive to everything in its trading environment that can affect its ability to maximise owner value: businesses must take into account the wishes of their customers and the activities of their competitors, interest rates, traffic conditions and the weather. But though businesses must take all those factors into account, business is not accountable to them. 'Being accountable' is not just a matter of physical functionality; it presupposes that the principal has some legitimate authority over the agent. Typically this authority arises because the powers exercised by the agent have been delegated to the agent by the principal, and have been delegated conditionally, for the specific purpose of achieving the outcome designated by the principal.

Business accountability typically arises in two main ways. First, a business is automatically accountable to its owners, because it belongs to them: it is their property. This is clearest in the case of businesses that are corporate in form, where there is a separation between ownership and control. In corporations, the corporate directors are accountable to the corporate owners – the shareholders in aggregate – for achieving the definitive corporate objective;[22] in a business corporation, that objective is maximising long-term owner value by selling goods or services.

Second, a business is accountable to those to whom it has specifically rendered itself accountable, by entering into particular, typically contractual, kinds of relationships. The contracts need not be written; the business might, for example, have bound itself by creating expectations that it now should honour.

Some businesses are not subject to either of these sorts of accountability. Consider a debt-free sole proprietor who sells services for cash. Since the manager is also the owner, there is no separate person to whom he is accountable. And the business is simple enough not to involve any of the other relationships that often give rise to accountability: it lacks, for example, investors and trade creditors. Such a business might, however, still be both financially successful and fully ethical. While accountability is often a useful attribute, it is far from being a necessary feature even of the best businesses.

REASONS FOR THE CONTEMPORARY IMPORTANCE OF TRANSPARENCY AND ACCOUNTABILITY

If transparency and accountability are not virtues, but merely contingently useful adjuncts, why are they deemed to be so important?

One reason is simply the size of many modern institutions. When organisations – be they governments, businesses or universities – grow large, powers usually need to be delegated. When they are, accountability becomes important to ensure that the delegated powers are exercised correctly, and in service of the correct ends. Similarly, transparency becomes more necessary when organisational procedures and processes need to be scrutinised by those who are not themselves directly involved in their operation. The problems of size are often exacerbated by corporate form; accountability is central to good corporate governance because of the separation of ownership and control.

A more dubious reason for the prominence of transparency and accountability is moral relativism. It is often doubted – or worse still, denied – that the substantive virtues of the 'old morality' have objective standing, or a rational basis. When such doubts prevail, however unjustifiably, procedural virtues may seem easier to justify. Precisely because they are compatible with all sorts of activities, virtuous and otherwise, transparency and accountability may seem more acceptable as standards; they suggest a tolerant acceptance of alternative value systems. Transparency might indeed be considered to be the organisational counterpart of sincerity; it shares sincerity's questionable moral worth.

The most troubling reason for the prominence of transparency and accountability, however, is their promotion by campaigners who seek to subvert whatever real value those qualities might have. By falsely extending the range of those concepts, and perverting their meanings, such attempts can also seriously undermine substantive objectives.

CONTEMPORARY PERVERSIONS OF PRINCIPAL: MULTIPLE ACCOUNTABILITY AND STAKEHOLDING

Increasingly, wider accountability is advocated precisely by those who are seeking to avoid its burdens, notably politicians and organisational managers. Lest this sound fanciful, consider again Mrs Beckett's pious wish:

> I would like companies to think more deeply about how they can be transparent and accountable to *all* those with an interest in their business.[23]

And consider as well who might be deemed to have an interest in their business. Given the interconnections made possible by modern technology, everyone and anything might affect, or be affected by, the operations of an organisation, and might thus be considered one of its 'stakeholders'.[24] But if companies were indeed accountable to all their stakeholders, as Mrs Beckett would have it, to whom would they actually be accountable? The answer is simple: to nobody. It is notoriously difficult to serve even two masters properly, far less an infinite number.[25]

Nevertheless, multiple accountability is at the core of the increasingly accepted but wholly pernicious stakeholder doctrine.[26] Sometimes called 'stakeholder theory', this is the doctrine that organisations, including corporations and particularly businesses, should be run not to serve the interests of their owners, but to benefit all their stakeholders. It is an essential tenet of stakeholder theory that organisations are accountable to all of their stakeholders, and that the proper objective of management is to balance stakeholders' competing interests.

Stakeholder theorists explicitly deny the essential duty that agents owe to principals. Consider the words of R. Edward Freeman, one of the creators and most prominent advocates of the stakeholder doctrine. According to Freeman,

> 'The Agency Principle'...says that any agent must serve the interests of *all* stakeholders.[27]

The stakeholder doctrine makes agency unworkable, by denying that agents have any particular duty to their principals.

Though widely advocated as a means of improving business conduct and business performance, the stakeholder doctrine is not a sensible model of, or even compatible with, either business or most other substantive objectives. And that is because the definitive stakeholder aim – balanced benefits for all stakeholders – precludes all objectives that favour particular groups. Business understood as the activity of maximising long-term owner value is automatically ruled out. So are the quite different aims of maximising value-added for customers and improving benefits for employees. Since all organisations with substantive ends aim at something other than 'balanced stakeholder benefits', they are all ruled out by stakeholder theory. According to stakeholder theory, there is only one legitimate organisational objective: balanced stakeholder benefits.

Supporters of stakeholder theory may now object: what they advocate is not dispensing with substantive objectives, but pursuing them while serving the interests of all the stakeholders. Unfortunately, their insistence on multiple accountability makes substantive objectives difficult to sustain.

Consider an organisation that purports to be a business, but attempts to operate in accordance with stakeholder theory. It differs from an ordinary business in several significant ways. First, whereas an ordinary business[28] is accountable to its owners,[29] a stakeholder business is supposed to be accountable to all of its stakeholders. This presumably means that the managers, employees and other agents of the stakeholder business are accountable to all of the business's stakeholders instead of just to the owners. But the managers, employees and other agents are themselves stakeholders of the business. The stakeholder doctrine would therefore seem to render them accountable *inter alia* to themselves, without offering any explanation of how such multiple self-accountability is meant to work.

Even more significantly, however, what is the outcome for which the business's agents are accountable to all of its stakeholders? By hypothesis, the objective of the stakeholder business will not be the ordinary business objective of maximising long-term owner value. At best it will be the business objective subject to the interests of all the stakeholders. In holding the organisation accountable, however, there is no reason to assume that all the stakeholders will give the business objective the same weight. Indeed, no stakeholder group has any particular incentive to advance the business objective instead of its own interests. Each group may therefore give its own interests priority over both the business objective and the interests of the other stakeholders: there is nothing in stakeholder theory to stop customers from seeking a free handout, or employees a sinecure.

In such circumstances, it becomes clear why the role of management is reduced to 'balancing stakeholders' benefits', without any reference to achieving substantive objectives. It is because, being accountable to all of the stakeholders, and preoccupied with the need to balance the stakeholders' conflicting interests, managements typically have neither occasion nor incentive to pursue substantive objectives. Despite what advocates of the stakeholder doctrine may claim, the multiple accountability that is an essential feature of the stakeholder doctrine systematically perverts substantive objectives.

Multiple accountability also renders unworkable the central notion of balancing stakeholder benefits. First, stakeholder theory offers no guidance as to how the appropriate individuals or groups should be selected. Since stakeholders are all those who can affect, or who are affected by, the organisation, the number of people whose benefits need to be taken into account is infinite. For a balance to be struck, however, their numbers must somehow be limited. But stakeholder theory offers no criterion for doing so.

Second, even if the stakeholder groups could be identified and restricted to a manageable number, stakeholder theory does not explain what should count as a benefit for the purposes of balancing benefits. Despite the simplifying and often presumptuous assumptions that are commonly made, even members of the same notional stakeholder constituency may have significantly different views as to what is beneficial.

Third, and most fundamentally, even if the relevant benefits could somehow be identified, stakeholder theory provides no guidance as to how the balance is to be struck. Given the divergent interests of the different stakeholder groups, that which benefits one group will often harm another; even within a notional stakeholder group, benefits may well conflict with each other. The stakeholder doctrine does not indicate which of these benefits is to be preferred, or how conflicting interests are to be balanced; it offers no clue as to how to rank or reconcile the normally conflicting interests of stakeholders.

It may now be protested that such problems are, nonetheless, routinely resolved in practice. And indeed they are. But the way that they are resolved is by using the substantive goal of the organisation as a decision criterion. If the purpose of a corporation is to maximise long-term owner value, that purpose enables managers to identify which groups need to be considered, and which of their perceived benefits are relevant and legitimate; it indicates how benefits are to be ranked, and how conflicts are to be resolved. The only way that stakeholder theory can be made workable is to employ the very substantive objectives that it explicitly rejects.[30] Like a parasite, stakeholder theory is viable only so long as its targets withstand its attacks.

Why then is so radical and pernicious a doctrine so popular? One reason is that its implications are seldom recognised. Another is that stakeholder theory appears to offer a free lunch. It particularly appeals to those with much to gain from undermining accountability, including not just business managers, but politicians who would like to have the power, prestige and perquisites of office without the concomitant responsibilities. In addition, stakeholder doctrine appeals to the promoters of worthy 'causes', who believe they would be the beneficiaries if business profits were diverted from business owners.

But they are mistaken: nothing comes from nothing. The

wealth – and power – that they want from business will not be available if the essential business objective of maximising long-term owner value is forsaken, and investors are not allowed to reap the benefits of their investments. In the spurious expectation of achieving vaguely 'nicer' business behaviour, stakeholder doctrine would sacrifice not only property rights[31] and accountability, but also the wealth-creating capabilities of business strictly understood. Such are the wide-ranging and deleterious effects of extending the range of principals to which organisations, and particularly businesses, are said to be accountable.

CONTEMPORARY PERVERSIONS OF OUTCOME

Noxious though stakeholding's effects are, it is not the only way in which demands for greater accountability are routinely used to undermine business. Serious damage also results from attempts to alter the outcomes for which business is said to be accountable, and from prescribing unsuitable methods for enforcing accountability.

A business is properly accountable to its owners for achieving the definitive business objective, and to its contractual counterparties for fulfilling its contracts. The methods appropriate for enforcing these different types of accountability are properly determined by the owners and contractors themselves, the better to reflect their varying interests, resources, risk/reward profiles, etc.

Increasingly, however, it is claimed that businesses should be accountable for all sorts of public policy objectives, which are supposed to take priority over, or indeed replace, the definitive business purpose. Businesses are being held responsible for housing the homeless and saving the whale, for ending discrimination and eliminating world poverty. But holding a business accountable for achieving extraneous ends does not make their attainment any more likely; it simply diverts resources from the business's proper purpose. Like many other political objectives, those imputed to business are frequently counterproductive, incompatible or inconsistent. Consider the requirements that UK universities simultaneously foster social inclusion and academic excellence, or that directors serving on company audit committees simultaneously be experienced, expert, independent, and diverse.

In addition to stipulating the wrong outcomes, public demands for accountability and transparency often prescribe specific – and radically inappropriate – methods for achieving those outcomes. Government guidelines are incapable of identifying the independence of character that is a genuine virtue of non-executive directors; they therefore substitute irrelevant criteria of age and length of service. Those surrogates often rule out truly independent candidates, while admitting precisely the cronies they are meant to exclude. Meanwhile, satisfying the regulatory criteria diverts energy and attention: resources employed in data collection, form filling, and other 'box ticking' and 'hygiene' matters are withdrawn from substantive concerns.

THE PROPER BUSINESS VIRTUES: 'DISTRIBUTIVE JUSTICE' AND 'ORDINARY DECENCY'

What business should be held accountable for, is simply achieving the definitive business objective ethically. Business is ethical when it maximises long-term owner value, subject to respecting those values that are presupposed by the activity of business.[32] Long-term views require confidence in a future, and confidence requires trust. Accordingly, the conditions of trust must be observed. Equally, owner value presupposes ownership and respect for property rights. In order not to be ultimately self-defeating, business must therefore be conducted with honesty, fairness, the absence of physical violence and coercion, and a presumption in favour of legality. Collectively, these constraints embody what may be called *ordinary decency*.

Furthermore, since business is more likely to achieve its definitive purpose when it encourages contributions to that purpose, and not to some other, classical distributive justice is also essential. What *distributive justice* requires is simply that within the business, contributions to the business objective be the basis for distributing business rewards: those who do most for the business deserve most from the business.

When business and business ethics are understood in this way, it can be seen that the real virtues of business are not transparency and accountability, but the skills necessary for maximising long-term owner value ethically. They include, for example, shrewd market understanding and efficient operations, and presuppose those substantive excellences that have always been necessary for productive interactions with reality.

Almost all of the 'old' virtues, moral and intellectual, are required for business. Start with the 'classical' virtues. Risk-taking is intrinsic to business; so is courage in insisting on getting things right. Fortitude and endurance are required in building a business, and in maintaining it over the long term. The 'Victorian' virtues of thrift and hard work are obviously useful in helping to maximise owner value; saving and investment are the keys to accumulating business capital. The 'administrative virtues' of honesty and fairness have already been identified as essential to ethical business; moreover, the business objective is most likely to be achieved if it is adhered to disinterestedly. Reliability, understood as honesty in action, is also intrinsic to business activity, to attracting and retaining the best stakeholders.

To the extent that the 'Christian' and 'conservative' virtues are genuinely virtues, even they are characteristic of business. Acknowledging errors, and allowing people opportunities even after they have failed, are both valuable in an activity that necessarily requires risk-taking...and hopes to learn from its mistakes. Furthermore, novelty is justified in business only to the extent that it genuinely maximises owner value...considered over the long term.

Finally, the 'prudential virtues' are essential. The need for judgement is inescapable; for business decisions properly to be directed at maximising long-term owner value, they must be guided by 'practical reason', the capacity for deliberating well.[33] The exercise of practical reason is essential for identifying, achieving, and integrating the many different activities that must be successfully pursued and co-ordinated for maximising long-term owner value.

THE ENTREPRENEUR AS MODERN MORAL HERO

Business may thus be the activity in modern life that offers the greatest scope for the moral and the intellectual virtues. As such, it is a promising arena for seeking a modern moral hero. Unlike politics and warfare, which the ancients considered the best realms for exercising virtue, business does not use coercive force to implement its decisions. It must appeal to reason to attract the willing support of all the customers and suppliers, employees and investors who are necessary to its survival. Furthermore, unlike politics or war, business is inherently creative: to maximise value, it must create value.

The most heroic figure in business is the entrepreneur. By discovering something new – a new product or a new service, or a new use for existing goods or services – and bringing it to market, the entrepreneur creates something valuable: a business. In creating a business, he produces benefits for all those who, directly and indirectly, are involved in the new item's production, distribution, financing and use. The entrepreneur produces wealth for himself and his investors, opportunities for employees and suppliers, and

215

improvements in the lives of his customers. He may even create opportunities for his competitors and successors, by creating an entire industry.

And the ethical entrepreneur achieves all this through creative action, rigorous reality testing and superior insight. Just as Aristotle's *megalopsychic*, the man of great soul, possessed all the Aristotelian virtues, and was their greatest expression,[34] so the entrepreneur is the embodiment of enterprise, and a plausible model of the modern moral hero. To paraphrase Winston Churchill, 'Never before in the course of human events has so much been owed by so many to so few.'

1   As of December 2004, Shell's website made no fewer than 258 mentions of transparency and 204 mentions of accountability.
2   It is noteworthy, however, that the UK government's concern to spread transparency and accountability does not extend to its own operations. The government's Panel for Regulatory Accountability, chaired by the Prime Minister, is conspicuously not open to public scrutiny: '"No outsider is told of its agenda, input from outside Whitehall is not welcomed, we have no idea what happens and there is no apparent action," today's report says...Ministers have consistently refused to disclose information on the panel's activities' (Jean Eaglesham, 'Industry concern at Whitehall practice', *Financial Times*, 16 August 2004, p. 4). Similarly, the UK Freedom of Information Act has been undermined both by a flurry of information destruction, and a weakening (by 23 exceptions and a ministerial override) of the provisions first promised.
    In contrast, transparency and accountability have reportedly increased in the US corporate sector. In a study by GovernanceMetrics International (a private corporate watchdog) of board accountability, transparency and shareholder rights in 2,588 companies from around the world, the 1,154 US companies received an average score of 7.23 out of 10, up from a 6.5 average in a similar study done in 2002. Reported in 'Corporate conscience, improved', *Christian Science Monitor*, 8 September 2004, p. 8.
3   In a 4 March 1998 speech at the Pensions Investment Research Consultants conference, 'After Hampel: the new governance agenda', p. 3; emphasis in original. Available online at www.pirc.co.uk/mbspeech.htm This objective remains in the White Paper *Company Law Reform* presented to Parliament by the Secretary of State for Trade and Industry on March 2005 (Cm 6456, p. 20).
4   Quoted in Glyn Barker, 'A chance to measure corporate health', *Financial Times*, 2 August 2004, p. 6.

5   Produced in December 2004 by Paul Myners; available online at www.hm-treasury.gov.uk/independent_reviews/myners_review/review_myners_index.cfm

6   Quoted from Hermes Database, 9 December 2004: 'Government consults on rules for union modernisation fund'; consultation paper available at www.dti.gov.uk/er/union_mod_fund.htm The Fund is the result of a new power created by the Employment Relations Act 2004 allowing the Secretary of State for Trade and Industry to make money available to help trade unions modernise their operations.

7   With the associated guidance notes issued by the International Accounting Standards Board; Peter Wyman, 'The new transparency', *The Times*, 5 September 2004, p. 10.

8   The Transparency Directive: Directive 2004/109/EC of the European Parliament and of the Council of 15 December 2004. Its purpose is to enhance transparency in EU capital markets by establishing rules on periodic financial reports and disclosure of major shareholdings for issuers whose securities are admitted to trading on a regulated market in the EU. The Directive must be incorporated into national law by all Member States no later than 20 January 2007.

9   M2 PressWIRE, 'ACCC moves to increase transparency, certainty and accountability in mergers decisions', 28 May 2004.

10 J. Wolfensohn, then President of the World Bank, reported in John Plender, 'Speak up for dialogue', *Financial Times*, 21 June 1999, p. 22. The World Bank also reportedly considers transparency and accountability essential to fairer and more effective management of natural resources: 'World Resources 2002–2004: Decisions for the Earth – balance, voice, and power', reported in M2 PressWIRE, 14 July 2003, 'WORLD BANK GROUP Landmark report urges governance reforms to arrest decline of world's environment.'

11 '...every virtue or excellence both brings into good condition the thing of which it is the excellence and makes the work of that thing be done well...' *Nicomachean Ethics*, Book II, Chapter 6, 1106a15–17. In Richard McKeon (ed.), *Introduction to Aristotle*, trans. W. D. Ross (New York: Modern Library, 1947), p. 338.

12 Karen Robinson, 'Estate agent with the comic touch', *Sunday Times*, 21 October 2001.

13 In 1971.

14 Roy Brooks, *Brothel in Pimlico* (London: John Murray, 2001).

15 At a 1991 address to the Institute of Directors.

16 This is itself indicative of a strange inversion of values: what was criticised was not the poor quality of the company's ornaments, but Ratner's honest description of them.

17 Stephanie Northen, 'Gerald Ratner's little gem', *The Times Educational Supplement*, 28 June 2002, p. 4.

18 Not all accountability involves strict agency: children are often accountable to their guardians, and dependants to those who support them, without agency necessarily being involved.

19 The perfect gentleman's gentleman, Jeeves was neither obedient nor more than ostensibly biddable; he interpreted his role as serving Bertie Wooster's best interests, not taking Wooster's orders.

20 Perhaps understood as the personal equivalent of 'manoeuvrability' in a motor car.

21 Teleopathy consists of getting the ends wrong, or of attempting to achieve the stipulated ends in ways that are counterproductive. For a fuller explanation of teleopathy and its consequences, see Elaine Sternberg, *Just Business: Business Ethics in Action* (2nd edition) (Oxford and New York: Oxford University Press, 2000), p. 4 and *passim*.

22 For an extended analysis of this conceptual notion of corporate governance, see Elaine Sternberg, *Corporate Governance: Accountability in the Marketplace* (2nd edition) (London: Institute of Economic Affairs, 2004).

23 See Note 3 above.

24 This definition was initially proposed by one of the most prominent propounders of the 'stakeholder' doctrine (R. Edward Freeman, *Strategic Planning: a Stakeholder Approach* (Boston: Pitman Publishing, 1984), p. 46). Among the stakeholders included in this definition are terrorists, generations yet unborn and nameless sea creatures. This definition is also the one adopted by, for example, both the Body Shop (Mark Suzman, 'The social audit', *Financial Times*, 24 January 1996, p. 20), and the European Union: 'Stakeholder: an individual, community or organisation that affects, or is affected by, the operations of a company' (EU Green Paper, *Promoting a European Framework for Corporate Social Responsibility* (European Commission Directorate-General for Employment and Social Affairs, Unit EMPL/D.1, July 2001, Concepts Annex, p. 28)).

25 Most of the criticisms would apply equally even if 'stakeholders' were restricted to the more plausible subset of shareowners, employees, suppliers, lenders, customers, and society.

26 For a comprehensive description and criticism of the stakeholder doctrine, see Sternberg, *Corporate Governance*, especially Chapter 6, pp. 126–54.

27 'A stakeholder theory of the modern corporation', in T. L. Beauchamp and N. E. Bowie, *Ethical Theory and Business* (6th edition) (Englewood-Cliffs, NJ: Prentice-Hall Inc., 2001), pp. 55–66; reprinted in Eugene Heath (ed.), *Morality and the Market: Ethics and Virtue in the Conduct of Business* (New York: McGraw Hill, 2002), p. 415; emphasis added.

28 Where the business is corporate in form, and thus legally distinct from its owners. In other organisational forms, where the business is legally identified with its owners, it is the business's agents, e.g. employees, managers, etc., who are accountable to the owners.
29 And other parties to which it has rendered itself accountable through (typically) contractual arrangements.
30 Or to justify some other principle of allocation.
31 The stakeholder doctrine also undermines private property, because it denies owners the right to determine how their property will be used. Insofar as assets are held or utilised by organisations, stakeholder theory stipulates that those assets should be used for the balanced benefit of all stakeholders. The owners of those assets are thereby prevented from devoting their property unequivocally to the ends of their choice.
32 For a full explanation, justification and illustration of this view of business ethics, see Sternberg, *Just Business*.
33 Aristotle, *Nicomachean Ethics*, Book VI, Chapter 5, 1140a25–b30 and Chapter 7, especially 1141b7–21.
34 *ibid.*, Book IV, Chapter 3, 1124a1–3.

CHAPTER 12

THE INTELLECTUAL VIRTUES: BEING CRITICAL

ROGER KIMBALL

The modern world is full of the old Christian virtues gone mad.
The virtues have gone mad because they have been isolated from
each other and are wandering alone. Thus some scientists care for
truth; and their truth is pitiless. Thus some humanitarians only care
for pity; and their pity...is often untruthful.[1]   G. K. Chesterton

We seem to have reached a point where if the word 'real' can be
used at all, then the only world which is 'real' for us, as in the world
in which all of us, including scientists, are born, work, love, hate
and die, is the primary phenomenal world as it is and always has
been presented to us through our senses, a world in which the sun
moves across the sky from east to west, the stars are hung like lamps
in the vault of heaven, the measure of magnitude is the human body
and objects are either in motion or at rest.[2]   W. H. Auden

'DIRECTIONLESS QUIBBLE'?

'We must never', Bismarck warned, 'look into the origins of laws or
sausages.'[3] Sage (and I like the pun) advice, I've always thought – but
how much at odds it is with the dominant current of modern
thought, which is to say Enlightenment thought. Immanuel Kant,
a great hero of the Enlightenment, summed up the alternative to
Bismarck's counsel when, in an essay called 'What is Enlightenment?',[4]
he offered '*Sapere aude*', 'Dare to know!', as a motto for the movement. Enlightened man, Kant thought, was the first real adult: the
first to realise his potential as an *autonomous* being – a being, as the
etymology of the word implies, who 'gives the law to himself'. As
Kant stressed, this was a moral as well as an intellectual achievement, since it involved courage as much as insight: courage to put
aside convention, tradition, and superstition (how the three tended
to coalesce for Enlightened thinkers!) in order to rely for guidance
on the dictates of reason alone.

Bismarck's observation cautions reticence about certain matters; it implies that about some things it is better not to inquire too closely. What Walter Bagehot said about the British monarchy – 'We must not let in daylight upon magic'[5] – has, from this point of view, a more general application. The legend 'Here be monsters' that one sees on certain antique maps applies also to certain precincts of the map of our moral universe. Enlightened man, by contrast, is, above all, a creature *who looks into things*: he wants to 'get to the bottom' of controversies, to dispel mysteries, to see what makes things 'tick', to understand the mechanics of everything from law to sausages, from love to society. Who has the better advice, Bismarck or Kant?

Of course, it is not a simple choice. For one thing, it might be argued that Kant's own attitude toward the imperative 'Dare to know!' was complex. In a famous passage towards the beginning of *The Critique of Pure Reason*, for example, Kant tells us that he was setting limits to reason in order to make room for faith.[6] Exactly what Kant meant by this... what to call it? this admission? this boast? this concession?... Well, whatever Kant meant by his invocation of faith, it has been an abiding matter of debate. Nevertheless, it is fair to say that Kant's 'critical philosophy' is itself a monument of Enlightenment thought, as much in its implied commendation of the 'critical attitude' as in the 'Copernican revolution' he sought to bring about in philosophy.

Today, we can hardly go to the toilet without being urged to cultivate 'critical thinking'. Which does not mean, I hasten to add, that we are a society of Kantians. Nevertheless, what we are dealing with here is an educational watchword, not to say a cliché, that has roots in some of the Enlightenment values that Kant espoused. It's a voracious, quick-growing hybrid. A search for the phrase 'critical thinking' using the Google search engine brings up 2,290,200 references in 0.08 seconds. The first match, God help us, is with something called 'The Critical Thinking Community', whose goal is 'to promote essential change in education and society through the cultivation of fair-minded critical thinking'.[7] (Why is it, I wonder, that the conjunction of the phrase 'critical thinking' with the word 'community' is so reliably productive of nausea?)

Everywhere you look, in fact, you will find the virtues of 'critical thinking' extolled: colleges and universities claim to be stuffed with the thing, and even high schools – even, *mirabile dictu*, primary schools – brag about instilling the principles of 'critical thinking' in their charges. There's 'critical thinking' for bankers, for accountants, for cooks, gardeners, haberdashers, and even advanced toddlers. Last summer, my wife and I took our 5-year-old son to an orientation meeting for parents considering sending their children to a local kindergarten. School officials enthusiastically told us about how they would bring the principles of critical thinking to Sally's colouring book and little Johnnie's sport. Absolutely everyone is enjoined to scrutinise his presuppositions, reject conventional thinking, and, above all, to be original and/or 'creative'. (Ponder, if your stomach is strong enough, a 'Creative Critical Thinking Community'.)

To some extent, we owe the infestation of 'critical thinking' to that great twentieth-century movement to empty minds while at the same time inflating the sense of self-importance, or, to give it its usual name, Progressive Education. It was John Dewey, thank you very much, who told us that 'education as such has no aims', warned about 'the vice of externally imposed ends', urged upon his readers the notion that 'an individual can only live in the present'. (The present, Dewey said, 'is what life is in leaving the past behind it', i.e., a *nunc stans* of perfect ignorance.)[8] So much for the Arnoldian ideal of a liberal arts education as involving the disinterested pursuit of the 'best that has been thought and said'.[9]

The first thing to notice about the vogue for 'critical thinking' is that it tends to foster not criticism but what one wit called 'criticismism': the 'ism' or ideology of being critical, which, like most *isms*, turns out to be a parody or betrayal of the very thing it claims to champion. In this sense, 'critical thinking' is an attitude guaranteed to instil querulous dissatisfaction, which is to say ingratitude, on the one hand, and frivolousness, on the other. Its principal effect, as the philosopher David Stove observed, has been 'to fortify millions of ignorant graduates and undergraduates in the belief, to which they are already only too firmly wedded by other causes, that the adversary posture is all, and that intellectual life consists in "directionless quibble"'.[10]

The phrase 'directionless quibble' is from Jacques Barzun's *The House of Intellect*, and a fine book it is, too, not least in its appreciation of the ways in which unanchored intellect can be 'a life-darkening institution'.[11] I suggest, however, that the phrase 'directionless quibble' is not entirely accurate, since the habit of quibble cultivated by 'critical thinking' does have a direction, namely against the status quo. The belief, as Stove puts it, 'that the adversary posture is all' is at the centre of 'critical thinking'.[12] Lionel

Trilling spoke in this context of 'the adversary culture' of the intellectuals.[13] Only today, I received word of a long article in *Teachers College Record*, a journal from Indiana University that describes itself as 'the voice of scholarship in education'. The featured article is a 30,000-word behemoth by a professor of 'inquiry and philosophy' called 'Ocularcentrism, Phonocentrism and the Counter Enlightenment Problematic: Clarifying Contested Terrain in our Schools of Education'. I am too charitable to subject you to a sample of its almost comically reader-proof prose,[14] but it is worth pausing to note that such work is *absolutely typical* in the academic establishment today. It really is 'the voice of scholarship', or what's become of scholarship.

PREJUDICE AGAINST PREJUDICE

How we got here makes for a long story. I'd like to dip into a few chapters of that story and then speculate briefly about what an alternative might look like.

It seems obvious that 'critical thinking' (I employ the quotation marks because the activity in question is neither critical nor, in any robust sense of the word, thinking) is a descendant or re-enactment of the Enlightenment imperative 'Dare to know!' In this sense, it is a precursor or adjunct of that 'hermeneutics of suspicion' that the French philosopher Paul Ricoeur invoked when discussing the intellectual and moral demolition carried out by thinkers like Darwin, Marx, Freud, and Nietzsche.[15] It would be hard to exaggerate the corrosive nature of these assaults. Often, indeed, what we encounter is less a hermeneutics of suspicion than a hermeneutics of contempt. The contempt expresses itself partly in a repudiation of the customary, the conventional, the habitual, partly in the cult of innovation and originality. Think, for example, of John Stuart Mill's famous plea on behalf of moral, social and intellectual 'experiments in living'.[16] Part of what makes that phrase so obnoxious is Mill's effort to dignify his project of moral revolution with the prestige of science – as if, for example, his creepy relationship with the married Harriet Taylor was somehow equivalent to Michael Faraday's experiments with electromagnetism. You see the same thing at work today, when young hedonists in search of oblivion explain that they are 'experimenting' with drugs.

It is worth pausing over Mill's brief on behalf of innovation. You've heard it a thousand times. But familiarity should not blind us to its fatuous malevolence. Throughout history, Mill argues, the authors of such innovations have been objects of ridicule, persecution, and oppression; they have been ignored, silenced, exiled, imprisoned, even killed. But (Mill continues) we owe every step of progress, intellectual as well as moral, to the daring of innovators. 'Without them', he writes, 'human life would become a stagnant pool. Not only is it they who introduce good things which did not before exist; it is they who keep the life in those which already exist.'[17] Ergo, innovators – 'developed human beings'[18] is one phrase Mill uses for such paragons – should not merely be tolerated, but should positively be encouraged as beacons of future improvement.

David Stove called this the 'They All Laughed at Christopher Columbus' argument. In a penetrating essay in his book *Cricket versus Republicanism*, Stove noted that 'the Columbus argument' (as he called it for short) 'has swept the world':

> With every day that has passed since Mill published it, it
> has been more influential than it was the day before. In the
> intellectual and moral dissolution of the West in the twentieth
> century, every step has depended on conservatives being
> disarmed, at some critical point, by the Columbus argument;
> by revolutionaries claiming that any resistance made to them
> is only another instance of that undeserved hostility which
> beneficial innovators have so regularly met with in the past.[19]

The amazing thing about the success of the Columbus argument is that it depends on premises that are so obviously faulty. Indeed, a moment's reflection reveals that the Columbus argument is undermined by a downright glaring weakness. Granted that every change for the better has depended on someone embarking on a new departure: well, so too has every change for the worse. And surely, Stove writes, there have been at least as many proposed innovations which 'were or would have been for the worse as ones which were or would have been for the better'.[20] Which means that we have at least as much reason to discourage innovators as to encourage them, especially when their innovations bear on things as immensely complex as the organisation of society. As Lord Falkland admonished, 'when it is not necessary to change, it is necessary not to change'.[21]

The triumph of Millian liberalism – one of the main 'active ingredients' in 'critical thinking' – shows that such objections have fallen on deaf ears. But why? Why have 'innovation', 'originality', etc. become mesmerising charms that neutralise criticism before it even gets started, when so much that is produced in the name of innovation is obviously a change for the worse? An inventory of the fearsome social, political and moral innovations made in this past century alone should have made every thinking person wary of unchaperoned innovation. One reason that innovation has survived with its reputation intact, Stove notes, is that Mill and his heirs have been careful to supply a 'one-sided diet of examples'.[22] You mention Columbus, but not Stalin; Copernicus, but not the Marquis de Sade; Socrates, but not Hegel. Mill never missed an opportunity to expatiate on the value of 'originality', 'eccentricity', and the like. 'The amount of eccentricity in a society', he wrote, 'has generally been proportional to the amount of genius, mental vigour, and moral courage it contained.'[23] But you never caught Mill dilating on the 'improvement on established practice' inaugurated by Robespierre and St Just, or the 'experiments in living' conducted by the Marquis de Sade.

Still, in order to understand its world-conquering success, one has to go beyond simple credulity and an abundance of one-sided examples. Flattery comes into it. Mill was exceptionally adroit at appealing to his readers' moral vanity. When he spoke (as he was always speaking) of 'persons of decided mental superiority',[24] he made it seem as though he might actually be speaking about *them*. Mill said that there was 'no reason that all human existence should be constructed on some one or some small number of patterns'. Quite right! Even if persons of genius are always likely to be 'a small minority', still we must 'preserve the soil in which they grow'. Consequently, people have a duty to shun custom and nurture their individual 'self-development' if they are not to jeopardise 'their fair share of happiness' and the 'mental, moral, and aesthetic stature of which their nature is capable'.

Mill's blandishments went even deeper. In *On Liberty*, Mill presented himself as a prophet of individual liberty. He has often been regarded as such, especially by liberal academics, who, of course, have been instrumental in propagating the gospel according to Mill. And 'gospel' is the *mot juste*. Like many radical reformers, Mill promised almost boundless freedom, but he arrived bearing an exacting new system of belief. In this sense, as Maurice Cowling argues, *On Liberty* has been 'one of the most influential of modern political tracts', chiefly because 'its purpose has been misunderstood'. Contrary to common opinion, Cowling wrote, Mill's book was:

not so much a plea for individual freedom, as a means of ensuring that Christianity would be superseded by that form of liberal, rationalising utilitarianism which went by the name of the Religion of Humanity. Mill's liberalism was a dogmatic, religious one, not the soothing night-comforter for which it is sometimes mistaken. Mill's object was not to free men, but to convert them, and convert them to a peculiarly exclusive, peculiarly insinuating moral doctrine. Mill wished to moralise all social activity...Mill, no less than Marx, Nietzsche, or Comte, claimed to replace Christianity by 'something better'. Atheists and agnostics, humanists and free-thinkers may properly give thanks to Mill.[25]

This tension in Mill's work – between Mill the libertarian and Mill the moralistic utilitarian – helps to account for the vertiginous quality that suffuses the liberalism for which *On Liberty* was a kind of founding scripture. Mill's announced enemy can be summed up in words like 'custom', 'prejudice', 'established morality'. All his work goes to undermine these qualities – not because the positions they articulate are necessarily in error, but simply because, being customary, accepted on trust, established by tradition, they have not been subjected to the acid-test of his version of the utilitarian calculus. The tradition that Mill opposed celebrated custom, prejudice and established morality precisely because they had prevailed, and given good service, through the vicissitudes of time and change; their longevity was an important token of their worthiness. Let us by all means acknowledge, as Edmund Burke acknowledged, that 'a state without the means of some change is without the means of its conservation'.[26] Still, Burke was right to extol prejudice as that which 'renders a man's virtue his habit...Through just prejudice, his duty becomes a part of his nature.'[27]

Mill overturned this traditional view. Indeed, he was instrumental in getting the public to associate 'prejudice' indelibly with 'bigotry'. He epitomised what the German philosopher Hans-Georg Gadamer called the Enlightenment's 'prejudice against prejudice'.[28] For Mill, established morality is suspect first of all *because* it is established. His liberalism is essentially corrosive of existing societal arrangements, institutions and morality. At bottom, Mill's philosophy is a kind of inversion of Alexander Pope's optimism: 'Whatever is, is suspect' might have been Mill's motto. He constantly castigated such things as the 'magical influence of custom' ('magical' being a negative epithet for Mill), the 'despotism of custom [that] is every-where the standing hindrance to human advancement', the 'tyranny of opinion' that makes it so difficult for 'the progressive principle' to flourish. According to Mill, the 'greater part of the world has, properly speaking, no history because the sway of custom has been complete'.

Such passages reveal the core of moral arrogance inhabiting Mill's liberalism. Liberty was always on Mill's lips; a new orthodoxy was ever in his heart. There is an important sense in which the libertarian streak in *On Liberty* is little more than a prophylactic against the coerciveness that its assumption of virtuous rationality presupposes.

Such 'paradoxes' (to put it politely) show themselves wherever the constructive part of Mill's doctrine is glimpsed through his cheerleading for freedom and eccentricity. Mill's doctrine of liberty begins with a promise of emancipation. The individual, in order to construct a 'life plan' worthy of his nature, must shed the carapace of inherited opinion. He must learn to become adept at 'critical thinking', to subject all his former beliefs to rational scrutiny. He must dare to be 'eccentric', 'novel', 'original'. At the same time, Mill notes, not without misgiving, that:

> As mankind improves, the number of doctrines which are no longer disputed or doubted will be constantly on the increase; the well-being of mankind may almost be measured by the number and gravity of the truths which have reached the point of being uncontested. The cessation, on one question after another, of serious controversy is one of the necessary incidents of the consolidation of opinion – a consolidation as salutary in the case of true opinions as it is dangerous and noxious when the opinions are erroneous.[29]

In other words, the partisan of Millian liberalism undertakes the destruction of inherited custom and belief in order to construct a bulwark of custom and belief that can be inherited. As Mill put it in his *Autobiography* (posthumously published in 1873):

> I looked forward, through the present age of loud disputes but generally weak convictions, to a future…[in which] convictions as to what is right and wrong, useful and pernicious, [will be] deeply engraven on the feelings by early education and general unanimity of sentiment, and so firmly grounded in reason and

in the true exigencies of life, that they shall not, like all former and present creeds, religious, ethical, and political, require to be periodically thrown off and replaced by others.[30]

So: a 'unanimity of sentiment' (a.k.a. custom) is all well and good so long as it is grounded in the 'true exigencies of life' – as defined, of course, by J. S. Mill.

MORAL DYNAMITE

Mill's utilitarianism provides one major model for 'critical thinking'. Another is found in the work of that modern Thrasymachus, Friedrich Nietzsche. In a celebrated epigram, Nietzsche wrote that 'we have art lest we perish from the truth'.[31] His disturbing thought was that art, with its fondness for illusion and make-believe, did not so much grace life as provide grateful distraction from life's horrors. But Nietzsche's real radicalism came in the way that he attempted to read life *against* truth.

Inverting the Platonic–Christian doctrine that linked truth with the good and the beautiful, Nietzsche declared truth to be 'ugly'[32] – a statement that, even now, has the capacity to bring one up short. Suspecting that 'the will to truth might be a concealed will to death', Nietzsche boldly demanded that 'the value of truth must for once be experimentally *called into question*'.[33] This ambition to put truth itself under the knife of human scrutiny is, as it were, the moral source of all those famous Nietzschean formulae about truth and knowledge – that 'there are no facts, only interpretations',[34] that 'to tell the truth' is simply 'to lie according to a fixed convention',[35] etc. As Nietzsche recognised, his effort to provide a genealogy of truth led directly 'back to the moral problem: *Why have morality at all* when life, nature, and history are "not moral"?'[36]

Nietzsche's influence on contemporary intellectual life can hardly be overstated. 'I am dynamite',[37] he declared, shortly before sinking into irretrievable madness. He was right. In one way or another, his example is an indispensable background to almost every destructive intellectual movement the last century witnessed: deconstruction, post-structuralism, just about anything followed by the word 'studies' (gender studies, science studies, post-colonial studies) – all trace a large part of their pedigree to Nietzsche's obsession with power, in particular his subjugation of truth to scenarios of power. Foucault's insistence that truth is always a coefficient of 'regimes of power',[38] for example, is simply Nietzsche done over in black leather.

And where would our deconstructionists and post-structuralists be without Nietzsche's endlessly quoted declaration that truth is 'a moveable host of metaphors, metonymies, and anthropomorphisms'?[39] The philosopher Richard Rorty summed up Nietzsche's importance when he enthusiastically observed that 'it was Nietzsche who first explicitly suggested that we drop the whole idea of "knowing the truth".'[40] Add a dollop of Marx for the appropriate degree of politicisation and presto: you have the formula for contemporary redactions of critical thinking.

Conceptually, such signature Nietzschean observations as 'everything praised as moral is identical in essence with everything immoral'[41] add little to the message that Thrasymachus was dispensing twenty-five hundred years ago. They are the predictable product of nominalism and the desire to say something shocking, a perennial combination among the intellectually impatient. Nietzsche's real radicalism arises from the grandiosity of his hubris. His militant 'God is dead' atheism had its corollary: the dream of absolute self-creation, of a new sort of human being strong enough to dispense with inherited morality and create, in Nietzsche's phrase, its 'own new tables of what is good'.[42] This ambition is at the root of Nietzsche's goal of effecting a 'transvaluation of all values'.[43] It is also what makes his philosophy such an efficient solvent of traditional moral thought.

Truth versus life: it was Nietzsche's startling conclusion that science was at bottom allied with nihilism because of its uncompromising commitment to truth. 'All science', he wrote, 'has at present the object of dissuading man from his former respect for himself.'[44] In order to salvage life from science 'the value of truth must for once be experimentally *called into question*'. It is one of the curious features of Nietzsche's mature thought that he wished to question the value of truth while upholding honesty as his one remaining virtue. Traditionally, as my epigraph from Chesterton suggests, the moral virtues have been all of a piece. For example, Aquinas observes that 'nearly all are agreed in saying' that the moral virtues are interconnected, that 'discernment belongs to prudence, rectitude to justice',[45] and so on. It is worth asking whether honesty, sundered from the family of virtues, remains a virtue – whether, in the end, it even remains honest. Untempered by other virtues, honesty functions not so much to reveal truth, as to expose it. Is that honest?

Nietzsche clung to honesty after abandoning the other virtues because it allowed him to fashion the most ruthless instrument of interrogation imaginable. Difficulty, not truth, became his criterion of value. Thus he embraced the horrifying idea of the Eternal Recurrence primarily because he considered it 'the hardest possible thought'[46] – whether it was also true didn't really matter.

Nietzsche *opposed* honesty to truth. He looked to art as a 'countermovement'[47] to nihilism, not because he thought that art could furnish us with the truth, but because it accustomed us to living openly with untruth. Ultimately, Nietzsche's ideal asks us to transform our life into a work of art. Accepting Schopenhauer's inversion of the traditional image of man, Nietzsche no longer finds human life dignified in itself: if man is essentially an expression of irrational will, then in himself he is morally worthless. This is the dour irony that attends Nietzsche's effort to burden man with the task of *creating* values rather than *acknowledging* them. And it is here, too, that Nietzsche's aestheticism and his rejection of morality intersect. For Nietzsche, man is not an end in himself, but only 'a bridge, a great promise'.[48] In order to redeem that promise, man must treat life with the same imperiousness and daring that the artist brings to his work. If, as Nietzsche argued, 'life itself is *essentially* appropriation, injury, overpowering what is alien and weaker; suppression, hardness…and at least, at its mildest, exploitation',[49] then it is hardly surprising that the perfect aesthete will also be the perfect tyrant.

Nietzsche never tired of pointing out that the demands of traditional morality fly in the face of life. One might say, yes, and that is precisely why morality is so valuable: it acknowledges that man's allegiance is not only to life but also to what ennobles life – that, indeed, life itself is not the highest court of appeal. But for Nietzsche the measure of nobility is the uninhibited pulse of life: hence his penchant for biological and physiological metaphors, his invocation of 'ascending' and 'descending' forms of art and life. He defines the good as that which enhances the feeling of life. If 'to see others suffer does one good, to make others suffer even more',[50] then violence and cruelty may have to be granted the patent of morality and enlisted in the aesthete's palette of diversions. In more or less concentrated form, Nietzsche's ideal is also modernity's ideal. It is an ideal that subordinates morality to power in order to transform life into an aesthetic spectacle. It promises freedom and exaltation. But, as Novalis points out, it is really the ultimate attainment of the barbarian.[51]

NIHILISM WITHOUT TEARS

The impulse of 'critical thinking' comes in a variety of flavours, from bitter to cloyingly sweet, and it can be made to serve a wide range of philosophical outlooks. That is part of what makes it so dangerous. One of the most beguiling and influential American practitioners is Richard Rorty. Once upon a time, Rorty was a serious analytical philosopher. Since the late 1970s, however, he has increasingly busied himself explaining why philosophy must jettison its concern with outmoded things like truth and human nature. According to him, philosophy should turn itself into a form of literature or – as he sometimes puts it – 'fantasizing'. He is set on 'blurring the literature–philosophy distinction and promoting the idea of a seamless, undifferentiated "general text"', in which, say, Aristotle's *Metaphysics*, a television programme, and a French novel might coalesce into a fit object of hermeneutical scrutiny. Thus it is that Rorty believes that 'the novel, the movie, and the TV program have, gradually but steadily, replaced the sermon and the treatise as the principal vehicles of moral change and progress'.[52]

As almost goes without saying, Rorty's attack on philosophy and his celebration of culture as an 'undifferentiated "general text"' have earned him many honours. Indeed, Richard Rorty is widely regarded today as he regards himself: as a sort of secular sage, dispensing exhortations on all manner of subjects, as readily on the op-ed page of major newspapers as between the covers of an academic book of philosophical essays.[53] The tone is always soothing, the rhetoric impish, the message nihilistic but cheerful. It has turned out to be an unbeatable recipe for success, patronising the reader with the thought that there is nothing that cannot be patronised.

Rorty does not call himself a utilitarian or a Nietzschean. That might be too off-putting. Instead, he calls himself a 'pragmatist' or, more recently, a 'liberal ironist'.[54] What Rorty wants, as he explained in his book *Philosophy and the Mirror of Nature*, is 'philosophy without epistemology',[55] that is, philosophy without truth. In brief, Rorty wants a philosophy (if we can still call it that) which 'aims at continuing the conversation rather than at discovering truth'.[56] He can manage to abide 'truths' with a small 't' and in the plural; truths that we don't take too seriously and wouldn't dream of foisting upon others; truths, in other words, that are true merely by linguistic convention; truths, that is to say, that are not true. What he cannot bear – and cannot bear to have us bear – is the idea of Truth that is somehow more than that.

Rorty generally tries to maintain a chummy, easygoing persona. This is consistent with his role as a 'liberal ironist', i.e. someone who thinks that 'cruelty is the worst thing we can do' (the liberal part) but who, believing that moral values are utterly contingent, also believes that what counts as 'cruelty' is a sociological or linguistic construct. (This is where the irony comes in: 'I do not think', Rorty writes, 'there are any plain moral facts out there…nor any neutral ground on which to stand and argue that either torture or kindness are [sic] preferable to the other.')[57]

Accordingly, one thing that is certain to earn Rorty's contempt is the spectacle of philosophers without sufficient contempt for the truth. 'You can still find philosophy professors', he tells us witheringly, 'who will solemnly tell you that they are seeking *the truth*, not just a story or a consensus but an honest-to-God, down-home, accurate representation of the way the world is.'[58] That's the problem with liberal ironists: they are ironical about everything except their own irony, and are serious about tolerating everything except seriousness.

As Rorty is quick to point out, the 'bedrock metaphilosophical issue' here is whether we have any non-linguistic access to reality. Does language 'go all the way down'?[59] Or does language point to a reality beyond itself, a reality that exercises a legitimate claim on our attention and provides a measure and limit for our descriptions of the world? In other words, is truth something that we invent? Or something that we discover?

The main current of western culture has overwhelmingly endorsed the latter view. But Rorty firmly endorses the idea that truth is merely a human invention. He wants us to drop 'the notion of truth as correspondence with reality altogether' and realise that there is 'no difference that makes a difference' between the statement 'it works because it's true' and 'it's true because it works'.[60] He tells us that '[s]entences like…"Truth is independent of the human mind" are simply platitudes used to inculcate…the common sense of the West.' Of course, Rorty is right that such sentences 'inculcate…the common sense of the West'. He is even right that they are 'platitudes'. The statement 'the sun rises in the east' is another such platitude.

Rorty looks forward to a culture – he calls it a 'liberal utopia' – in which the 'Nietzschean metaphors' of self-creation are finally 'literalized', i.e. made real. For philosophers, or people who used to be philosophers, this would mean a culture that 'took for granted that philosophical problems are as temporary as poetic problems, that there are no problems which bind the generations together in a single natural kind called "humanity"'.

Rorty recognises that most people are not yet liberal ironists. Many people still believe that there is such a thing as truth independent of their thoughts. Some even continue to entertain the idea that their identity is more than a distillate of biological and sociological accidents. Rorty knows this. Whether he also knows that his own position as a liberal ironist crucially depends on most people being *non*-ironists is another question. One suspects not. In any event, he is clearly impatient with what he refers to as 'a particular historically conditioned and possibly transient' view of the world, that is, the pre-ironical view, for which things like truth and morality still matter. Rorty, in short, is a connoisseur of contempt. He could hardly be more explicit about this. He tells us in the friendliest possible way that he wants us to 'get to the point where we no longer worship *anything*, where we treat *nothing* as a quasi divinity, where we treat *everything* – our language, our conscience, our community – as a product of time and chance'.[61] What Rorty wants is philosophy without philosophy. The 'liberal utopia' he envisions is a utopia in which philosophy, as traditionally conceived, has conveniently emasculated itself, abandoned the search for truth, and lives on as a repository of more or less bracing exercises in fantasy.

In his book *Overcoming Law*, the jurist and legal philosopher Richard Posner criticises Rorty for his 'deficient sense of fact' and 'his belief in the plasticity of human nature',[62] noting that both are 'typical of modern philosophy'. They are typical, anyway, of certain influential strains of modern philosophy. And it is in the union of these two things – a deficient sense of fact and a utopian belief in the unbounded plasticity of human nature – that the legacy of Nietzsche bears its most poisonous fruit.

The cognitive pessimism espoused by figures such as Rorty has moral as well as intellectual implications. When Rorty, expatiating on the delights of his liberal utopia, says that 'a postmetaphysical culture seems to me no more impossible than a postreligious one, and equally desirable',[63] he perhaps speaks truer than he purposed. For despite the tenacity of non-irony in many sections of society, there is much in our culture that shows the disastrous effects of Nietzsche's dream of a postmetaphysical, ironised society of putative self-creators. And, of course, to say that such a society would be as desirable as a postreligious society amounts to saying also that it would be just as *un*desirable.

Like his fellow liberal ironists, Rorty takes radical secularism as an unarguable good. For him, religion, like truth – like anything that transcends our contingent self-creations – belongs to the childhood of mankind. Ironists are beyond all that, and liberal ironists are beyond it with a smile and a little joke.

APPEARANCE VERSUS REALITY?

But, of course, whether our culture really is 'postreligious' remains very much an open question. That liberal ironists, such as Richard Rorty, make do without religion does not tell us very much about the matter. In an essay called 'The Self-Poisoning of the Open Society', the Polish philosopher Leszek Kolakowski observes that the idea that there are no fundamental disputes about moral and spiritual values is 'an intellectualist self-delusion, a half-conscious inclination by Western academics to treat the values they acquired from their liberal education as something natural, innate, corresponding to the normal disposition of human nature'.[64] Since liberal ironists like Richard Rorty do not believe that anything is natural or innate, Kolakowski's observation has to be slightly modified to fit him. But the general point remains, namely that 'the net result of education freed of authority, tradition, and dogma is moral nihilism'. Kolakowski readily admits that the belief in a unique core of personality 'is not a scientifically provable truth'. But he argues that, 'without this belief, the notion of personal dignity and of human rights is an arbitrary concoction, suspended in the void, indefensible, easy to be dismissed',[65] and hence prey to totalitarian doctrines and other intellectual and spiritual deformations.

The Promethean dreams of writers such as Nietzsche and Rorty depend critically on their denying the reality of anything that transcends the prerogatives of their efforts at self-creation. Traditionally, the recognition of such realities has been linked to a recognition of the sacred. It is a mistake typical of intellectuals to believe that this link can be severed with impunity. As Kolakowski notes elsewhere, 'Culture, when it loses its sacred sense, loses all sense.'

> With the disappearance of the sacred...arises one of the most dangerous illusions of our civilization – the illusion that there are no limits to the changes that human life can undergo, that society is 'in principle' an endlessly flexible thing, and that to deny this flexibility and this perfectibility is to deny man's total autonomy and thus to deny man himself.[66]

It is a curious irony that proponents of 'critical thinking' from Mill and Nietzsche to Richard Rorty are reluctant children of the Enlightenment. Remember Kant's motto for the Enlightenment: *Sapere aude*, 'Dare to know!' For the proponent of 'critical thinking', the liberal ironist, and other paragons of disillusionment, that motto has been revised to read 'Dare to believe that there is nothing to know.' The Enlightenment sought to emancipate man by liberating reason and battling against superstition. It has turned out, however, that when reason is liberated entirely from tradition – which means also when it is liberated entirely from any acknowledgment of what transcends it – reason grows rancorous and hubristic: it becomes, in short, something irrational.

Philosophy itself has been an important casualty of this development. It is no accident that so much modern philosophy has been committed to bringing us the gospel of the end of philosophy. Once it abandons its vocation as the love of wisdom, philosophy inevitably becomes the gravedigger of its highest ambitions, interring itself with tools originally forged to perpetuate its service to truth.

It is an axiom of 'critical thinking' that the extent of our disillusionment is a reliable index of our wisdom: the idea that somehow the less we believe the more enlightened we are. There is, however, a curious irony here. For there is an important sense in which philosophy *must* contribute to the reduction of human experience. At least, it must *begin* by contributing to it, and this for the same reason that philosophy cannot proceed without a large element of doubt. There is something essentially corrosive about the probing glance of philosophy: something essentially dis-illusioning. If our goal is a human understanding of the world, then the activity of philosophy must itself be part of what philosophy investigates and criticises.

Yet if philosophy begins by interrogating our everyday understanding of the world, all of its fancy conceptual footwork is for naught if it does not in the end lead us to affirm a fully human world. It is a delicate matter. In one sense, philosophy is the helpmeet of science. It aids in the task of putting our conceptual household in order: tidying up arguments, discarding unjustified claims. But in another sense, philosophy peeks over the shoulder of science to a world that science in principle cannot countenance. The problem is that we do not, cannot, inhabit the abstract world that science describes. Scientific rationality replaces the living texture of experience with a skeleton of 'causes', 'drives', 'impulses', and the like.

The enormous power over nature that science has brought man

235

is only part of its attraction. Psychologically just as important is the power it gives one to dispense with the *human* claims of experience. How liberating to know that kindness is just another form of egotism! That beauty is merely a matter of fatty tissues being arranged properly! That every inflection of our emotional life is nothing but the entirely predictable result of glandular activity! *Just another, merely, nothing but...*How liberating, how dismissive are these instruments of dispensation – but how *un*true, finally, to our experience.

In this sense, scientific rationality is a *temptation* as well as an accomplishment, because inherent in its view of the world is an invitation to forget one's humanity. By regarding all problems as *technical* problems, susceptible to human manipulation and control, 'critical thinking' fosters a species of Prometheanism – a form of 'rationalism' that, as the philosopher Michael Oakeshott observed, dreamed of 'thought free from any authority save the authority of "reason"' as well as thought committed to the 'evanescence of imperfection'.[67] It is worth noting that it is precisely this Promethean aspect of scientific rationalism that links it with evil. As the Austrian novelist Robert Musil observed, the feeling that 'nothing in life can be relied on unless it is firmly nailed down is a basic feeling embedded in the sobriety of science; and though we are too respectable to call it the Devil, a slight whiff of brimstone still clings to it'.[68]

The antidote to 'critical thinking' involves the application of a paradox and the recognition of a reality. The paradox (or apparent paradox) revolves around the fact that the way out of the impasse of 'critical thinking' is not the abandonment of criticism but its more intelligent deployment, which means its deployment in accordance with the moral and intellectual limits of 'the good for man'. The recognition revolves around the acknowledgment that the human world is not the abstract world distilled by the operation of reason, but a world of appearances, a world of tangible realities that have myriad historical tendrils and interconnections. Reaffirming that world challenges not only the cult of 'critical thinking' but also the scientism that glorifies technology and seeks to realise Descartes's dream of rendering man 'the master and possessor of nature'.[69] In this sense, to challenge 'critical thinking' is also to challenge the Kantian ideal of man as an autonomous being: it is, in short, to recognise that, in a deep sense, man does not 'give the law to himself' but must depend upon something that transcends him.

Reason allows us to distinguish between appearance and

reality; but *our* reality turns out to be rooted firmly in the realm of appearance. As the English philosopher Roger Scruton observed,

> The scientific attempt to explore the 'depth' of human things is accompanied by a singular danger. For it threatens to destroy our response to the surface. Yet it is on the surface that we live and act: it is there that we are created, as complex appearances sustained by the social interaction which we, as appearances, also create. It is in this thin top-soil that the seeds of human happiness are sown, and the reckless desire to scrape it away – a desire which has inspired all those 'sciences of man', from Marx and Freud to socio-biology – deprives us of our consolation.[70]

Consolation? Indeed, more: it threatens to deprive us of our humanity. In Plato's phrase, philosophy turns out in the end to be an effort to 'save the appearances'.

We all of us inhabit a world irretrievably shaped by science; we know that the sun does not *really* move from east to west, just as we know that the stars are not *really* hung like lamps from the sky. And yet... As the epigraph from Auden suggests, we recognise the legitimacy of that reality – our reality – every time we wake and find that the sun, once again, has risen. Enlightenment is a grand idea. But Bismarck was right about laws and sausages.

1   G. K. Chesterton, *Orthodoxy* (New York: Doubleday, 1990), p. 30.
2   W. H. Auden, *Secondary Worlds* (London: Faber & Faber, 1968), p. 126.
3   Well, Bismarck is said to have issued this warning about laws and sausages. This proverbial admonition – sometimes in the form 'If you like laws and sausages, you should never watch either one being made' – is widely attributed to the Iron Chancellor, but generally with the proviso 'unverified'.
4   Immanuel Kant, 'What is Enlightenment?' in *The Philosophy of Kant: Immanuel Kant's Moral and Political Writings*, ed. Carl J. Friedrich (New York: Modern Library, 1977), pp. 132–9.
5   Walter Bagehot, 'The English constitution' in *The Collected Works of Walter Bagehot*, ed. Norman St John-Stevas (London: The Economist, 1974), p. 243.
6   Immanuel Kant, *Critique of Pure Reason*, trans. Norman Kemp Smith (New York: St Martin's Press, 1965), p. 29.
7   http://www.criticalthinking.org/about/mission.shtml

8   John Dewey, *Democracy and Education* (New York: Free Press, 1944), pp. 107, 108, 75.

9   Matthew Arnold, 'The function of criticism at the present time' in *The Portable Matthew Arnold*, ed. Lionel Trilling (New York: The Viking Press, 1972), p. 248.

10   David Stove, *Scientific Irrationalism: Origins of a Postmodern Cult* (New Brunswick: Transaction, 2001), p. 185.

11   Jacques Barzun, *The House Of Intellect* (New York: Harper and Brothers, 1959), pp. 119, 251.

12   Stove, *Scientific Irrationalism*, p. 185.

13   Lionel Trilling, *The Moral Obligation To Be Intelligent: Selected Essays*, ed. Leon Wieseltier (New York: Farrar, Straus, Giroux, 2000), p. 552.

14   But you can see for yourself at this URL: http://www.tcrecord.org/Content.asp?ContentID=11546

15   Paul Ricoeur, *Freud and Philosophy: An Essay on Interpretation* (New Haven: Yale University Press, 1972), pp. 32ff.

16   J. S. Mill, *On Liberty, and Other Writings,* ed. Stefan Collini (Cambridge: CUP, 1995), p. 81.

17   *ibid.*, p. 64.

18   *ibid.*

19   David Stove, 'The Columbus argument' in *Cricket Versus Republicanism and Other Essays* (Sydney: Quakers Hill Press, 1995), pp. 58–9. This essay is also available in David Stove, *On Enlightenment*, ed. Andrew Irvine (New Brunswick: Transaction, 2003).

20   *ibid.*, p. 59.

21   Lucius Carey, Viscount Falkland, 'A speech concerning episcopacy' in *Discourse of Infallibility* (London: William Nealand, 1660), p. 3.

22   Stove, 'Columbus argument', p. 60.

23   Mill, *On Liberty*, p. 67.

24   *ibid.*

25   Maurice Cowling, *Mill and Liberalism*, 2nd edition (Cambridge: CUP, 1990), p. il.

26   Edmund Burke, *Reflections on the Revolution in France,* ed. Conor Cruise O'Brien (New York: Penguin, 1986), p. 106.

27   *ibid.*, p. 183.

28   Hans-Georg Gadamer, *Truth and Method* (New York: Seabury Press, 1975), p. 240.

29   Mill, *On Liberty*, p. 45. The paeans to 'eccentricity', 'originality' and the like occur throughout the text, but especially in Chapter 3, 'Of Individuality, as one of the elements of well-being'.

30   John Stuart Mill, *Autobiography*, ed. John M. Robson (New York: Penguin, 1990), p. 100.

31 Friedrich Nietzsche, *The Will To Power*, ed. Walter Kaufmann (London: Weidenfeld & Nicolson, 1968), p. 435.

32 *ibid.*

33 Friedrich Nietzsche, 'On the genealogy of morals' in *Basic Writings of Nietzsche*, ed. Walter Kaufmann (New York: Basic Books, 1968), p. 589.

34 Nietzsche, *Will to Power*, p. 267.

35 Friedrich Nietzsche, 'On truth and lies in a nonmoral sense' in *Philosophy and Truth: Selections from Nietzsche's Notebooks of the Early 1870s*, ed. Daniel Breazeale (Atlantic Highlands, NJ: Humanities Press, 1979), p. 84.

36 Friedrich Nietzsche, *The Gay Science*, ed. Walter Kaufmann (New York: Vintage Books, 1974), p. 282.

37 Friedrich Nietzsche, 'Ecce homo' in *Basic Writings*, p. 782.

38 Michel Foucault, 'Truth and power' in *The Foucault Reader*, ed. Paul Rabinow (New York: Vintage Books, 1984), p. 73.

39 Nietzsche, *Philosophy and Truth*, p. 84.

40 Richard Rorty, *Contingency, Irony, and Solidarity* (Cambridge: CUP, 1989), p. 27.

41 Nietzsche, *Will to Power*, p. 155.

42 Friedrich Nietzsche, 'Thus spoke Zarathustra', Part 3, No. 12 'On old and new tablets' in *The Portable Nietzsche*, ed. Walter Kaufmann (New York: The Viking Press, 1968), pp. 308ff.

43 Nietzsche, *The Will to Power*, p. 45. See also 'On the meaning of ascetic ideals', No. 27 in 'On the genealogy of morals'.

44 Nietzsche, 'On the genealogy of morals', pp. 591–2.

45 St Thomas Aquinas, 'Summa theologica', Q. LXV, Art. 1, in *Basic Writings of St Thomas Aquinas*, Vol. II, ed. Anton C. Pegis (New York: Random House, 1944), p. 496.

46 Nietzsche, *The Will to Power*, p. 545.

47 *ibid.*, p. 419.

48 Nietzsche, 'On the genealogy of morals', p. 521.

49 Nietzsche, 'Beyond good and evil' in *Basic Writings*, p. 393.

50 Nietzsche, 'On the genealogy of morals', p. 503.

51 Novalis quoted in Thomas Mann, 'Nietzsche's philosophy in the light of recent history' in *Essays of Three Decades*, trans. H. T. Lowe-Porter (New York: Alfred A. Knopf, 1947), p. 166.

52 Rorty, *Contingency, Irony, and Solidarity*, pp. xiii–xvi.

53 Richard Rorty, *Consequences of Pragmatism* (Minneapolis: University of Minnesota Press, 1982), p. xxxix.

54 Rorty, *Contingency, Irony, and Solidarity*, p. xv.

55 Richard Rorty, *Philosophy and the Mirror of Nature* (Princeton: Princeton University Press, 1980), p. 357.

56 *ibid.*, p. 373.

57 Rorty, *Contingency, Irony, and Solidarity*, p. 173.

58 Richard Rorty, 'Deconstruction and circumvention' in
Essays on Heidegger and Others (Cambridge: CUP, 1991), p. 86.

59 Rorty, *Consequences of Pragmatism*, p. xxxvi.

60 *ibid.*, p. xxix.

61 Rorty, *Contingency, Irony, and Solidarity*, p. 22.

62 Richard Posner, *Overcoming Law* (Cambridge, MA: Harvard
University Press, 1996), p. 444.

63 Rorty, *Contingency, Irony, and Solidarity*, p. xiv.

64 Leszek Kolakowski, 'The self-poisoning of the open society' in
Modernity on Endless Trial (Chicago: Chicago University Press, 1990),
p. 171.

65 *ibid.*, p. 172.

66 Leszek Kolakowski, 'The revenge of the sacred in secular culture'
in *Modernity on Endless Trial*, p. 72.

67 Michael Oakeshott, 'Rationalism in politics' in *Rationalism in
Politics and Other Essays* (Indianapolis: Liberty Fund, 1991), pp. 6, 10.

68 Robert Musil, *The Man Without Qualities*, Vol. I, trans. Sophie
Wilkins (New York: Alfred A. Knopf, 1995), p. 327.

69 René Descartes, 'Discourse on method' in *The Philosophical Works
of Descartes*, trans. Elizabeth S. Haldane and G. R. T. Ross, Vol. 1
(Cambridge: CUP, 1979), p. 119.

70 Roger Scruton, *Modern Philosophy: An Introduction and Survey*
(London: Sinclair-Stevenson, 1994), p. 244.